LEFT BRAIN–RIGHT BRAIN DIFFERENCES:
Inquiries, Evidence, and New Approaches

James F. Iaccino
Illinois Benedictine College

LEA **LAWRENCE ERLBAUM ASSOCIATES, PUBLISHERS**
1993 Hillsdale, New Jersey   Hove and London

Lawrence Erlbaum Associates, Inc., Publishers
365 Broadway
Hillsdale, New Jersey 07642

Library of Congress Cataloging-in-Publication Data

Iaccino, James F.
    Left brain–right brain differences : Inquiries, evidence, and new
approaches / James F. Iaccino.
        p.   cm.
    Includes bibliographical references and index.
    ISBN 0-8058-1340-3
    1. Cerebral dominance. I. Title.
    [DNLM: 1. Dominance, Cerebral. WL 335 I104L]
QP385.5.I23   1993
612.8′25–dc20
DNLM/DLC
for Library of Congress   92-49108
                                                                CIP

Books published by Lawrence Erlbaum Associates are printed on acid-free
paper, and their bindings are chosen for strength and durability.

Printed in the United States of America
10 9 8 7 6 5 4 3 2 1

Most especially dedicated to:
Michele, Jonathan, and Nicole,
for patiently enduring and being there
for this sometimes weary "split-brain" author!
My thanks for having such a wonderful family!

Contents

Preface

Ever since my undergraduate schooling in psychology, I have been interested in doing experimental research on the topic of human cerebral asymmetries (i.e., left brain–right brain differences). In fact, my senior independent study involved a basic replication of one of Curry's (1967) classic dichotic listening designs to determine if a left-ear advantage (LEA) or right-hemisphere superiority existed for nonverbal inputs.

Although my findings yielded nonsignificant differences between ear sides, I was not discouraged so easily and continued my research endeavors in asymmetries while in graduate school and beyond. Since 1988, my experimental methodologies have become more controlled and precise; further, the results obtained from these numerous studies have shown some interesting differences in hemispheric processing, not only between the genders, but also across hand-dominant groups.

Therefore, one of the reasons for my writing this text is to share my most recent findings with other colleagues in this specialized area of study. More importantly, it is my opinion that cerebral asymmetries effectively encompass a number of fields in psychology—from perceptual to physiological and comparative to even the cognitive—to address the age-old questions of human nature: Why are cerebral asymmetries present to such a strong degree in this particular species and how are these asymmetries activated both in the laboratory and in everyday situations? You may derive some answers from this work set before you.

This book basically examines those issues most central to human cerebral asymmetries. It is not intended to be an exhaustive research account, nor is it designed to provide the reader with definitive statements on the subject. One needs only to familiarize oneself with the literature to realize that inconsistencies and conflicting results are more the norm than the exception. Rather, the text was primarily written to: (a) give the reader a more coherent and logical framework to continue the scholarly pursuit of cerebral asymmetries either experimentally, clinically, or just for intrinsic satisfaction purposes; (b) present more up-to-date research findings in brain lateralization with normal subjects (with particular emphasis on gender and handedness factors); and (c) discuss newer models of asymmetry that recently have surfaced in the literature (e.g., the revised "attention set" theory formerly attributed to Kinsbourne and Bryden).

The book adopts a traditional inquiry approach. Although hardly a creative way to present the information, it seems surprising that few texts utilize this method to emphasize key points in brain differences. Specifically, a research question relevant to asymmetries is posed at each chapter's beginning (e.g., "Are split-brain patients truly divided in cognitive functions?"). Experimental evidence is then presented to support a particular position. Concluding comments are provided in a summary section at the end of each chapter.

The chapters are organized around a series of four major parts: an introductory part designed for the novice or less advanced students (chapters 1–3); a more detailed part on clinical brain asymmetries, involving neuropsychological, split-brain, and other pathological disorders (chapters 4–6); a very thorough investigation of more normal brain lateralization studies, including gender, handedness, and developmental factors (chapters 7–10); and a concluding part that discusses current approaches, revised theories, and future perspectives on cerebral asymmetries (chapter 11).

The text is written so that each chapter (or part) can be read independently of any other. It is up to the reader to decide how much of the material is relevant for his or her purposes. Further, it is hoped that undergraduates, as well as higher-level students in psychology and other related disciplines, can use this book (or any of its sections) as a supplementary resource for more advanced physiological, neurobiological, or specialized topics courses. The writing is intended to be quite clear and straightforward, without sacrificing the detail and complexity of the multiple research reports and experimental articles I have reviewed throughout the 1980s and beyond.

ACKNOWLEDGMENTS

I am indebted to the following authors for their excellent works: Bradshaw and Nettleton (*Human Cerebral Asymmetry*, 1983); Springer and Deutsch (*Left Brain, Right Brain*, 1989); and Geschwind and Galaburda

(*Cerebral Lateralization: Biological Mechanisms, Associations, and Pathology*, 1987). Without their guidance, I would not have been able to refine this text into its present form. I also thank my psychology undergraduate majors for assisting me with the multiple data analyses for many of the asymmetry studies conducted at Illinois Benedictine College in Lisle over the past few years. My spouse, Michele, and my two lovely children, Nicole and Jonathan, were also quite supportive during this intensive period of writing, and so I especially dedicate this book to them.

James F. Iaccino

PART ONE

INTRODUCTION
TO CEREBRAL ASYMMETRIES

Part I is designed to acquaint the reader with the topic of cerebral asymmetries in several stages. Chapter 1 highlights the morphological and functional left–right asymmetries associated with the human brain. Chapter 2 discusses the degree to which these asymmetries are unique to the human being via cross-species comparisons. Finally, chapter 3 explores the two types of cognitive styles (sequential vs. holistic processing) in relation to the respective left and right cerebral hemispheres. Through these initial chapters, it is hoped that the reader will become proficient enough with asymmetries to master the more advanced parts contained within the text.

CHAPTER ONE

Are Brain Symmetries
A Common Misconception?

In its most literal definition, *asymmetry* refers to the concepts of *not well balanced*, *unevenly proportioned*, or *unequally represented*. Most of the world can be described according to this asymmetrical *imbalance*.

CULTURAL ASYMMETRIES

Many cultures have employed an asymmetrical type of organization to dichotomize reality into polar opposites, with the sacred, warm, good, and male linked to a *right* perspective; and the profane, cold, dark, and female associated with a *left* (or more sinister) orientation (Bradshaw & Nettleton, 1983). Even in the Christian tenet of salvation, according to Bradshaw and Nettleton, the blessed will sit at God's right hand. However, the cursed will continue to remain at their left-sided, or sinful, orientation to the Creator.

Architecture, like religious belief, is an expression of the culture's dichotomized view of life. In Eastern traditions, the dome construction pervades and highlights the Gestalt expansiveness (or *right* mode) of knowledge, which has no beginning or end. However, Western societies have more focused buildings (i.e., spiral towers) pointing upward to the heavens; these structures symbolize the orderly, finite, and more rational left side of knowledge (Ashbrook, 1988).

BODY ASYMMETRIES

When examining the microcosm of society, the human being, symmetry appears to be only skin deep. Beneath the surface, a number of paired organs, bones, and other structures have shown small, yet consistent, left–right asymmetries in size and shape. For instance, the male right testicle is usually larger and higher than its left counterpart (McManus, 1976). The female breasts show such variations as well. When it comes to disease states, investigations have yielded even more compelling evidence. Many diseases apparently strike one side of the human body more frequently than the other. For example, left-sided tumors are reported more often in various bilateral organs such as the breast, kidney, ovary, testis, and nasal cavity (Robin & Shortridge, 1979).

Handedness Differences

One very pronounced asymmetry is in hand dominance. Hand dominance is the ability to use one hand over the other across a large range of manual activities (e.g., unscrewing a jar, writing with a pencil, and throwing a baseball). We are predominantly a right-handed species: Cross-cultural studies average the incidence of right-hand use to be approximately 90% in comparison with the 7–8% figure frequently reported for left-hand use. Based on a number of reports, it also appears that right- and left-handed asymmetries have remained relatively stable over time (Coren & Porac, 1977).

Control of hand dominance is governed by the two cerebral hemispheres. For right-handers, the left hemisphere takes control over the right via the contralateral (or crossed-over) nerve pathways leading to the right side of the body. More numerous motor fibers have been identified in this pathway system, signifying its importance to right-handed dominance. For left-handers, the ipsilateral (or same-sided) pathway sometimes takes charge over the contralateral, suggesting that the left brain mainly regulates human hand preference (Springer & Deutsch, 1989).

Eye, Ear, and Foot Differences

Left–right asymmetries seem to be the strongest for handedness, followed by footedness, eyedness, and earedness, respectively. A large-scale study conducted by Coren and Porac (1981) revealed that many humans use the right foot over the left across a number of tasks (e.g., kicking a ball or grasping a small object with the toes). Even 17-day-old infants move the right leg forward before the left. If anything, the left foot is used as a support, whereas the manual activities are engaged in by the right (Peters & Petrie, 1979).

With respect to eye preferences, humans typically align their sight with the right eye when tracking an object, even when both eyes are kept open. The image from the left eye apparently is suppressed so that a double image of the target is not perceived (Porac & Coren, 1976). The weakest of all body side preferences involves the ears. Auditory acuity rarely seems to be dependent on the ear-side tested, as assessed in a variety of threshold experiments (Coren & Porac, 1981).

MORPHOLOGICAL BRAIN ASYMMETRIES

At first glance, each cerebral hemisphere looks like the mirror image of the other, both anatomically and structurally. For a number of decades, a symmetrical brain organization was assumed, with the left hemisphere basically controlling the right 50% of the body and the right hemisphere governing the remaining left 50%. However, as indicated with handedness, the left brain apparently is in charge in a majority of cases, regardless of the body side. Therefore, the cerebral hemispheres should be examined in greater detail to determine if any morphological (i.e., physical) asymmetries exist along with suggested functional ones.

Sylvian Fissure Asymmetries

The *sylvian fissure*, a major lateral groove separating the temporal and parietal lobes of the brain, is generally longer on the left side (Rubens, 1977). This fissure also continues farther along horizontally before terminating, typically at a lower level in the left brain (refer to Fig. 1.1).

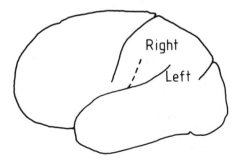

FIG. 1.1. Left and right sylvian fissures with right fissure superimposed on left hemisphere. From *Human Cerebral Asymmetry* (p. 22) by J. Bradshaw and N. Nettleton, 1983, Englewood Cliffs, New Jersey: Prentice-Hall. Copyright 1983 by Prentice-Hall. Reprinted by permission.

The higher termination point of the right sylvian fissure is usually apparent by the fourth month in the fetal brain (LeMay & Culebras, 1972).

Temporal Planum Asymmetries

Cerebral differences also have been found with the *temporal planum*, a language-related area that includes much of the Wernicke region and through which the sylvian fissure passes. Recent studies have shown that the left temporal planum is larger than the right in a majority of cases, and is evident as early as the 31st week of gestation (Chi, Dooling, & Gilles, 1977). In particular, the superior portion of the superior temporal gyrus seems to be the most affected part of the left temporal planum.

Another area close in proximity to the planum, the parietal operculum, is also larger on the left side in cases where planum asymmetries have been reported (LeMay & Culebras, 1972). In addition, microscopic-level research has indicated more pronounced cell layers in the temporal lobe close to the vicinity of the left temporal planum (Galaburda, Sanides, & Geschwind, 1978).

Prefrontal Asymmetries

With respect to the brain's prefrontal regions, the left areas (especially Broca's motor-speech area) apparently are smaller than the right areas. Anatomists have speculated that hemispheric folding may be greater in these left prefrontal regions, suggesting that the total cortical surface may still be larger in this particular hemisphere (Wada, Clarke, & Hamm, 1975).

Fetal brain evidence would further support this claim. Right-hemispheric folding proceeds much earlier, by as much as 2 weeks ahead of the left. Eventually, the slower developing left-hemisphere areas attain a greater complexity of organization either by an increase in size and/or more intricate cortical foldings (Galaburda, 1984). The reported left–right asymmetries shown in the prefrontal regions, as well as the sylvian fissure and temporal planum, all involve brain areas mediating language functions in humans.

Venous System Asymmetries

Specific vein locations also have been mapped to identify possible morphologic asymmetries between the hemispheres. The major vein in the left hemisphere (i.e., the Vein of Labbe) lies very close to the language areas, whereas the predominant vein in the right hemisphere (i.e., the

Vein of Trolard) traverses the superoparietal region, a location involved with nonverbal spatial processing (Hochberg & LeMay, 1975).

However, left–right asymmetries in blood flow have demonstrated some inconsistent results. At times, greater pressure is reported in the left frontal and precentral regions (Springer & Deutsch, 1989). In contrast, more current and intensive studies have indicated stronger right-sided pressure, especially when subjects are engaged in attention-demanding tasks (Deutsch, Papanicolaou, Bourbon, & Eisenberg, 1987). To compound the issue, hemispheric changes in blood flow seem to be largely dependent on which hand is tested in these tasks, with left-hand movement increasing the flow in the right hemisphere's motor region, and, correspondingly, right-hand movement slightly elevating the flow in the left hemisphere area (Halsey, Blaunstein, Wilson, & Wills, 1979). One conclusion certainly can be derived from these complex findings: Blood flow does not appear to be symmetrically distributed between the two cortical sides.

Gross Brain Asymmetries

If one examines the entire brain configuration, a nonsymmetrical shape between the hemispheres is clearly evident. The right hemisphere's frontal and central regions are wider, with the frontal pole generally extending beyond the left (Fig. 1.2). In contrast, the left hemisphere's anteroparietal and posterooccipital regions are larger, with the occipital pole protruding more posteriorly than its right counterpart (Chui & Damasio, 1980). The wider right frontal and left occipital lobes give the human brain a counterclockwise torque appearance. These gross asymmetries (particularly in the left hemisphere) are shown in fetal as well as neonatal brains (LeMay & Geschwind, 1978).

FUNCTIONAL BRAIN ASYMMETRIES

Based on the aforementioned distinctions, the question arises: Are left–right morphologic asymmetries related to the more functional asymmetries historically associated with the hemispheres (i.e., linguistic processing on the left side and spatial processing on the right)? Some researchers have concluded that the correlation between the morphologic and functional asymmetries is a strong one, especially when linguistic functions are considered (Walker, 1980). Their reasoning is that many of the structures reported to be larger (and/or more folded) on the left side are mainly responsible for language control and its comprehension.

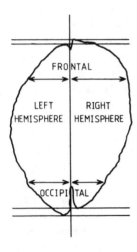

FIG. 1.2. Gross asymmetries in left and right hemispheres. From *Human Cerebral Asymmetry* (p. 25) by J. Bradshaw and N. Nettleton, 1983, Englewood Cliffs, New Jersey: Prentice-Hall. Copyright 1983 by Prentice-Hall. Reprinted by permission.

The next section reviews the specific functions traditionally linked with each hemisphere, keeping in mind that lateralization in function might have a physical base in the human brain.

Left Hemisphere: Language Functions

Clinical studies have shown that patients with cerebral lesions in the left hemisphere experience a wide variety of language disorders or *aphasias*, from articulation to comprehension deficits. Recent evidence by Zurif (1980) suggested that certain language dysfunctions, such as Broca's aphasia, involve not only articulation problems but comprehension ones as well, indicating that certain sites in the left brain regulate more than one linguistic function. It could be that such regions (e.g., Broca and Wernicke's) encompass wider cortical areas than previously supposed. Thus, the left hemisphere might contain an extensive number of neural tracts and structures associated with linguistic inputs (Dimond, 1980).

Research work with normal subjects also has demonstrated some consistent findings with language-related stimuli. Words and letters presented tachistoscopically have produced striking right visual-field (RVF) advantages (i.e., left hemisphere superiorities), whereas dichotically spoken digits and words have produced the corresponding right-ear, left-hemisphere advantages (REA) (Bryden, 1965; Kimura, 1967; Zurif & Bryden, 1969). These field and ear advantages do not appear to be limited to meaningful utterances, however, because nonsense syllables ("pa" and "ga"), nonwords ("goze" and "cipe"), and even speech played backward have generated similar superiorities within the left hemisphere (Bradshaw & Gates, 1978; Krashen, 1977). Overall, the results of these studies suggest that the left brain is involved more heavily with the phono-logical (or verbalized) aspects of language rather than its syntactical and/or semantical construction, which might be more structurally specific.

Would these findings imply that the right hemisphere plays an insig-nificant role in mediating language-related behavior? Not necessarily so. Ross (1984) hypothesized that *prosody* is the right hemisphere's contri-bution to language. Prosody, by definition, involves a variation in emo-tional intonation when communicating a particular utterance (e.g., a rising inflection when using the questioning "yes"). Ross's (1984) patients who had right-hemispheric (as opposed to left-hemispheric) anterior lesions often spoke with a flattened intonation, whereas those who had right posterior lesions typically experienced more problems in determining the emotional tone of speech produced by others. More global right-hemisphere damage included both of these prosodic deficits. Ross's (1984) evidence clearly implicated the right hemisphere with some very impor-tant linguistic functions, especially ones involving communication and its appropriate expression.

Further studies have shown that patients experiencing major speech impairments (e.g., Broca's aphasics) eventually could learn to carry on short, meaningful conversations if they could convert word strings ini-tially to musical sequences, which, in time, gradually were deemphasized (Albert, Sparks, & Helm, 1973). It was presumed that the intact right hemisphere compensated for the left's linguistic impairment by using the melodic medium to acquire new language elements. Aspects of metaphor and qualities of humor also appeared to be mediated by the right hemisphere. Damage to this side usually resulted in patients who were overly literal in their interpretation of metaphors, stories, and even car-toons (Foldi, Cicone, & Gardner, 1983). One might conclude that the right hemisphere acts in a supportive role to the left, which primarily regu-lates the major components of language.

Right Hemisphere: Nonverbal Functions

Certain nonverbal functions have been found to be handled largely by the right hemisphere. Benton (1980) and others (Carey & Diamond, 1980) have identified a particular recognition failure (or *agnosia*) in right-hemisphere lesioned patients: prosopagnosia. This inability to recognize familiar faces is a clinical syndrome that almost always involves damage to posterior parietal-occipital areas of the right hemisphere and related regions in the left hemisphere as well. A more common agnosia, the failure to discriminate novel or unfamiliar faces, apparently results from more unilateral injury to the right hemisphere's posterior (and sometimes an-terior) regions.

Other visuospatial deficits linked with right-hemisphere damage include the inability to recognize familiar objects by touch (Fontenot & Benton, 1971); the failure to perceive three-dimensional spatial relations from two-dimensional representations such as in dot stereograms (Benton & Hecaen, 1970); and neglect of, or inattention to, the left side of one's body space (Hecaen & Albert, 1978; Walsh, 1978). Benton (1985) argued that the right hemisphere typically is involved in these simple visuospatial tasks, but that when more complex assignments need to be performed (e.g., drawing objects on command or copying line drawings) bihemispheric involvement is more often the case.

Amusia, or loss of musical ability, traditionally has been associated with patients who had right-hemisphere strokes (Gates & Bradshaw, 1977b). However, current studies with more normal subjects have indicated some left-hemisphere involvement in musical processing, especially with more complex sequences presented dichotically. A right-ear advantage (REA) often has been shown for these stimuli, whereas a right-hemisphere left-ear advantage (LEA) typically has occurred for simpler tonal sequences (Gates & Bradshaw, 1977a; Shanon, 1980). These dichotic findings seem to support Benton's (1985) position on task-level complexity and subsequent hemispheric involvement. Left-hemispheric REAs also have been found for musical properties, which share particular features with language, such as temporal order, duration, and rhythm (Carmon, 1978).

Simple nonverbal stimuli presented tachistoscopically to normal subjects (e.g., dot displays, line orientations, and photographed faces) have produced the typical left visual-field (LVF) or right-hemisphere advantages. However, when discrimination of targets involved one very specific feature, a shifting occurred from right- to left-hemisphere processing, as evidenced by the opposite superiority in the right visual field (Jones, 1979; Patterson & Bradshaw, 1975). In keeping with Benton's (1985) argument, these complex tachistoscopic identifications required more detailed, analytic processing, which only the left hemisphere could provide.

To summarize, the right hemisphere apparently mediates some very important nonverbal functions (e.g., facial discriminations and musical recognitions), yet it is assisted by the left hemisphere, especially in more complex visuospatial tasks. The functional asymmetries reported for each of the hemispheres suggest that the cortical differences are mainly ones of relative (rather than absolute) specialization: namely, the left hemisphere is more language oriented than the right, whereas the right is more visuospatial oriented than the left. Although relatively specialized for a particular input, each hemisphere still requires the other to complement its overall functioning.

Integration of Hemispheric Functions

How do the hemispheres effectively complement each other's functioning? The simple answer to this pertinent question is via the *corpus callosum*. The callosum is the largest of several commissures that connect regions of the left hemisphere with similar areas of the right hemisphere. (The anterior commissure is another hemisphere connector close in proximity to the corpus callosum.) This commissural band of nerve fibers takes time to attain its adult size (Fig. 1.3). It has been hypothesized that during this slow maturation process, the two sides of the brain develop at different rates, both morphologically as well as functionally (Trevarthen, 1974b).

The corpus callosum appears to play a major role in creating interhemispheric harmony in the normal brain, specifically by integrating the verbal and visuospatial functions into unified thought and subsequent action. The exact process by which this harmony is achieved is the more difficult question to answer. Some researchers have speculated that the corpus callosum duplicates the information in a carbon copylike fashion from one side to the other. Others have viewed the callosum as mainly inhibiting the overall activity in one hemisphere, thus allowing the other to take over for some task more suited to its respective processing mode (Levy, 1985).

A more promising model of callosal functioning involves the process of *topographic inhibition*. As Cook (1984a, 1984b) explained, the same neuronal message is not carried over from a point in one hemisphere to a similar point in the other hemisphere. What happens instead is that surrounding areas of the transmitted-to point become activated, representing the original neuronal input in a more generalized or contextually related format. A more precise example of how topographic inhibition works follows: If the word *mouse* activates a particular cortical point in the left hemisphere, the corresponding point for *mouse* in the right hemisphere would be inhibited. However, other regions surrounding the inhibited mouse point would be excited and would provide background information related to mouse, such as "is one of several rodents" or "is a natural prey of cats," through the more specialized visuospatial medium.

As Cook (1984a, 1984b) contended, callosal topographic inhibition apparently produced two different patterns of nerve excitation within the brain for the same information. Hence, both hemispheres "turned on" for whatever input, complementing (not copying) each other by processing the material according to their own specialized mode, be it more verbal or more visuospatial. Clearly Cook's (1984a, 1984b) approach was a unique one in examining functional asymmetries via the corpus callosum and, at the very least, provided a good physiological accounting as to why each hemisphere functions differently from the other.

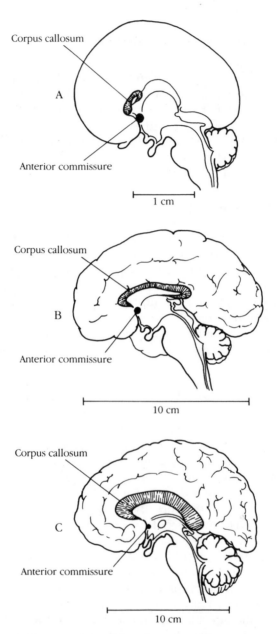

FIG. 1.3. Corpus callosum at three stages of development. A. Fetal (16 weeks), B. at birth (40 weeks), C. Adult. From "Cerebral Embryology and Split Brain" by C. Trevarthen in *Hemispheric Disconnection and Cerebral Function* (pp. 228–229) by M. Kinsbourne and W. L. Smith, 1974, Springfield, Illinois: Charles C. Thomas. Copyright 1974 by Charles C. Thomas. Reprinted by permission.

THEORIES OF CEREBRAL ASYMMETRY

If asymmetries are evident in the human brain, when are these hemispheric differences first shown? Hahn (1987) attempted to answer this question by presenting the two major theoretical views that have emerged in the asymmetry literature, namely Lenneberg's (1967) experiential model and Kinsbourne's (1975) genetic theory. Both approaches are presented briefly here and explored in more depth when discussing developmental factors associated with brain lateralization (chapter 10).

Lenneberg's Experiential Model

According to Lenneberg (1967), both hemispheres are *equipotential* (i.e., symmetrically organized) for language during the first few years of childhood. Then, as the child becomes more experienced in the use of language, the left brain acquires a relative specialization for this function. It is estimated that lateralization for language would be complete by the onset of puberty.

Lenneberg's (1967) conclusions primarily were based on findings by Basser (1962), who showed that children with damage to the right side of the brain experienced some speech disturbances (although not as many as left-side damaged subjects). However, this pattern of impairment was different for older groups (i.e., teenagers and adults), who rarely experienced aphasic disturbances after injury occurred to their right hemisphere. On the basis of Basser's (1962) clinical evidence, Lenneberg (1967) derived his lateralization time frame, which started during language acquisition (approximately age 2) and ended by puberty, the period when right-hemisphere aphasics were more infrequent.

Kinsbourne's Genetic Theory

Kinsbourne (1975), on the other hand, theorized that lateralization of linguistic functions is already present in the newborn brain, and perhaps even earlier. Reviewing Basser's (1962) cases, Kinsbourne (1975) found that in right-hemisphere damaged children who had aphasias, left-hemisphere injuries also were apparent. Thus, there probably is a strong genetic factor that gives the left hemisphere a greater language-acquisition ability at birth, making it possible for this side to slowly acquire relative dominance over the right throughout the early lifespan of the human.

The morphological evidence presented earlier indicates that the language areas of the left hemisphere are not the same size as the right, and that these anatomical differences are present even during fetal life. Perhaps

Kinsbourne's (1975) genetic predisposition factor for left-sided language involved a spatial programming element so that more cortical area was devoted to the hemisphere more involved with that particular function (Hahn, 1987; LeMay, 1982). Whatever the nature of this genetic factor, one thing remains clear: Both hemispheres are not equipotential for language at birth or, for that matter, even before birth. Human beings are programmed to display these functional (and morphological) cerebral asymmetries very early in development.

SUMMARY AND CONCLUSIONS

A brief review of human brain research was presented in this initial chapter to address this major inquiry: Are cerebral symmetries a common misconception? Based on the empirical evidence provided, the following conclusions were derived:

1. Morphological (i.e., physical) asymmetries were found to exist between the cerebral hemispheres, with the left language-related areas showing a more pronounced size and more intricate foldings.

2. Functional asymmetries also were reported between the hemispheres, with the left side being more specialized for linguistic materials and the right side more specialized for nonverbal, visuospatial stimuli. The corpus callosum allowed both sides to achieve an interhemispheric harmony with the respective inputs via a topographic inhibitory process, as postulated by Cook (1984a, 1984b).

3. Finally, in keeping with Kinsbourne's (1975) argument, a strong genetic predisposition for these left–right asymmetries was hypothesized, particularly for greater language-acquisition ability within the left hemisphere at birth or even earlier during fetal development.

Although both hemispheres resemble each other superficially, important distinctions can be noted at the structural and functional levels. Thus, a symmetrical brain organization is not really the true state of affairs; rather, cerebral asymmetry is the rule rather than the exception in understanding how the human brain operates. Whether lower level organisms display similar left–right cerebral differences to the same degree as the human species is the next logical inquiry to be addressed in chapter 2.

CHAPTER TWO

Are Cerebral Asymmetries
Unique to the Human Species?

In chapter 1, it was noted that the brain was lateralized for particular functions, with language more left centered and visuospatial skills more right based. In the past, certain researchers have regarded this lateral specialization of the brain as quite unique to the human species, having evolved from language acquisition and use (Ornstein, 1977). In fact, some (Levy, 1974; Levy-Agresti & Sperry, 1968) have stated that these cognitive processes were so incompatible with those employed for more visuospatial functions that they had to develop in opposite hemispheres of the brain; otherwise, such opposing modes of information processing would interfere seriously with each other if housed within the same hemisphere, either right or left.

However, other theorists have speculated that brain lateralization in humans is tied more directly to hand dominance. Kimura and Archibald (1974) proposed that human cerebral asymmetries did not evolve from language, but from particular motor skills that were employed in basic communication functions. Thus, the right hand served as the initial communication medium (via gestures and other manipulations), specializing the contralateral hemisphere for these physical expressions. Later on, vocalization became the more dominant mode of communication, and the already lateralized left hemisphere appropriately exercised control over this new function.

The spatial skills of the right hemisphere also could have developed in much the same manner as the left, by the emergence of another type of motor skill suited to the manipulation of three-dimensional relationships of the world apprehended by vision and grasped through touch (e.g., following a specific travel route from start to finish). Presumably the left hand acquired control of these operations, lateralizing the respective right hemisphere for the visuospatial input (Kimura & Archibald, 1974).

According to this approach, language use is viewed as a by-product of cerebral lateralization rather than its precursor. Studying the hand preference of an organism appears to be the more important factor in examining cerebral asymmetries (at least in humans). If this is the case, do lower lever creatures show hand preferences similar to humans, and, ultimately, similar left–right brain differences? The first section of this chapter addresses this key issue.

ANIMAL PAW AND CLAW PREFERENCES

Most animals show strong and consistent paw preferences when considering individual members of the same species. For instance, cats and mice generally use one paw in reaching for objects and grasping food (Collins, 1968; Warren, Abplanalp, & Warren, 1967). It also has been observed that many members of the rhesus monkey species often use one paw when engaging in manual types of tasks (Beck & Barton, 1972; Lehman, 1980). Although these limb preferences are similar to ones identified in humans, substantial variability exists between animal members of the same species, with the breakdown being approximately 50% right-pawed and 50% left-pawed. As Walker (1980) noted, humans appear to be the only species with lateral preferences biased toward one hand, with approximately 90% of the population being right-handed.

Collins (1969) suggested that the even distribution of right- and left-pawed animal preferences is due to chance factors initially determining which limb is to be the dominant one. Experience helps to establish a stronger permanence to the random paw preference by repeated usage of that selected limb across a wide range of manual activities.

Collins (1977) ruled out genetic factors in determining paw dominance after he performed a number of selective breeding experiments, in which mice who shared the same paw preference were mated consistently across three generations. Collins' (1977) last generation proportion surprisingly demonstrated the same even split of right- and left-pawed dominance as the initial generation percentage he started out with in his studies. Although selective breeding has not been performed on other animal species to date, it would seem that the direction of paw preference is not influenced heavily by genetic components (especially because Collins' [1977] ratios had not changed across successive generations).

The only species that has deviated from this even split of right- and left-limb preference is the parrot. Recent reports (Rogers, 1980) indicated that these birds predominantly use their left claw over their right when reaching for food. Humans and particular species of bird resemble each other the most when it comes to determining limb dominance, although the pattern of claw preference is reversed in parrots. Based on these overall findings, one can conclude that the relationship between limb preference and predicted brain lateralization is a weak one when examining lower level species. Keeping this in mind, I turn to other ways of assessing possible brain asymmetries in animals.

MORPHOLOGICAL BRAIN ASYMMETRIES IN ANIMALS

Similar to human brain research, one can look at the various structures within each of the hemispheres of the animal brain to determine if any morphological asymmetries are present. Some anatomical left–right differences have been reported recently in the brains of particular species that resemble those found in the human cortex.

Sylvian Fissure Asymmetries in Apes

The right sylvian fissure of the great apes typically curls upward at the posterior end and terminates in a higher position than its left counterpart. Of the animals studied, this effect was strongest in the orangutan, followed by the chimpanzee and gorilla, respectively (LeMay & Geschwind, 1975). Additional research has shown that the left sylvian fissure in chimps is generally longer than the right (Yeni-Komshian & Benson, 1976). Many of these fissure differences are quite comparable to those seen in the human brain (refer to chapter 1 for more detail).

Temporal Planum and Frontal Lobe Asymmetries in Apes

Cross-species similarities also have been identified with the temporal planum. The left planum is typically larger than the right in chimpanzees as well as humans (Witelson, 1977a). Further, the frontal lobe of the baboon species is reported to be wider in the right hemisphere, as in humans (Cain & Wada, 1979). Many of the anatomical asymmetries cited here for apes are not as strong as ones for humans. For instance, the size of the human left temporal planum can exceed the right in size by as much as 10 times. Asymmetries of this magnitude rarely are seen in the various ape species (Geschwind & Galaburda, 1987). One should exercise some caution when making these cross-species comparisons; although the direction of lateral disparity may be similar, the degree still remains somewhat unique to humans.

Cerebral Cortical Asymmetries in Rats

Consistent asymmetries in structure also have been demonstrated in the rat brain. Diamond, Dowling, and Johnson (1981) found that the male rat cortex was significantly thicker in several places within the right hemisphere (particularly in the posterior regions), whereas in the female cortex, the left hemisphere areas were thicker overall. In females ovariectomized at birth, the male pattern was seen. In a more recent study conducted by Diamond (1984), reversed thickness asymmetries occurred in male rats who had their testis removed shortly after birth.

Current anatomical work also has revealed that certain structures in the right hemisphere of the normal rat brain are typically of a larger size; these include the neocortex, sensorimotor cortex, and primary visual area. The hippocampus (a structure heavily involved with memory formation) exhibits laterality effects as well, with male rats displaying a thicker right hippocampus very early on in development. However, as these males get older, the differences become insignificant. Female rats show the reverse asymmetry with the hippocampus, but the pattern varies with the age of the organism (Geschwind & Galaburda, 1987). These gender differences suggest that hormones play an extremely critical role in the development of the rodent brain, which, as is discussed in chapter 8, is also the case with the human cortex.

PHARMACOLOGICAL BRAIN ASYMMETRIES IN ANIMALS

In addition to cortical asymmetries, chemical differences have been identified in the left and right hemispheres of the rat brain. More specifically, varying concentrations of particular neurotransmitter substances have been reported between the two brain sides; thus, attention is directed to these striking and very consistent results.

Dopamine Concentration Asymmetries in Rats

In a number of studies performed by Glick, Jerussi, and Zimmerberg (1977), Glick, Meibach, Cox, and Maayani (1979), and Glick and Ross (1981), a higher concentration of the *dopamine* neurotransmitter was found in the side of the brain contralateral to the direction of the rat's turning preference. In other words, rodents who preferred turning to the right had more significant dopamine levels (approximately a 15% increase) in their left hemisphere, whereas rodents who were turn biased to the left had correspondingly higher concentrations in the respective right hemisphere. These turn-biased behaviors were split evenly between the organisms, like the paw preferences mentioned earlier.

Similar results were obtained with other rat movements, such as direction of running, nocturnal circling, and even tail turning (which seemed to be a good predictor of later turning preference). Dopamine is a neurotransmitter that significantly regulates movement in organisms via the nigrostriatal pathway (a bundle of nerve fibers coursing throughout the entire cortex from hind- to forebrain regions). As Glick and colleagues suggested, it is not surprising to find movement preferences connected to dopamine imbalances in the nigrostriatal bundle of particular hemispheres, because this chemical primarily governs such behaviors in the rodent species.

Catecholamine Concentration Asymmetries in Humans

Asymmetries in neurotransmitter concentrations also have been shown in the human brain. Glick, Ross, and Hough (1982) obtained a lateralization pattern with dopamine levels that remarkably resembled the one in rodents, namely higher concentrations in the left hemisphere of right-hand-dominant subjects. Apparently, movement preferences are correlated strongly with specific chemical changes in the contralateral hemisphere of human and nonhuman species (like the rat).

Dopamine is not the only catecholamine that is represented unequally in the human cortex. To complement the excess dopamine on the left side, increased *norepinephrine* has been evident on the right side in particular structures such as the thalamus (Oke, Keller, Mefford, & Adams, 1978). It has been speculated that these catecholamine variations are responsible for the functional asymmetries reported in humans. More precisely, dopamine governs the finely controlled motor skill of speech in the left hemisphere, whereas norepinephrine regulates the more visuospatial abilities represented in the right hemisphere (Pribram & McGuinness, 1975; Tucker & Williamson, 1984). Because dopamine is the precursor substance to norepinephrine, the two hemispheres of the human brain should be regarded appropriately as functional complements, with right-sided lateralization perhaps developing from the left in much the same way as particular catecholamines (like norepinephrine from dopamine).

Whether a similar chemical-based evolutionary pattern holds for animals has yet to be determined. The information that is known about functional (i.e., behavioral) asymmetries in lower level species is reviewed next.

BEHAVIORAL BRAIN ASYMMETRIES IN ANIMALS

It already was shown that turning behaviors in rats were correlated highly with biochemical asymmetries in the brain. Behaviors in other animals also have been studied extensively across a wide variety of experimental tasks to determine whether functions are represented laterally in the cortex, which is similar to the human species (refer to chapter 1 for more detail on functional asymmetries in humans). Some of the more striking comparative findings have indicated brain lateralization of auditory functions across a number of species, including birds and monkeys.

Vocal Brain Asymmetries in Apes and Birds

Like humans, Japanese macaque monkeys have displayed right-ear advantages (REA) for sounds presented dichotically. In this case, the dichotic stimuli consisted of vocalizations unique to the macaque species. Each monkey tested was able to identify the calls much more accurately if they were fed into the right ear, meaning that the left hemisphere was more lateralized for these sounds. Monkeys of other species failed to show these ear asymmetries with the macaque calls, suggesting that lateralization of sounds was also species specific (Petersen, Beecher, Zoloth, Moody, & Stebbins, 1978).

Vocal control in several species of songbird has evidenced this same lateralization pattern. When Nottebohm (1977) sectioned (i.e., cut) the left hypoglossus nerve in adult male chaffinches and canaries, normal singing was replaced by either silent mouthing of calls or vocalization of a few properly placed elements of the call sequence. (The sound organ for songbirds—the syrinx—is innervated mainly by the hypoglossus, which feeds into the ipsilateral hemisphere.) With chaffinches, left-hypoglossal sectioning caused a permanent loss in singing, whereas with canaries, the effect was temporary and more a function of the organism's age, with younger birds recovering most of their singing via the undamaged right hypoglossus. When the right nerve was cut instead of the left, normal singing remained intact in all bird species. Nottebohm (1977) concluded that the left hypoglossal hemispheric pathway handles many of the vocalization functions in songbirds.

A morphological body side distinction would appear to be related to this functional asymmetry. Nottebohm (1979) found that the hypoglossus typically had a greater muscle mass on the left side. Supposedly larger muscles equip songbirds to more effectively vocalize their calls to other members of their species. It is no coincidence that larger brain areas associated with sound functions have been reported on the left side in apes and humans. Perhaps many animal species share a forerunner to human language involving internalized calls, which are lateralized (both functionally and spatially) within the left hemisphere (Geschwind, 1985). I return to the topic of theories of animal asymmetry at a later point in this chapter.

Other Functional Asymmetries in Animals

Studies with Monkeys. Behavioral asymmetries with monkeys also have been examined in other tasks. In one cross-modal matching study (Dewson, 1977), animals initially learned to press a red-lit panel if a tone was presented, and alternately a green-lit one when the animal discriminated noise. Afterward, unilateral lesions to the left or right auditory cortex (located within the temporal lobe) were performed. Amount of relearning on the same cross-modal matching task was assessed subsequently. Greater performance deficits were identified within the left-lesioned group, hence it was reasoned that the left hemisphere regulated important auditory integration functions in monkeys. However, several researchers (Hamilton, 1977; Walker, 1980) have critiqued Dewson's (1977) results because too small an *n* (i.e., subject number) was employed, lesions covered too wide an area, and the experimental design was a relatively simplistic one.

Deficits in the relearning of more complex auditory discriminations after unilateral lesions have typically occurred in monkeys, but, surprisingly, such impairments did not appear to be hemisphere specific (Dewson, Cowey, & Weiskrantz, 1970). Other tasks involving visual discrimination training of color, shape, and orientation dimensions also have shown similar results (Ettlinger & Gautrin, 1971; Warren & Nonneman, 1976). Apparently the absence of hemispheric asymmetries in these experiments implies that if any functions are lateralized in monkeys, they would tend to be fairly specialized ones (e.g., species-specific call identifications of macaques).

Studies with Birds. I already have indicated that vocal control is lateralized in the left hemisphere of certain species of songbirds. Other complex behaviors also display an associated lateralization in the brain of particular avian species. According to Rogers (1980), the left chick forebrain controls the behaviors of imprinting, visual discrimination learning, and auditory habituation, whereas the right forebrain regulates responses to novel or threatening stimuli as well as attack and copulatory behaviors. This behavioral distinction between more learned (left-hemispheric) and more reflexive (right-hemispheric) responses is probably due to the position of chick embryos favoring the right body side so that input to be learned is more effectively processed via the more active right eye and ear. A similar argument can be made for asymmetrical head turning in neonates to the right side upon tactile stimulation (Turkewitz, 1977).

It seems plausible that the brains of avian and human species are preprogrammed to handle information through a particular hemisphere (i.e., the left). Surprisingly, if chicks are raised in the dark before hatching, the aforementioned lateralizations are not evidenced, suggesting that environmental cues are essential for this asymmetry program to be activated (Rogers, 1980). Future research should be directed to the avian species, because some of the strongest brain-function correlates can be identified with these particular organisms.

Studies with Rats.   Denenberg, Garbanati, Sherman, Yutzey, and Kaplan (1978) reported that early environmental experiences have an effect on the rodent brain. Specifically, increased handling and enriched types of environments influenced rats' subsequent motor activity in open fields and through mazes, especially after the right hemisphere was damaged. Either the handled animals were overactive or remained virtually immobilized by the right lesions, with activity patterns being contingent on whether the rats were raised with cage mates or separately, respectively. Further studies revealed that right-damaged animals that were handled killed mice much more slowly than those that had lesions restricted to the alternate hemisphere, indicating that emotional responses such as aggression were regulated mainly by the right cortex, as with birds (Denenberg, 1981; Sherman, Garbanati, Rosen, Yutzey, & Denenberg, 1980).

The aforementioned results can be related to the morphological asymmetries already described in rats, where right cortical thickness is pronounced especially in the male members (Diamond et al., 1981). Activity and aggression behaviors might be dependent on hormonal factors that have been found to influence the physical configuration of the male rat's right brain.

Split-Brain Functions in Animals

Split-brain experiments also have been employed to examine lateralization of functions in various species. With respect to humans, the split-brain operations have worked quite successfully in containing epileptic seizures to one brain side. Specifically, the surgery consists of cutting those bands of nerve fibers (i.e., the commissures) that connect the two hemispheres together. On the whole, results have shown that patients display normal behavior except in laboratory-contrived situations where these subjects experience divided brain functions (Springer & Deutsch, 1989). Right-hemisphere spatial responses can be elicited if the left body side is stimulated, whereas left-hemisphere verbalizations can occur if the right side is activated. Typically, both types of responses cannot be displayed simultaneously, because the hemispheres are disconnected; therefore, each brain side operates somewhat independently of the other (see chapters 3 and 5 for more detail on human split-brain studies).

In animal species, these split-brain operations can be performed on relatively healthy subjects that have two fairly intact hemispheres. Myers and Sperry (1958) were among the first researchers to execute this surgery on cats. They discovered that when the corpus callosum and the optic chiasm were both sectioned (leaving the input contained on the ipsilateral side), cats initially trained on a visual discrimination assignment with one eye open and the remaining eye patched subsequently were unable to execute the task if the eye patch was switched. In fact, the animals had to learn the visual discriminations all over again. Obviously, the split-brain cats differed from their normal counterparts in that each hemisphere was isolated from the other, only receiving input from the one uncovered eye. Thus, by severing the corpus callosum, any discrimination could not be transferred to the alternate hemisphere. More current split-brain research with the cat species (Gulliksen & Voneida, 1975; Robinson & Voneida, 1973) indicated that whereas impairments do occur as a result of the surgery, behavioral deficits appear to be unrelated to hemisphere side, unlike the human findings.

Hamilton's (1977) work with rhesus monkeys confirmed this lateralization distinction between the animal and human species. Employing a variation of the Myers–Sperry surgical procedure, Hamilton (1977) taught split-brain monkeys to solve simple two-choice visual discriminations. Hemispheric differences were not evidenced, because speed of learning the discriminations was comparable for each brain side. Even when the stimuli were more difficult spatial compositions (i.e., detailed faces, two-dimensional drawings, and specific line orientations), hemispheric asymmetries were not apparent, although the tasks did take longer to learn. Hamilton's (1977) monkeys showed a left-hemisphere preference for more complex patterns, especially photographs of their own species as well as human faces. Definitely more research is required in the split-brain area before any conclusions can be derived from these picture brain preferences in monkeys.

Based on the preceding findings, one certainly can posit that humans behave differently from other organisms after split-brain surgery, display-ing very strong functional cerebral asymmetries upon recovery. As Hamil-ton (1977) advised, tasks used to examine asymmetries in split-brain animals should be modeled after human experiments if accurate infer-ences are to be made about future cross-species comparisons.

CURRENT REFLECTIONS ON ANIMAL ASYMMETRIES

Returning to the original question, "Are cerebral asymmetries unique to the human species?", a review of the literature has suggested that mor-phological, pharmacological, and/or functional brain asymmetries do ex-ist in a number of animal species. However, these differences are not as strong as those identified in humans, qualitatively speaking. The reader might then logically inquire, is the asymmetrical brain arrangement of humans truly a distinctive one within the evolutionary chain of develop-ment? Probably the best way to approach this issue is to decide whether language is a distinctively human activity or whether it contains prever-bal components that are present in lower level species.

Linguistic Uniqueness in Humans

As mentioned at the beginning of this chapter, a number of theorists (Lim-ber, 1977; Ornstein, 1977) have been strong advocates of the view that lateralization of the human brain proceeded from the use of speech, which became necessary when social units evolved. According to this position, no other species can (or ever will) acquire this unique ability because it: (a) does not have the vocal apparatus to produce the full range of speech sounds, (b) does not possess the same type of hemispheric configuration as the human, (c) does not cognitively process inputs through this highly advanced symbolic representation of thought processes into words, and (d) does not have a genetic predisposition to show these verbalizations because natural selection apparently only has designated the human spe-cies for this function over the course of time.

From a religious perspective, some (Ashbrook, 1988) even would con-tend that humans are the sole species lateralized for language to commu-nicate with the Creator and understand "The Word." In fact, the argument goes that humans are fashioned in the very image and likeness of that one reality; namely, the words represented in our left hemisphere contain those symbolic elements of the Creator's own language (or Lo-gos), which we continually seek to comprehend. It seems unlikely that other animal species are able to approach this transcendental plane of existence that the human can reach through the complex patterns of human speech.

Prelinguistic Commonalities Across Species

Another way to address the asymmetry problem is to acknowledge initially that speech is an activity reserved to humans alone, and then ask whether there are any preverbal forms of communication that some species share. If commonalities are found across species, it can be reasoned that the brain structures involved are functionally similar to each other, and that any asymmetrical differences are mainly ones of degree rather than radical departures from one species to the next.

As suggested earlier by Kimura and Archibald (1974), motor skills can be employed as a prelinguistic communication medium, in which various hand movements can represent a wide assortment of needs and expressions. *American Sign Language* (ASL) is a fine example of this technique in which the deaf learn to produce signs that symbolically represent the verbal units of English. The most current reports (Poizner, Klima, & Bellugi, 1990) have revealed that with deaf signers who experience unilateral lesions to the left hemisphere, marked ASL deficits occur, particularly in the sequencing of signs and the selection of appropriate grammar. Conversely, those subjects with right-hemisphere damage show the typical visuospatial impairments (e.g., incorrect orientations of the hand in making particular signs). Because these functional asymmetries were found in deaf signers, it can be concluded that hearing and speech are not necessary components for the development of hemispheric specialization. Therefore, the sounds of a language are not the critical factor in determining brain lateralization, as previously theorized.

Geschwind (1985) and Geschwind and Galaburda (1987) took this argument a step further. They distinguished between the external communicative aspects of language (i.e., the verbalizations) and those more internally based relevant neural codes, claiming that many animal species possessed this internal "preverbal wiring" even before speech evolved. The strongest support for this position comes from research studies executed on chimpanzees that have been trained specially in ASL.

Gardner and Gardner's (1975b) chimp, Washoe, clearly acquired a number of signs over a 4-year period and even combined signs to create new expressions. Data also indicate that ASL sentence construction is possible in ape species (Gardner & Gardner, 1975a; Terrace, 1980; Terrace, Petitto, Sanders, & Bever, 1979). The question immediately raised by critics is whether the animals are really employing a language system, understanding all the signs used as well as comprehending their meaning. However, these critics overlooked a more crucial issue. Because ASL resembles normal language with respect to its lateralization, any species that can acquire ASL is presumably representing important features of it by specialized neuronal codings within a particular hemisphere, as Geschwind (1985) proposed.

Thus, humans may not be the solitary species within the evolutionary chain that possesses cerebral asymmetries; lower level organisms might share the same structural codes as humans, and hence the basic asymmetrical blueprint for thought and subsequent action. Although Geschwind's (1985) ideas are still highly speculative, they do serve as signposts to future neuroscientists who are just beginning to discover the answer to whether animal asymmetries are directly comparable to human ones.

SUMMARY AND CONCLUSIONS

To summarize the major points of this chapter, although hand preference in lower lever species was not a good predictor of brain lateralization (as it was in humans), the following animal asymmetries were obtained in a number of experiments:

1. Morphological differences were primarily evidenced in apes and rats, with language-related areas being larger and cortical hemispheres being typically thicker, respectively.

2. Pharmacological differences also were shown, with higher concentrations of dopamine residing in the hemisphere contralateral to the turning preference side in rats and dominant hand in humans.

3. Behavioral asymmetries, particularly in the lateralization of auditory functions within the left hemisphere (e.g., vocalizations and singing), were reported in specific species of monkey and songbird. Other acquired behaviors and discriminations of avian species were regulated by the left hemisphere as well. Conversely, emotional expressions and activity levels mainly were controlled by the right hemisphere in rats and chicks. However, split-brain studies to date have produced the least encouraging results in functional lateralization across species.

4. Finally, preverbal components of human speech were identified in those animal species who learned the symbolic sign language of the deaf (i.e., ASL). Hemispheric specialization for particular ASL components recently has been found for brain-damaged deaf signers and a similar lateralization has been claimed for ape signers, with the signs being coded in the left hemisphere and their physical expression being represented in the right hemisphere.

At several points within this chapter, it was indicated that the strength of these animal asymmetries was not as pronounced as human types. This does not imply that hemispheric differences are especially unique to the human species. Quite the contrary, several researchers like Geschwind (1985) have proposed that an internal, neural blueprint for brain lateralization exists for most species. Researchers presumably need to design tasks that can most effectively tap into this preverbal code to accurately assess which asymmetries show the strongest correlation across species, as Hamilton (1977) contended. Therefore, the uniqueness associated with particular asymmetries should reflect a relative rather than an absolute brain difference as research work continues to proceed on cross-species comparisons.

Chapter 3 explores cerebral asymmetries from another perspective, namely different cognitive styles, with sequential and holistic information processing being represented in the left and right cerebral hemispheres, respectively.

Two Brains, Two Cognitive Styles?

So far I have primarily differentiated left and right hemispheric functions in terms of the traditional verbal–nonverbal dichotomy. However, as stated in chapter 2, nonverbal organisms can learn a symbolic language (i.e., ASL) that apparently is coded in much the same manner as our verbal type of communication, with sign acquisition represented in the left hemisphere and sign expression in the right (Poizner, Klima, & Bellugi, 1990). Therefore, verbal ability does not seem to be the only function mediated by the left brain side.

At this point, it might be more appropriate to discuss hemispheric functions by another distinction, namely, a *left-analytic* versus a *right-holistic* mode of information processing. According to this more useful dichotomy originally posited by Ornstein (1977), each hemisphere is specialized for a different type of thinking or *cognitive style*, with the left side employing a more sequential, analytic thought process and the right a more holistic, gestalt frame of reference. Subscribers to this view further noted that the left cognitive style is more representative of the logical, rational type of thinking exercised in Western societies, whereas the right style is more applicable to the intuitive, mystical thinking of cultures and religions in the East. Table 3.1 puts the aforementioned distinctions into a better perspective.

Ornstein's (1977) cognitive approach is discussed in further detail, specifically by describing how each mode operates and then by providing sufficient evidence from clinical and normal brain studies in support of this recently theorized dichotomy.

TABLE 3.1
Cognitive Styles Associated with Cerebral Hemispheres

Left Hemisphere	Right Hemisphere
Verbal	Nonverbal, visuospatial
Sequential, temporal	Simultaneous, gestalt
Analytic	Synthetic
Rational	Intuitive
Western thought	Eastern thought

From *Left Brain, Right Brain* (p. 284) by S. P. Springer and G. Deutsch, 1989, New York, W. H. Freeman. Copyright 1989 by W. H. Freeman. Adapted by permission.

THE TWO COGNITIVE MODES CHARACTERIZED

The Left-Analytic Mode

The cognitive style of the left hemisphere has been called analytic, basically because this brain side breaks stimulus information down into its separate components or features. The parts are then processed, one at a time, in a very orderly, sequential fashion (Galin, 1979). Another way to define this cognitive style is that the left hemisphere uses a serial (rather than parallel) type of processing to analyze the relevant components. It logically follows that the greater the number of items presented, the longer the period of time required to process these complicated stimulus arrays (Cohen, 1973). Garner (1978) even suggested that some stimuli are more amenable to this serial analysis over others, especially ones that possess very salient dimensions or highly discernible features.

A primary function of this left-analytic mode involves the temporal ordering of relevant inputs abstracted from the array. That is, the placement of these features within a particular sequence is extremely important. What comes first, second, third, and so on makes a difference in the way the information is processed and eventually stored in memory.

For temporal ordering to occur, the following conditions have to be satisfied: succession, duration, and causality (Ornstein, 1977). *Succession* refers to a specific past, present, and future time frame in which the information is arranged linearly. *Duration* deals with the relative period of time devoted to each abstracted item within this past–present–future continuum. This processing period is an extremely malleable one, continually being restructured from our most recent memories to ones more permanently established on episodes in the past. The final condition, *causality*, has its underpinnings in the first two requirements. Simply put, *causality* means that the occurrence of present as well as future events is determined by ones that already transpired in the past.

With respect to analytic processing, identification and recognition of key stimuli are highly dependent on whether the previously presented arrays contained a number of similar as opposed to different, more discriminable features. Ornstein (1977) and other proponents of this view (Galin, 1979) argued that the left hemisphere is more functionally adept than the right at handling this temporal ordering of inputs, with its associated dimensions of succession, duration, and causality.

This linear conceptualization of time not only shapes the thought processes of the left hemisphere, but is shaped by the cultural context. It has been observed that Western society is oriented very heavily around the "clock perspective," where time is broken down into smaller and smaller units that can be measured very precisely. Thus, the left-linear mode of consciousness is grounded strongly in the environment wherein one is reared, with an analytic frame of reference being molded from these experiential encounters (Bergson, 1965). Heredity does not play an insignificant role in the development of this cognitive style asymmetry. Rather, the hemispheric specialization of the left hemisphere for sequential (or propositional) thinking works hand in hand with relevant cues identified within the more technologically advanced Western culture, such as learning to abstract central from incidental features in highly complex information patterns (Bogen, 1975).

The Right-Holistic Mode

There is another cognitive style linked with the right hemisphere that, until recently, was relegated to minor status (in fact, texts deliberately used the word *minor* in reference to this mode and its associated hemisphere). The style is, of course, right-holistic, and the main reason that it has been treated in such an irrelevant (often irreverent) fashion over the decades has more to do with sociological-based distinctions than neurological. According to Ornstein (1977, 1978), Western culture has placed a good deal of emphasis on the verbal-analytic style of information processing, because this was the reasoning most prized in that particular society. However, Ornstein (1977, 1978) affirmed that societal conceptions are changing toward the more practical view that both modes are needed to understand human cognitions, and that, depending on one's point of view, each hemisphere's cognitive style is major to the total comprehension process.

The right-holistic mode is particularly good at grasping patterns of relations between the component parts of a stimulus array, integrating many inputs simultaneously to eventually arrive at a complete configuration (i.e., a gestalt). Cohen (1973) indicated that one of the unique aspects of this mode is that processing time is not dependent on the number of features that make up the overall pattern (as was the case with the left-analytic mode), and so the argument follows that the right hemisphere exhibits a parallel rather than a serial type of processing in apprehending the stimulus configuration.

Garner (1978) further mentioned that certain stimuli possess characteristics that are more compatible with right-holistic processing, as opposed to left-analytic processing. Some of the more common stimulus properties include simple wholes or blobs, which cannot be subdivided into specific features; templates, which represent the idealized examples of particular classes of objects; and plus configurations, which represent more than the sum of their individual parts.

Another very interesting function of this mode is stimulus closure: From incomplete patterns or missing elements, a whole configuration still can be abstracted in the same way that humans bridge experiential gaps to form spatial-cognitive maps of their surroundings (Nebes, 1978). A physiological distinction even has been advanced by some theorists to differentiate right processing from left. In effect, spatial and topographic skills are represented more diffusely in the right hemisphere, thus allowing even infrahuman organisms to form a single, supramodal gestalt from a variety of sensory inputs. Conversely, motor skills and language are seen to be represented more focally or localized in the left hemisphere, enabling only certain species (humans) to handle these functions competently (Semmes, 1968).

One characteristic not found in right-holistic processing is the temporal ordering of elements. Rather, a present centeredness or timeless experience has been associated with this cognitive mode in which all events are perceived to occur immediately and simultaneously. This style of thinking is reflected across many Eastern cultures where no distinction is made between past and present, and time is considered to be an ontological absurdity. The nonlinear mode is cultivated deliberately in these Eastern, mystical traditions for the purpose of arriving at a more accurate picture of reality not based on time, linear consciousness, or the physical changes of this illusory world (Lee, 1973).

Ornstein (1977) suggested that Westerners only can reach this timeless dimension by altering their state of consciousness from the more normal one in which analytic reasoning is invested heavily. Psychedelic drugs often produce this altered infinite present experience, specifically by increasing the amount of information to be registered by the brain. Marijuana and mescaline users typically report lengthier (and sometimes indefinite) durations in which more stimulation is perceived each and every moment. Occasionally a complete indifference to the altered time perceptions has been found, with subjects remarking that the "plentiness and fullness" of time are totally irrelevant to the ongoing state of mind in which they are existing (Huxley, 1979; Tart, 1971).

Another altered state that directly taps into the right-holistic mode is one experienced every night when asleep: dreaming. While in this state, the subject is loosened from the temporal and spatial constraints of the everyday world. Past and future can now exist side by side with the indistinct present, and time no longer flows forward as in linear consciousness (Webb, 1979). Dream researchers have commented that this altered state is regarded by many as very mysterious, chiefly because of a different medium being employed that is quite unusual and unfamiliar: thinking in pictures (or gestalts). Upon awakening, the subject's left-analytic mode cannot express in words what the right-holistic mode has experienced that previous night (Hall, 1979). It would appear that brief encounters with the right-cognitive style shows that another reality can exist, in which an entirely different type of thinking dominates (at least for the short duration).

EXPERIMENTAL EVIDENCE FOR THE COGNITIVE MODE DICHOTOMY

The laboratory findings with split- and normal-brain subjects in relation to this analytic–holistic processing dichotomy are now considered. Although some of the research work is sparse, certain trends in the literature can still be noted, which affirm the existence of distinct cognitive styles in particular brain hemispheres.

Clinical Brain Studies

Holistic Closure in the Right Hemisphere.   Perhaps the strongest case can be made for holistic processing in the right hemisphere when stimulus closure is investigated in split-brain patients. Levy-Agresti and Sperry (1968) were among the first to show that these subjects were able to choose the appropriate two-dimensional representations for completed three-dimensional solids when the left hand (right hemisphere) was involved more often. More current studies by Nebes (1978) and others (Zaidel & Sperry, 1974) have replicated these results: commissurotomy subjects demonstrate a right-hemispheric holistic superiority in tasks that require them to (a) tactually select components that would complete visually perceived designs, (b) match a given part of a geometric form (e.g., an arc of a circle) to the appropriately sized shape, or (c) decide which solid alternative corresponds to a fragmented figure.

In many of these tasks, the right hand (left hemisphere) adopts a more analytic style, concentrating on the specific features or details of the configuration (e.g., length of lines or size of angles) instead of the entire pattern. This strategy apparently results in the left hemisphere's less accurate matching of parts to their respective whole.

Although the right hemisphere is more capable of perceiving the holistic pattern to elements, a gradient of lateralization still exists in part-to-whole matching. With shapes that are less free form and more rule bound, the left hemisphere shows a striking superiority to the right in abstracting overall configurations from their given features (Franco & Sperry, 1977). Therefore, one must exercise some caution in designating all holistic processing to the right hemisphere. Some of this thinking can be performed by the left side of the brain, primarily with components that are arranged structurally to form only certain shapes.

Nonetheless, the commissurotomy studies indicated that the right hemisphere is generally better at perceiving part-to-whole identifications, especially ones involving more free-form shapes. The strongest cognitive asymmetries are evidenced further in tasks requiring active touch (i.e., continual handling and manipulation of the objects by the left hand), with weaker ones being displayed in nontactual, visual discriminations (Gazzaniga & LeDoux, 1978; Harris & Carr, 1981).

Image Formation: Cognitions Restricted to One Hemisphere.
A right-hemispheric involvement has been proposed recently for the formation of images, because they possess a unique visual, nonverbal nature and they are structured on an overall pattern (or gestalt) of relevant features. Although a review of the split-brain literature does not support this asymmetrical view (Erlichman & Barrett, 1983), specific studies have shown that, depending on the nature of the particular task, one hemisphere appears to be more specialized than the other in processing various images.

For instance, Farah, Gazzaniga, Holtzman, and Kosslyn (1985) found that commissurotomy patients did much better on imaging the lower-case versions of uppercase letters when the inputs were presented in the right visual field (left hemisphere). More current work by Corballis and Sergent (1988) replicated these results. However, when the task required split-brain subjects to mentally rotate their images to decide whether the letters were in normal form or backward, the left visual field (right hemisphere) was faster and more accurate in making the judgments.

Based on this research, one might conclude that mental imagery is not a cognitive function solely restricted to a single hemisphere. Rather, it contains components more suitable for right-holistic processing (e.g., overall pattern rotation) and others more appropriate for left-analytic processing (e.g., detailed discriminations of lowercase letters).

Left-Hemispheric Temporal Ordering in the Brain Damaged. Although few studies have investigated the factor of information sequencing in split-brain subjects, reports have come in from other clinical groups, primarily those with unilateral brain damage. Early findings revealed that left-hemisphere (not right-hemisphere) damage seriously interfered with subjects' perception of temporal ordering (Carmon & Nachshon, 1971). Reviews of the clinical evidence to date also tend to confirm the left hemisphere's specialization for sequential processing and the temporal resolution of information, irrespective of its spatial complexity (Carmon, 1978; Mills & Rollman, 1980).

Over the years, it has been known that laterality differences in music perception exist in the brain damaged, with judgments involving tonal memory, melodic pattern, loudness, and associated timbre more a function of the right hemisphere (Bogen & Gordon, 1971; Milner, 1962), and discriminations involving musical duration, sequencing, and rhythm more restricted to the left (Alajouanine, 1948). Thus, even temporal and nontemporal aspects of music perception can be divided along this cognitive mode continuum, extending from left analytic to right holistic, respectively.

Dream Deficits Following Surgery: A Case for Duality. The right–left cognitive duality also can be applied, on a very limited scale, to the dreams of particular clinical populations. Researchers have noted that one complaint common to many split-brain patients is that they no longer dream after the surgery, apparently because they are no longer able to verbalize (let alone analyze) the various details of this holistic state via the left hemisphere, because it is disconnected from the right (Springer & Deutsch, 1989). However, further research has indicated that commissurotomy subjects can provide some descriptions of their dreams if they are awakened immediately upon entry into the rapid eye movement (REM) state (Greenwood, Wilson, & Gazzaniga, 1977). Their recall of the dream content still remains at a lower level than untreated epileptics', suggesting that some memory deficits do occur as a result of the surgery (Zaidel & Sperry, 1974). Damage to the right parietal lobe of the brain also produces similar dream impairments (Humphrey & Zangwill, 1951).

When normal hemispheric functioning is disrupted, analytic processing may become so dissociated from the holistic that an even more non-recallable dream state is produced. Or, in all the studies cited, the patients may have started with poorer memories. As Springer and Deutsch (1989) advised, more work needs to be performed with clinical subjects before, as well as after, surgery to determine if general memory abilities are affected, along with more specific recall of dreams. Only then can more accurate assessments be made with respect to the analytic–holistic dichotomy.

Normal Brain Studies

Visual Processing of Facial Stimuli.   A left-visual field (LVF) superiority already has been reported in normal subjects for the recognition of photographed faces as well as schematic drawings of faces (Patterson & Bradshaw, 1975; Suberi & McKeever, 1977). These tasks basically had subjects match a laterally presented test face with a target face that was viewed previously. However, the reverse superiority (a RVF advantage) occurred when the test face closely resembled the target, with the exception of a single feature that had to be discerned. The experimenters of these field studies (Bradshaw, Taylor, Patterson, and Nettleton, 1980) concluded that subjects had switched from a holistic type of processing to one that was more analytic (i.e., left hemispheric or right field) as the task requirements changed from general facial recognitions to more specific feature discriminations. According to Bradshaw and Sherlock (1982), even nonfacelike stimuli (e.g., bugs) have produced similar holistic left-field and analytic right-field advantages, with the asymmetries typically more pronounced in subjects who had familiarized themselves sufficiently with the task.

More supportive evidence for the cognitive mode dichotomy comes from chimeric facial studies. Specifically, each chimeric figure (or split face) has the right half of one face fused with the left half of a completely different face at the midline. Normal subjects generally experience perceptual completion of these figures (i.e., the two distinct facial sides are combined into a composite pattern in which only one face is perceived). Further, when subjects are asked to select the face that most closely resembles the chimeric figure, they generally prefer the picture based on the left-field half and more often point to it with either hand (Schwartz & Smith, 1980). Earlier findings with split-brain patients tend to confirm these LVF advantages (Levy, Trevarthen, & Sperry, 1972), highlighting the right hemisphere's holistic style of processing the split-face inputs.

Auditory Processing of Tonal Sequences and Melodic Arrangements.   Asymmetries also have been identified with particular tonal sequences: simple arrangements have been known to elicit a left-ear advantage (LEA) in normal subjects, whereas more complex types have produced an alternate REA (Halperin, Nachshon, & Carmon, 1973; Robinson & Solomon, 1974). Based on these quite consistent results, several researchers have commented that the left hemisphere (via the right ear) is more capable of processing the internal structure of very complex tones arranged sequentially across time (Davis & Wada, 1977b; Gordon, 1978). Some authors (Mills & Rollman, 1980; Schwartz & Tallal, 1980) even speculated that this specialized timing mechanism in the left hemisphere is a vital component to the perception of speech, because it allows for more efficient processing of rapidly changing acoustic patterns (of which language is basically composed). Thus, the left hemisphere's superiority for language might be derived from its unique ability to analyze temporally ordered inputs.

More extensive studies involving musical sequences have provided additional support for this left analytic–right holistic dichotomy. Bever and Chiarello (1974) were among the first to show that laterality differences in music perception are strongly dependent on the level of subjects' listening skills. In their research, more experienced musicians demonstrated a REA (or left-hemisphere advantage) for melodic presentations, whereas less skilled nonmusicians exhibited a LEA (or right-hemispheric advantage) for the same sequences. To explain these results, Bever and Chiarello (1974) suggested that more educated listeners perceive melodies as primarily consisting of harmonious, yet complex sets of component parts, whereas more naive subjects only are able to focus on the simpler, overall contours of the melodies. Comparable findings have been reported in recent years (Bever, 1980; Kellar & Bever, 1980), revealing that particular aspects of music perception can be handled by the left hemisphere, especially those that involve more complex, linearly related dimensions (such as ordering, sequencing, and rhythm).

I propose that the normal brain hemispheres operate according to an informational complexity–internal strategic interactive model for auditory processing. Specifically, the right hemisphere is more involved with simpler sequences and more basic subject listening capabilities. Alternately, more left-hemispheric processing occurs with very complex auditory patterns combined with a higher level of listening strategies. Ornstein's (1977) cognitive mode dichotomy fits into this framework, with the analytic operation being more a function of highly detailed, complex processing and the holistic operation more a general, somewhat simpler type of abstraction. Level of subject aptitude with music can be another way to distinguish hemispheric functions, with greater aptitude more conducive to left-style processing and weaker aptitude more to right-style processing (Gaede, Parsons, & Bertera, 1978). Whatever terminology is adopted, one conclusion is clearly evident: The left hemisphere handles auditory (as well as visual) inputs with a very different set of cognitions than the right. Some attentional components that comprise each of the distinctive hemispheric styles will now be considered.

Lateral Eye Movements: An Accurate Measure of Cognitive Functioning?

Kinsbourne (1974) and Trevarthen (1972) argued that auditory as well as visual asymmetries in normal subjects actually reflect an attentional reallocation toward the body side contralateral to the hemisphere that is more specialized to register that particular input. For instance, speech requires an analytical type of processing. Thus, the respective left hemisphere, which is more primed to receive this material, focuses more attention onto the contralateral right ear. Trevarthen (1972) specifically likened this "covert attentional shift in body space" to an orientation-type reflex that is governed exclusively by the more activated hemisphere.

Conjugate lateral-eye movements (or CLEM) appear to be a vital component of Trevarthen's (1972) contralateral orienting response. That is, the cognitive activity occurring in one hemisphere triggers the respective eye movements on the opposite body side. Therefore, left looking would reflect more right-hemisphere activity, whereas right looking correspondingly would show more left-hemisphere involvement (Bakan, 1969; Gur & Gur, 1977). Various types of questions have been employed across many studies to assess the direction of these eye movements, and, subsequently, hemispheric cognitions. As predicted, those that involved more analytic inquiries (e.g., provide this term's definition, solve this simple arithmetic problem, spell this word) have produced more right CLEMs, whereas ones of a more holistic nature (e.g., identify this melodic pattern, visualize this geometric form, locate self in this diagram) have generated more left CLEMs (Galin & Ornstein, 1974: Kocel, Galin, Ornstein, & Merrin, 1972). The direction of these eye movements also has been fairly consistent within subjects, providing some index of preferred cognitive style, with more left looking reflecting a greater imaginative, right type of personality, and more right looking reflecting a stronger rational, left type (Day, 1964).

However, almost half the studies to date have been unable to produce this CLEM effect with particular questions (Shevrin, Smokler, & Wolf, 1979; Takeda & Yoshimura, 1979). This raises an interesting problem: are CLEMs really an accurate measure of hemispheric activation in normal subjects? Ehrlichman and Weinberger (1978) reported that there are so many factors determining ocular movements that any conclusion reached is, at best, a gross oversimplification. A further deficiency noted by these reviewers is that a single operational definition for what constitutes a CLEM has not been reached. Is it the first or last ocular movement? Is it the longest lasting fixation or the number of fixations over a given period? Is it always a zeroing in on an imagined target straight ahead of the viewer? Others have remarked that before one claims that a certain direction of looking is indicative of a favored cognitive style, some relevant external variables need to be considered. In particular, Gur, Gur, and Harris (1975) found that where the experimenter is located critically affects the pattern of the eye movements, with position in front of the subject rarely producing the lateralized ocular behaviors. Rosenberg (1980) even advocated the use of external stimuli (e.g., moving stripes) to avoid many of the problems currently inherent in the CLEM technique.

At the present time, the relationship between eye movements and cognitive preference is regarded as a fragile one; perhaps future experimentation will solidify this weak link, but perhaps not. Only further investigations with CLEMs will reveal the true story about cognitive functioning in the normal brain hemispheres.

The Serial–Parallel Distinction: A Critical Reexamination. As theorized previously by Cohen (1973), the left hemisphere is said to employ a slower, serial type of processing, whereas the right hemisphere is unaffected by the number of features that comprise the overall configuration and so processes all parts in a faster, parallel fashion. Although Cohen's (1973) serial–parallel processing distinction between hemispheres intuitively sounds like a reasonable variation of Ornstein's (1977) analytic–holistic dichotomy, it has not received strong support in the normal brain literature. Only one study performed by Ohgishi (1978) suggested the possibility that the left hemisphere might, in fact, be a serial analyzer. Other findings have indicated, surprisingly, that both hemispheres process information (whether configurational or letter stimuli) in the same manner. Even parallel processing has been attributed to the left as well as right hemisphere in some of the experimental tasks (Polich, 1980; Umilta, Salmaso, Bagnara, & Simion, 1979).

Bradshaw, Bradley, and Patterson (1976) and Bradshaw and Nettleton (1983) also made the convincing argument that the serial–parallel distinction may not be as useful as the Ornstein (1977) dichotomy. Although their studies have shown faster identify matching by the right hemisphere for test and target stimuli that are the same and slower judgments by the left hemisphere for stimuli that are different, not all *same* and *different* decisions can be classified so nicely by parallel right- and serial left-side processing, respectively. Variations from this pattern include the following: Facial test stimuli that completely differ from their targets produce a right-hemisphere (not left-hemisphere) superiority, and those configurations that can be identified only by their separate features demonstrate a left-hemisphere superiority for both same and different judgments.

Based on these conflicting results, it probably is a good idea to abandon Cohen's (1973) classification and adhere to the more empirically supported analytic–holistic one in further references to hemispheric styles.

HEMISPHERICITY: A RELIANCE ON ONE COGNITIVE STYLE

A related topic to cognitive styles is the concept of *hemisphericity*, a term first introduced by Bogen (1969a, 1975). He basically defined *hemisphericity* as an individual's greater reliance on one cognitive style of processing over another, with either the left hemisphere's propositional–analytic mode of thought dominating or the right hemisphere's appositional–holistic type. Bogen's (1969a, 1975) *hemisphericity* is further examined with respect to individual, occupational, cultural, as well as educational preferences with particular cognitive styles.

Individual Preferences

As mentioned earlier in this chapter, some individuals favor one cognitive mode more than another to solve particular problems, with left-hemisphere-oriented people employing a more verbal–analytic approach and right-hemisphere-oriented people using a more spatial–holistic strategy. Characteristics also have been attributed to such individuals: Left-moders typically are described as more logical and rational, whereas right-moders are more imaginative and creative (Arndt & Berger, 1978; Zenhausen, 1978).

In addition, certain mood patterns have been associated with these cognitive styles. A "tarnishing of reality" often is attributed to a recessive analytic style. When damage occurs to the left hemisphere, individuals often report that they are tottering on the edge of a catastrophe or that they have "been done in" by what has transpired (Bear & Fedio, 1977). It would seem that the left-analytic style does more than just rationally problem solve; it also smooths over any major problems or traumas experienced in reality. Moreover, research has shown that an overly positive view of the world can be linked with the respective right-holistic style. Right-moders usually overestimate good feelings and drastically underestimate experienced negative circumstances. Thus, the right style is claimed to polish perceptions to such a point that happy feelings will dominate over sad ones (Mandell, 1980).

Another way to look at these results is to say that the analytic style reasons out the mood that will be expressed, realizing the self-destructive nature of feelings such as depression and worry. On the other hand, the holistic style attempts to present a more optimistic view of life (sometimes to the point of nonrationality) for the express purpose of motivating individuals to live each day completely and to the *fullest*. Researchers definitely find some appeal in the idea that differences in individuals' perceptions of reality may be related to differences in the degree to which they use the two cognitive styles, because studies continue to be published in this area.

Occupational Preferences

Early work conducted by Bakan (1969) indicated that, depending on the major, college students utilize one cognitive style of processing over another. Those who majored in science, math, and engineering fields at one university generally looked more to the right (left-hemisphere dominance), whereas those who pursued literature or one of the other areas in humanities showed more left lateral eye movements (right-hemisphere dominance). Apparently the scientific disciplines elicited more analytic processing in the students, whereas the liberal arts were processed by the more imaginative, holistic mode. However, Springer and Deutsch (1989) critique Bakan's (1969) findings, claiming that CLEMs may not be a reliable measure of hemisphericity (as already pointed out).

A later study by Dabbs (1980) was much more supportive of occupational preferences in cognitive style, which basically were assessed by the amount of blood flow distributed to each cerebral hemisphere in various college student majors. As predicted by Dabbs (1980), those who declared English as a major had a greater blood flow in the left hemisphere, whereas those who majored in such creative disciplines as architecture had a correspondingly higher level in the right hemisphere. The less active brain sides generated lower temperatures for each of these majors, suggesting that interest in a particular career path could distribute cognitive activity asymmetrically, with greater hemispheric processing being devoted to compatible fields of study.

Subjects already within particular professions also have been examined by several experimenters with respect to hemisphericity. Galin and Ornstein (1974) discovered that lawyers, as opposed to ceramists, exhibited greater fluctuations in EEG left-hemisphere activity when tasks changed from language-related assignments to ones of a more spatial nature. A similar study by Arndt and Berger (1978) revealed that, whereas lawyers and sculptors showed the same visual-field advantages, the type of task dictated which hemisphere was more active across subjects (with more left activity for letter stimuli and more right for facial patterns). Clearly, more work needs to be performed on occupational hemisphericity before one can say assuredly that certain professions require a particular type of cognitive processing. For now, the most that can be said is that some patterns of hemispheric activity change as a function of occupation and/or given assignment. Whether these differences are truly indicative of cerebral organizational ones still remains a mystery to be solved by future scientists. Perhaps a new direction in which to orient one's attention is whether hemisphericity can be measured by paper-and-pencil tests designed to determine one's preferred cognitive style by means of major and/or career interest inventory questions (Torrance & Reynolds, 1980). Only time can tell whether this approach will prove to be a fruitful one.

Cultural Preferences

Researchers have examined other cultures to determine if ways of thinking are affected by the background in which one is reared. The Hopi Indian culture is one such background that has been looked at extensively by Bogen, DeZare, TenHouten, and Marsh (1972) and Rogers, TenHouten, Kaplan, and Gardiner (1977). Based on their findings, it would appear that Hopi Indians are strongly right-thought oriented in comparison with other groups (e.g., rural and urban Whites). On one test that measured the extent to which subjects completed figures from separated parts shown to them (*The Street Gestalt Completion Test*), Hopi Indians holistically scored the highest, followed by urban Black women and urban Black men, respectively. Greater brain activity in the right hemisphere also has been recorded in Hopis when they listened to stories in their native language as opposed to English, further confirming the claim that this particular culture is more right modal.

Other American Indian cultures have been studied as well, with some interesting inconsistencies being reported across various tasks. Navajo subjects typically show LEAs (right-hemisphere dominance) for consonant–vowel syllables presented dichotically. However, they show the same RVF advantages (left-hemisphere dominance) as Anglo college students when asked to name outlines of objects presented tachistoscopically (Scott, Hynd, Hunt, & Weed, 1979). McKeever (1981) attempted to make sense of these seemingly contradictory findings by suggesting that English vocalization was required in the tachistoscopic assignment, unlike its predecessor, which did not sufficiently control for ear-order presentations. He argued that there is no solid evidence for right-hemispheric specialization for language in Navajo Indians. Of course, the native language of these subjects was not assessed as had been done in some of the aforementioned Hopi studies (Rogers et al., 1977). Hence it might be plausible to suggest that a holistic dominance still exists, at least for the Navajo's own tongue.

As Ornstein (1977) remarked, American Indian cultures and other less technologically advanced societies (e.g., the Trobrianders and other island people) do not possess the same linear construction of time as we do. Their speech patterns are, at best, jerky and very disconnected (e.g., "thou-bring-here-we-plant-coconut"); microscopic time frames are almost entirely absent (the period it takes to boil rice might be the smallest unit); and a rootedness in each present moment is clearly visible (e.g., "this-here-it-emerge-sprout-cut-eat"). Anthropologists certainly would agree with Ornstein (1977) that only by looking at the native language of these various cultures can one hope to understand their cognitive styles, which might be more right holistic than our conventional experiments would suggest (Zook & Dwyer, 1976).

Eastern religions and cultures (i.e., Indian, Buddhist, and Sufi) emphasize right-modal thinking over left. Past research has shown that calm, restful right-brain alpha rhythms can be produced while inside the Yogi meditative state. Yogis can respond further to a series of repetitive stimuli at the same reaction level when not meditating (Anand, Chhina, & Singh, 1972). Zen masters apparently can still remain "tuned in" to objects even during their contemplative state; Westerners, on the other hand, display the usual habituation "tune out" response to continual, repetitive stimulation (Kasamatsu & Hirai, 1972). This habituation behavior, according to Ornstein (1977) and more recently by Ashbrook (1988), seems to be a function of left-mode thinking. Therefore, one must "free oneself" from this state of consciousness, redirect attention to the right cognitive style, and eventually experience objects "afresh" each and every moment without habituation "setting in."

This Eastern *dishabituation* or *deautomatization* process can be learned by Westerners, but it is not an easy one to achieve. An entire "shakeup of cognitive structures and current conceptualizations" must be performed by subjects, because it is only in the destructuring of present reality that the right reality can be experienced (Grinder & Bandler, 1976). One technique that has proved to be useful in changing Western cultural hemisphericity involves focusing attention onto a single object within the environment (e.g., a blue vase). By continual concentration on every feature of the stimulus, an almost hypnotic (sometimes mystical) state is achieved, in which a blanking out of the left reality occurs, to be replaced by a consciousness of "unity and oneness" (Deikman, 1972). After the subject reenters the left reality, he or she will carry back some of those right-modal experiences and perceive everyday objects in an entirely new fashion.

Other deautomatization methods can be employed besides this type of concentrative meditation: fasting, ritualistic dancing, and remaining within unchanging *ganzfeld* environments. Even ingesting psychoactive drugs and other compounds can produce similar experiences. All these techniques have one common ingredient, namely the disruption of the linear mode of consciousness of everyday life. It is encouraging to know that any Westerner can deconstruct present reality to arrive at a more right-minded experience. All it takes is time and the desire to achieve this timeless, desireless state. As Ashbrook (1988) and Tart (1990) mentioned, Westerners are not locked into a particular cultural hemisphericity. In fact, not only can we change our dominant left way of thinking, but we also can synthesize it with the more Eastern, holistic style.

Educational Preferences

Bogen (1975, 1977) has done some extensive writing on the educational aspects of hemisphericity, indicating that Western society has overemphasized the three Rs (reading, writing, and arithmetic) in the school system and subsequently has educated students "lopsidedly" toward left-propositional thinking rather than right-appositional thinking. Bogen (1975, 1977) suggested that educators should encourage more right-hemisphere learning in the classroom so that the other half of the student's potential can be actualized (i.e., the artistic and musical talents, the creative insights, as well as the spatial problem-solving abilities). Bogen (1975, 1977) particularly advocated the use of different instructional techniques to boost right-hemisphere thinking; to this end, more hands-on laboratories and field experiences should be included in the educational curriculum, at the expense of the more traditional (yet always favored) lectures and seminars.

Other writers have taken Bogen's lead and have listed some alternative holistic approaches to solve this educational problem. Edwards (1979) recommended that students be involved in the fine arts, particularly drawing. Her exercises specifically consist of students copying objects that are presented upside-down. Edwards's (1979) view is that the left hemisphere will not be able to label or analyze the "topsy-turvy" items because they will be, for the most part, unrecognizable. Thus, the right hemisphere will be able to exercise its holistic style fully, without being inhibited by its analytic counterpart. Wheatley (1977) suggested that the right hemisphere can be more involved in the less creative, more logical disciplines such as mathematics if spatial relationships are emphasized to a greater extent, through the use of various puzzles, mosaics, and other geometrical forms (e.g., tessellations, tangrams, cubes, and pentominoes), which can be included easily into the child's curriculum.

Although Prince's (1978) ideas on developing right-brain thinking were directly applicable to the business world, they can be extended logically to the educational environment. For instance, having a musical background to complement any material that is delivered, as well as guessing the major topic that is described in fairly lengthy detail, are two ways that the student population can acquire a holistic style more effectively. With respect to the teaching of reading skills in the classroom, linguistic processing (via the "phonetic" method) also should be balanced more properly with the right-spatial type. To achieve this, a "whole word" method should consist of children visualizing an entire image of each word, in which the size, shape, and phonemic features are included. This visualization-and-say strategy not only will benefit the neglected right side, but it also will help the left in attaining a greater mastery in word pronunciation (Southgate & Roberts, 1970). Carmon, Gordon, Bental, and Harnes (1977) found the visualization-and-say method quite effective with dyslexics who have suffered from left-hemisphere damage. In fact, reading scores improved in such groups as the nondamaged right hemisphere gradually adopted this more visual, holistic strategy.

More recently, Stanish and Singletary (1987) and Stanish (1989) attempted to integrate analytic and holistic instructional styles into any educational content area. They based their "ambidextrous" or balanced-brain approach on many of Eberle's (1982, 1987) creative games designed to develop the imagination. In Stanish's most current curriculum targeted at Grades 2–8, a series of exercises is provided to teachers so that the student's creative right-thought processes are stimulated further.

Two examples of these exercises are illustrated in Figs. 3.1 and 3.2. In the "finish drawing this animal" assignment, the student is required to visualize holistically the figure and "close" the portion already provided, and also is asked to image an entirely new creature never encountered before in reality. The analytic style then comes into play, taking its cue from the right half: features are filled in, a name (or label) is assigned to the drawn-in animal, and a specific color is provided. In the "put together a prototype" exercise, right-modal thinking is emphasized again; a "marvelous invention" has to be constructed from the cut-out parts and a holistic strategy has to be used once more. The left-analytic style logically flows from the right when the student is required to write a descriptive paragraph about the prototype for patent purposes. It would appear that Stanish (1989), like Bogen before him, wanted to correct the imbalance within the educational system by prioritizing right thinking and viewing left processing, if anything, as a logical extension of the right and not vice versa. It remains to be seen whether, in the long run, such educators' efforts will pay off for students.

Finish Drawing This Animal

Make it an unusual one-of-a-kind mammal.
Draw in some interesting features.
Give it a name.
Give it some color.
Give it some fleas.
Give it some friends.
Draw and color in some background environment.
Tell some additional things about it.

- *fluency*
- *originality*
- *elaboration*
- *visualization*
- *transformations*
- *probable flexibility*

FIG. 3.1.   An example of one of Stanish's (1989) educational exercises, "Finish Drawing This Animal," involving both holistic and analytic cognitive styles. From *Ambidextrous Mind Book* (p. 19) by B. Stanish, 1989, Carthage, IL: Good Apple. Copyright 1989 by Good Apple. Reprinted by permission.

Dichotomania: The Dangers of Overdichotomizing

Although I lean toward the left analytic–right holistic approach to understanding the functions of the human brain, not all researchers feel comfortable subscribing to this dichotomy. In fact, some would say that a dichotomania exists in our country to view many things, including the brain, in terms of the polar opposites of rationality and intuition. Individuals, occupations, cultures, and educational systems have been classified voguishly according to one of these opposites, when this might not be the true state of affairs. Therefore, one must be careful not to overextend this theorized dichotomy beyond the research findings (Gardner, 1978). In fact, brain synthesis and integration could be viewed as viable alternatives to the speculated hemispheric dichotomy and division, which has been popularized lately.

As some experimenters have suggested, if a dominant cognitive style exists, it might not be desirable to change the person's associated per-

Put Together a Prototype

Cut out the pieces and on white paper glue together a marvelous invention. Think about the functions and benefits it could serve. Then write a descriptive paragraph or two about it for the patent office.

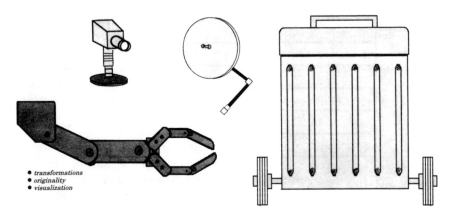

- *transformations*
- *originality*
- *visualization*

FIG. 3.2. Another one of Stanish's (1989) educational exercises, "Put Together a Prototype," using holistic and analytic strategies. From *Ambidextrous Mind Book* (p. 29) by B. Stanish, 1989, Carthage, IL: Good Apple. Copyright 1989 by Good Apple. Reprinted by permission.

ceptions, because a particular way of processing inputs will always be desirable to some task or situation. The recommendation of these researchers has been put simply: "leave well enough alone" (Ausburn & Ausburn, 1978). Only time and further study will determine whether this advice is sound.

SUMMARY AND CONCLUSIONS

Chapter 3 showed us that the verbal–spatial distinction between left and right hemispheres is not the only way to classify cerebral functions. The analytic–holistic dichotomy also would seem to be an appropriate categorization to explain how brain hemispheres process various types of inputs. The main points of this chapter can be summarized as follows:

1. Clinical studies have revealed that split-brain patients and other brain-damaged groups temporally order information via the left-analytic mode, whereas part-to-whole match via the right-holistic mode.

2. Research with normal subjects has provided additional support for distinct cognitive styles in each hemisphere. Chimeric facial identifications and simple tonal arrangements seem to involve right-brain cognitions to a greater extent than left. Conversely, more complex auditory patterns and specific feature recognitions appear to be more dependent on left-sided cognitions.

3. Finally, hemisphericity (i.e., the reliance on one cognitive style) was approached from a number of perspectives: individual, occupational, cultural, and educational preferences. Although differences were noted in all areas, with particular attention paid to Western society's emphasis on the left-analytic style, it was advised not to overgeneralize the findings in light of the prevailing dichotomanic trend sweeping the country. However, the evidence still remains compelling enough to continue to use the analytic–holistic distinction when referring to cerebral asymmetries (see Sperry, 1985, for more information).

Now that a general knowledge of brain differences has been provided, I can focus on the more complicated chapters within the text. The first such challenging topic is on understanding asymmetrical brain functions in subjects who have specific neurophysiological disorders.

CLINICAL EVIDENCE FOR CEREBRAL ASYMMETRIES

Part II presents compelling evidence from clinical brain studies on the functional asymmetries associated with left and right cerebral hemispheres. Specifically, chapter 4 focuses on such neuropsychological disorders as the aphasias, agnosias, and other related impairments so that the reader will be in a better position to understand how these behavioral dysfunctions relate to hemispheric disturbances. Chapter 5 approaches the asymmetry issue from another clinical perspective, namely split-brain research, to determine how cognitive functions are affected grossly when the hemispheres can no longer communicate with each other through the typical callosum channel. This part concludes with chapter 6, in which a highly detailed analysis of brain differences in the pathologies and developmental disabilities is presented for further scrutiny. It is expected that the reader will be able to extract relevant information from these clinical findings so that applications to more normal brain functioning (and associated asymmetries) can be achieved directly.

CHAPTER FOUR

What Do Neuropsychological Disorders Reveal About Brain Asymmetries?

Research on cerebral asymmetries actually started in the 19th century, when clinicians noted functional disturbances in patients who had damage restricted solely to one cortical hemisphere. What follows is a brief historical account of these earliest findings, so that more current neuropsychological studies can be placed in the proper perspective.

HISTORICAL OVERVIEW

Franz Gall, a German anatomist, and Jean Baptiste Bouillaud, a French professor of medicine, were among the first theorists to propose that linguistic functions were localized in the frontal lobes of the brain. Their speculations spurred Marc Dax in his investigations to such an extent that he delivered a paper on hemispheric localization of functions to his medical colleagues at a meeting in Montpellier, France in 1836. Dax reported that of his "40-plus" brain-damaged patients who suffered from serious speech disturbances, not a single case involved damage to the right hemisphere. He concluded that each hemisphere of the brain regulated different functions, with speech being controlled primarily by the left side (Fancher, 1990; Gibson, 1962). It is to Dax's credit that the scientific study of cerebral lateralization began to be taken seriously, especially by French surgeon Paul Broca, who attended the meeting.

51

Broca's Aphasia

Broca (1864) observed that one of his patients named Tan had suffered from a loss of speech for many years. In fact, the only sounds he could make were the monosyllables "tan tan." Upon autopsy, Broca discovered that Tan's brain had a lesion in the posterior–inferior portion of the left frontal lobe. Lesions within the same general area soon were found in other patients who experienced related speech disturbances (Fig. 4.1). Based on this accumulated evidence, Broca finally concluded that the faculty of language was dependent on an intact, healthy left hemisphere. Moreover, he suggested that if the frontal part of this hemisphere was injured, aphasic symptoms would result (see Critchley, 1970).

All of *Broca's aphasics* displayed the same symptomatology: little speech production; nonfluent and poorly articulated vocalizations when evidenced; a greater reliance on agrammatical, telegraphic components of language that included concrete nouns and, to a lesser extent, verbs (e.g., "window . . . break," "boy, man . . . anger"); and, finally, the substitution of incorrect sounds for correct ones in words that were expressed (i.e., phonemic paraphasias). The ability of these patients to name objects was quite poor, but prompting did help them attain the correct pronunciations, suggesting that this deficit was not simply one of articulation. (Many times Broca remarked that the damaged area was located just in front of the primary speech-motor regions, which apparently were spared in this disorder.) In the most severe cases of the aphasia, patients often vocalized one or two words over and over again to convey a wide variety of ideas. However, most of Broca's aphasics understood the spoken or written word, further indicating that the difficulty was mainly

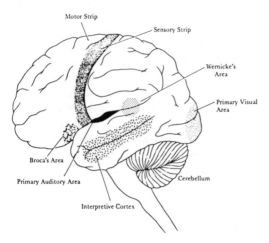

FIG. 4.1.   Broca (1864) and Wernicke's (1874) areas of the left hemisphere. From *Pioneers of Psychology* (p. 89) by Raymond E. Fancher, 2nd ed., 1990, New York: W. W. Norton. Copyright 1990 by W. W. Norton. Reprinted by permission.

an expressive (motor output) type instead of a receptive (comprehension) disorder (Critchley, 1970).

In 1868, British neurologist John Hughlings Jackson applied Broca's clinical findings to his theory of cerebral dominance, which, simply put, elevated the left side of the brain to a superior status regulating most cognitive activity. According to Jackson (1958), there was no higher mental process than speech, and so the left hemisphere was conceptualized as "willfully" leading the right automatically along in many important functions. Thus, the tone was set to regard the right hemisphere as the minor side—a view that, until recently, has persisted across many decades.

Wernicke's Aphasia

By the 1870s, other types of language disorders became associated with damage to the left hemisphere. Karl Wernicke, a German neurologist, claimed to have found a second language center in the left temporal lobe immediately posterior to the primary auditory cortex (Fig. 4.1). In his group of 10 clinical patients who suffered injury to this Wernicke area, an apparent loss of memory occurred for the auditory images of words. Thus, although these subjects heard what was said to them, they could not remember what the words meant. Because comprehension of speech · was affected grossly, typical patient utterances were fluent and rapid, but generally contained meaningless jargon and often were totally devoid of content (Wernicke, 1874).

Many of *Wernicke's* (1874) *aphasics* generated output that resembled something akin to a word salad, or potpourri of verbosity. For instance, when one patient was asked by Bradshaw and Nettleton (1983) how he felt, he replied, "I felt worst because I can no longer keep in my mind from the mind of the minds to keep me from my mind and up to the ear which can be to find among ourselves" (p. 38). Wernicke's (1874) aphasics often seemed unaware that they had this speech disturbance and continued to talk as if nothing were wrong. When these aphasics were given books, they attempted to read the texts aloud, but only succeeded in producing gibberish while their eyes rapidly scanned the pages. Wernicke (1874) further observed that the patients' speech salad was marked by numerous mispronunciations, apparently because they were unable to monitor their words and correct themselves as they went along rapidly.

The type of disturbance just described has been called sensory (or receptive) aphasia to distinguish it from the motor (or expressive) aphasia previously identified by Broca (1864). The major difficulty with the Wernicke (1874) type is not in speaking. Rather, it lies in the patients' understanding of their spoken language.

Conduction Aphasia

Wernicke (1874) has been credited with predicting another type of aphasia that could be produced if damage occurred to the neural pathways connecting the centers for speech production (Broca's area) and speech comprehension (Wernicke's area), namely *conduction aphasia*. Although spontaneous speech and subsequent understanding remained intact, patients were unable to repeat aloud what was immediately heard, because the connections between their auditory and motor word memories had been disrupted. Neurologists (Geschwind, 1972) soon identified several cases of this milder type of aphasia and eventually found the locus of the disturbance in the arcuate fasciculus, which, as predicted, linked both Broca's and Wernicke's areas together. Because of Wernicke's (1874) work, many scientists have arrived at a more realistic view of the way complex functions such as language were mediated by the brain; several interactive areas in the left hemisphere (i.e., Broca's motor, Wernicke's sensory, and the associative regions) became implicated with language rather than just one overall, controlling site as was speculated previously.

Apraxia

By the turn of the century, reports were being published concerning another neuropsychological disorder referred to as *apraxia*. Some patients were unable to perform simple hand movements on command but were able to execute the very same acts spontaneously without difficulty. For instance, they could brush their teeth as part of their normal bedtime routine but could not reproduce the same movements when instructed to "pretend brush." Over the years, it was shown that apraxic subjects understood the experimental commands quite well, suggesting a nonlinguistic difficulty. Upon postmortem examination, most often damage to the left parietal lobe was evidenced. It was concluded that the left hemisphere regulated deliberate, purposeful movements as well as linguistic functions but that the cortical areas involved for these behaviors were located in different lobes (Pinel, 1990).

Alexia and Agraphia

As noted previously with the aphasic disorders, patients displayed some problems with reading and writing. A particular place seemed to be implicated with *alexic* (inability to read) and *agraphic* (inability to write) disturbances. Specifically, neuronal pathways connecting the primary visual cortex with the left angular gyrus (an area posterior to Wernicke's) were damaged extensively. According to Pinel (1990), the angular gyrus was primarily responsible for the comprehension of language-related material received directly from the left visual cortex; when this pathway was disrupted, visuolinguistic skills (i.e., reading and writing) subsequently were impaired.

There have been some clinical cases reported in which the writing function is spared, a condition known as *alexia without agraphia*, so that patients can write sentences spontaneously or from dictation, but cannot read their own writing. These patients not only had damage to their left occipital lobe and the angular gyrus, but also the neuronal tracts of their corpus callosum, which connected the lobe and the gyrus (Albert & Friedman, 1985).

As the 1900s rapidly approached, linguistic functions were regarded as involving much more than simple speech patterns localized within a frontal section of the left hemisphere. Broca's area was just one small part of a much larger picture of language representation within the brain. In the 1960s, Geschwind attempted to integrate all the previously identified brain components into a much more unified system for understanding linguistic behaviors.

For example, reading aloud behaviors were described in the following fashion: First, the primary visual cortex was activated; then information was transmitted immediately to the angular gyrus, which translated the visual image to an auditory code; next, the adjoining Wernicke area comprehended the auditory code and relayed this verbal understanding to the arcuate fasciculus, Broca's area, and the motor cortex, respectively, where the appropriate speech sounds were elicited (Geschwind, 1965).

Although the Geschwind (1965) model mainly operated in a serial, step-by-step fashion, the complexity of these linear operations still should be noted. Activity in the left hemisphere for linguistic behaviors now extended from anterior to posterior regions, with more and more of the cortical surface being implicated in these actions.

Amusia

Although the left hemisphere historically has been associated with language and other types of analytic abilities, the right hemisphere has been portrayed as the "silent partner," obedient to the dominant hemisphere. Yet, certain discoveries made several centuries ago highlighted some of the skills this brain side possessed. One of these was in singing. Dalin (1745) noted that in the most severe cases of aphasia, patients still were able to carry tunes rather successfully (see Benton & Joynt, 1960). Similar observations were reported in the early 1900s, suggesting that the singing function was spared in aphasic subjects.

Gates and Bradshaw (1977b) reviewed the clinical cases that came in over the decades and found additional support for the right hemisphere's involvement in music. Apparently, when this side of the brain was damaged, a loss in musical ability (or amusia) occurred. Often patients were unable to recognize individual tones, common melodies, or rhythms. Destruction to the left hemisphere rarely produced this particular disorder.

Visuospatial Disorders Including the Agnosias

In 1876, Jackson argued that the right, or minor, hemisphere possessed particular visuospatial abilities that were localized in the posterior (i.e., occipital) lobe. One of his patients who suffered from a tumor at this particular site experienced problems in identifying people, objects, and locations. This recognition failure (or *visual agnosia*) was, for the most part, ignored by investigators who primarily devoted attention to left-hemisphere disorders (see Jackson, 1958).

However, in the 1930s, the first massive clinical study on unilateral hemispheric damage was executed by Weisenberg and McBride (1935). They showed that the right-brain side had its own unique functions (which were equally important to the left's linguistic ones). Not surprisingly, left-hemisphere damage resulted in poorer patient performance on verbal types of tests. However, right-hemisphere injury also disturbed performance, most especially on tests that emphasized nonverbal skills (e.g., assembly of puzzles, completion of figures, and manipulation of geometric forms). Two visuospatial tasks that were affected by right-hemisphere lesions are depicted in Fig. 4.2. Both assignments required a strategic manipulation and completion of a figure that could not be executed satisfactorily by most subjects.

Weisenberg and McBride (1935) identified other visuospatial disturbances in patients with right-hemisphere damage. For instance, subjects were disoriented in space (i.e., they were unable to move within a familiar location such as their house without getting lost). Apparently, the ability to form and manipulate static topographical maps of their surroundings was impaired grossly. Moreover, a *neglect* (or hemispatial inattention) *syndrome* was evidenced, especially when posterior (i.e., parietal or parietooccipital) regions of the right hemisphere were disrupted extensively. Patients typically did not attend to their left spatial side and so missed objects presented to that region. Later work performed by Heilman and Watson (1977) replicated these findings. These researchers also showed that neglect patient drawings were very incomplete on the left side, suggesting that these subjects were actually blind (i.e., hemianopic) in their left visual field (Fig. 4.3). The other deficits that were noted by

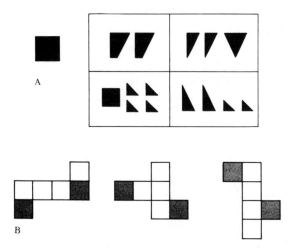

FIG. 4.2. Visuospatial tasks derived from Weisenberg and McBride (1935). A. Which boxed set(s) can form the square on the outside? B. If you fold these patterns into cubes, in which cube(s) will the dark sides meet at one edge? From *Left Brain, Right Brain* (p. 16) by Sally P. Springer and Georg Deutsch, 1989, New York: W. H. Freeman. Copyright 1989 by Sally P. Stringer and Georg Deutsch. Reprinted by permission.

Weisenberg and McBride (1935) involved the facial agnosias that were observed previously by Jackson more than a century ago.

Right-Hemisphere Aphasia

One idea initially proposed by Wernicke (1874) had to do with the recovery of language after left-hemisphere lesions. Supposedly, the right hemisphere took over some of the linguistic functions previously associated with the left side. Gowers (1893) and later Neilsen (1946) confirmed Wernicke's (1874) hypothesis by showing that language gradually recovered in left-hemisphere injured aphasics, and also that newly developed lesions in the right hemisphere contributed to relapse into partial to permanent aphasia.

Recent case studies (Cummings, Benson, Walsh, & Levine, 1979) verified recovery from left-hemisphere aphasia, even when the disturbance was so global as to involve total destruction of the temporal–parietal lobes. The right cerebral hemisphere is flexible enough to acquire new functions that were previously lost by unilateral left damage. However, this right functional plasticity is not a perfect (nor complete) replacement for the destroyed left; further, it is highly vulnerable to the same stressors that afflicted the left side. Thus, right-hemisphere aphasias may not

Model   Patient's Copy

FIG. 4.3.   Neglect patient drawings. A patient who suffered from a right-
hemisphere posterior stroke was asked to copy the model pictures. Note
the absence of detail in the left side of the patient's drawings. From *Left
Brain, Right Brain* (p. 193) by Sally P. Springer and Georg Deutsch, 1989,
New York: W. H. Freeman. Copyright 1989 by Sally P. Springer and Georg
Deutsch. Reprinted by permission.

be as uncommon as the linguistics have suggested throughout the 20th
century.

The Neglected Right Syndromes

Semmes (1968), Eccles (1973), and Springer and Deutsch (1989) attempted
to explain why right-hemispheric disorders (i.e., the amusias, agnosias,
and even aphasias) have remained unidentified for so long. One major
reason is that abilities in the right hemisphere seem to be more globally
represented, as opposed to functions in the left hemisphere, which are
more localized. According to Semmes (1968), right-brain skills are distributed over larger brain regions; therefore, the effects of any right-sided
impairments are expressed more subtly. On the other hand, linguistic

functions primarily are centered in particular areas of the left lobes. Thus, dysfunctions within this hemisphere tend to be more pronounced and not overlooked so easily by investigators.

The other factor responsible for right-sided neglect involves a societal cause, namely that the function (or hemisphere) implicated with language is regarded as all important by that cultural setting. Therefore, other abilities play a secondary role to the overglorified linguistic ones. Even today some neurologists still adhere to this view. But, as Springer and Deutsch (1989) advised, the complementary nature of both hemispheres should be acknowledged properly. In addition, if a disruption in functions should occur in either hemisphere due to unilateral damage, complex mental activity will be affected detrimentally, regardless of the brain side involved.

CLINICAL PROCEDURES

Two neurosurgical procedures were developed in the 1930s and 1940s to specifically determine which hemisphere mainly regulated speech patterns before brain operations were performed on severe cases of epilepsy. The *Penfield* and *Wada tests* made it possible to identify (and spare) important language centers of the brain, and also allowed scientists to see how the cerebral hemispheres were organized asymmetrically as they derived their cortical maps.

Penfield's Electrical Brain Stimulation Procedure

Penfield (1975) and Penfield and Roberts' (1959) technique of mapping the language areas of the brain involved moving an electrode through different cortical regions of the respective hemisphere while the subject was fully conscious, although locally anesthetized. At each site that was electrically stimulated, the patient saw a series of pictures and was then asked to identify the familiar object that was represented in each. If a speech area was found, aphasic arrest usually resulted (i.e., the subject was unable to speak, even though he or she tried to talk or move their mouth). Milder forms of the arrest included slurring and repetition of words, inability to name the particular objects while other verbalizations remained intact, and hesitation in responding with the proper object name. Diseased tissue areas caused by the epilepsy also were identified by Penfield (1975) with this electrical stimulation technique. If such an area were localized and stimulated by the electrode, the patient typically experienced auras (or early warning types of sensations) immediately preceding the epileptic attack. Penfield (1975) surgically removed these particular tissue spots unless they happened to lie near a language region where ablation would have produced the aphasic arrest.

The clinical data collected at the Montreal Neurological Institute over the years revealed that a large number of sites in the left hemisphere was associated with linguistic functions, confirming the previous findings by Wernicke (1874). Aphasiclike responses from the right hemisphere were more rare, although a few disruptions in vocalizations were evidenced, showing that language was not completely lateralized to one side of the brain (Pinel, 1990). Although Penfield's (1975) electrical stimulation procedure allowed the scientist to localize functions within a particular hemisphere, Wada's test (developed by Wada & Rasmussen, 1960) permitted a more complete examination of functions mediated between both hemispheres.

Wada's Sodium Amytal Technique

Wada and Rasmussen's (1960) procedure consisted of an injection of sodium amytal into the carotid artery on one side of the patient's neck. The barbiturate crossed the blood–brain barrier of the ipsilateral hemisphere and quickly anesthetized that side for approximately 5–10 minutes, producing a condition commonly referred to as *hemiparesis* (i.e., *hemisphere paralysis*). Functions within the contralateral hemisphere subsequently were assessed via verbal questions. Patients were asked to recite series of well-known elements (e.g., the days of the week, letters of the alphabet, and numbers backward in threes from 100) and to name very familiar objects. If the injected hemisphere was dominant for speech (as the left was), an abrupt aphasic arrest occurred that lasted until the drug's effects wore off completely. In contrast, when the nondominant speech hemisphere was tranquilized, mutism usually was not evidenced and patients continued to carry out the verbal tasks during the temporary right-sided paralysis (Wada & Rasmussen, 1960).

Over the years that the Wada test has been in use, it has proved to be especially valuable in localizing verbal functions in various handedness groups. Milner (1974) and Rasmussen and Milner (1977) showed that almost all *dextrals* (or right-handers) were left-hemisphere dominant for speech (92%) and that most *sinistrals* (left-handers) and ambidextrous subjects were also left-hemisphere dominant for that particular function (69%). If the left-handers experienced early left-hemisphere damage to the brain, however, this dominance decreased to approximately 30%. Milner's (1974) results clearly indicated that the right hemisphere was able to recover the left's lost ability, as was mentioned previously.

Extreme emotional reactions also have been reported consistently in several studies after sodium amytal was injected into the patient's carotid artery. Dysphoric (i.e., negative-catastrophic) reactions frequently accompanied left-sided injections, whereas indifference and even inappropriate euphoric responses were generated with right-sided injections. The Wada test can be used to identify particular emotional states of brain-lesioned subjects, such as pathological crying associated with left hemisphere damage and pathological laughing with right hemisphere injury (Rossi & Rosadini, 1967; Sackheim et al., 1982; Terzian, 1964).

The Wada test certainly has paved the way for other clinical techniques used to determine language laterality, particularly in depressed patients. For instance, the effects of unilateral electroconvulsive therapy (ECT) on depression have been shown to be very similar to those of unilaterally injected sodium amytal, except that left-sided ECT typically has produced a greater impairment in verbal tasks over an extended period of days with dextral subjects (Kriss, Blumhardt, Halliday, & Platt, 1975). Because of the Wada and earlier Penfield techniques, neurosurgeons are now in a much better position to avoid disturbing language centers and related verbal memory areas of the brain in a number of clinical populations.

RECENT EVIDENCE WITH NEUROPSYCHOLOGICAL DISORDERS

Current Findings with Aphasia

Recent findings by Zurif (1980) suggested that Broca's aphasics do not have relatively intact comprehension as was supposed previously. When complex syntax is involved, problems especially are noted in their comprehension ability. Zurif (1980) claimed that these aphasics only understand simple sentences because they make inferences about the meaning based on a sampling of the major lexical elements (i.e., nouns and verbs) involved, not because they grasp the sentence's overall syntactical structure. Dimond (1980) further argued that Broca's area may not be the only lateralized region associated with speech. Some subcortical areas probably are implicated as well (such as the thalamus), which primarily function as integration centers for frontal (Broca's) *and* posterior (Wernicke's) lobe input, thus explaining, to some degree, why the aphasia produces articulation and comprehension impairments.

Ojemann (1979, 1983) found some support for the Dimond (1980) position. Employing Penfield's (1975) electrical brain stimulation procedure on clinical cases, Ojemann (1979, 1983) found that when the left thalamus was stimulated, speech arrest problems occurred, especially in ob-

ject naming, reading of simple sentences, and ability to recognize pho-
nemes (individual speech sounds), coupled with the perseveration of the
initial syllable of words to be pronounced. Speech also was distorted,
slurred, and often slower in these subjects; accompanying comprehension impairments were evidenced as well. Ojemann (1979, 1983) concluded that language functions extended far beyond the boundaries of
the Wernicke-Geschwind regions, with subcortical areas being involved
directly in Broca's (1864) aphasia. More anterior and posterior cortical
regions were identified subsequently, with subjects showing incredible
variability in their lateralization of linguistic ability. According to Ojemann
(1979, 1983) and his colleagues, the left cortex might be organized like
a mosaic pattern for language, with articulation and comprehension functions being distributed widely throughout the hemisphere instead of being localized in the respective Broca's and Wernicke's areas as hypothesized traditionally.

Moreover, the most recent research conducted by Poizner et al. (1990)
verified Ojemann's (1979, 1983) findings. In deaf signers with left-
hemisphere lesions, pronounced language aphasias occurred similar to
nondeaf patients. However, even when signers had intact Broca's and
Wernicke's areas, comprehension loss in signing still occurred. This apparently was due to lesions within the left parietal lobe, with associated
subcortical damage that extended into the frontal lobe. As Poizner et al.
(1990) suggested, the physiological sites implicated with Broca's and Wernicke's aphasia may not be so well defined in deaf signers. For nondeaf
populations, the brain organization in the left hemisphere may not be
as specifically lateralized for language either, as Damasio (1983) and Grodzinsky (1990) implied.

With respect to right-hemispheric linguistic disturbances, it has been
reported consistently that such lesioned patients have difficulty determining the emotional tone of speech produced by others. Heilman,
Scholes, and Watson (1975) demonstrated that these subjects could not
point to the appropriate facial picture that best illustrated the tone of voice
the experimenter conveyed in an accompanying descriptive sentence. In
fact, right-hemisphere lesioned patients did much poorer than a comparison group of Broca's aphasics.

Interestingly, this intonational impairment seemed to operate independently of subjects' comprehension of different emotional states. Performance on tasks (Tucker, Watson, & Heilman, 1977) that required
verbal identification of an emotion conveyed by the contents of a read
story was not affected detrimentally, suggesting that these patients were
unable to discern relevant, external perceptual cues (such as facial expressions or experimenter's tone of voice) associated with the discrimination of particular emotions.

Ross (1981, 1984) discovered that this discrimination difficulty was linked to damage in the right hemisphere's posterior lobes, both temporal and occipital. Ross (1981, 1984) further noted a second, highly distinctive intonational impairment when lesions occurred in the anterior areas of the right brain, namely a flattened speech pattern (or affective aphasia). Because patients were not forceful enough in their articulations, they often resorted to additional wordage to express the strong feelings they were experiencing (e.g., "I'm angry [I really am]"). Because Broca's aphasics rarely suffered from either intonational problem, Ross (1981, 1984) concluded that linguistic tone (i.e., prosody) was a function exclusively reserved to the right hemisphere.

Based on this evidence, it would seem that although language primarily is mediated by the left hemisphere, the right side plays a contributory role, particularly in the way the language is expressed emotionally. Lateralization of the right-prosodic function also resembles the left linguistic, in that anterior cortical regions are associated more with self-generated outputs, whereas areas lying more posteriorly are involved more with comprehension of outputs generated by others. It remains to be determined whether prosodic deficits are holistically represented in the right hemisphere, as was recently found for the left-sided aphasias.

Current Findings with Apraxia and Alexia

Recent reports (Albert & Friedman, 1985) have indicated that lesions in the left hemisphere affect the execution of purposeful movements. In particular, two apraxias have been associated most with left hemisphere injury: *ideational apraxia* and *ideomotor apraxia*. With ideational apraxia, the subject cannot perform an appropriate sequence of acts (e.g., the patient may pick up a perfume bottle and move it to his or her mouth instead of nose). Ideomotor apraxia, on the other hand, involves the inability of the patient to execute acts on command (e.g., mime waving goodbye). If the actual objects are given within the appropriate context, however, the subject typically fares much better. Over the past few years, several investigators (Marshall, 1980; Poizner et al., 1990) have discovered that left-hemisphere aphasia and ideomotor apraxia do not necessarily reflect the same inability in comprehending symbols, and so can occur independently of each other.

One apraxia has been found to involve either damage to the left or right hemisphere. The expression of *constructional apraxia*, the inability to reproduce figures by drawing or assembly, appears to be dependent on which side of the brain the lesion is located. If the left hemisphere is damaged, patients' drawings usually reflect the overall configuration of objects, but details and relevant features are sorely lacking. On the other hand, with right-hemisphere lesions, features are discriminated correctly, but the parts show a scrambled type of organization. Assembling objects by hand generates a similar error pattern for each hemisphere.

These results definitely highlight the two major modes of information processing discussed in chapter 3, with either the left brain's analytic style being impaired or the right's holistic. It is speculated that damage to the pathways connecting the occipital and parietal lobes has occurred with this apraxia, and therefore subjects are unable to visualize the type of output that needs to be generated for the successful manipulation of objects (Dimond, 1980).

Although the reading disorder has been linked mainly to left-hemisphere injury with respect to alexia, a condition known as *deep dyslexia* sometimes is expressed where the right hemisphere apparently takes over some of the reading skills previously associated with the left side. In deep dyslexia, the patient might be asked to read aloud the printed word *table*, but will respond with *chair*. The patient's wrong response, termed a *paralexic error*, is more reflective of a phonological difficulty than a semantic one. Generally, comprehension of words is preserved, but subjects cannot pronounce or name the actual units accurately.

Coltheart (1979, 1980a, 1980b) proposed that the left hemisphere's normal reading mechanisms have been deactivated entirely under this condition. However, the right hemisphere remains intact and uses the semantic skills that it possesses to first comprehend the meaning of the pronounced word (especially if it is a high-frequency, concrete noun) and then communicates this meaning to the left side. This input is not sufficient for the left hemisphere to distinguish between synonyms or closely related words; therefore, phonological errors subsequently are made. Actually, deep dyslexia shows the limitations of linguistic functions in the right hemisphere; patients cannot comprehend the meaning of abstract words—only concrete ones—and demonstrate little (if any) response to the former items.

Current Findings with Amusia and the Visual Agnosias

Originally, amusia was viewed as a right-hemisphere disorder. Even in the 1970s, research had shown this to be the case. The Bogen and Gordon series of studies revealed that if intracarotid sodium amytal was administered to the right brain, the patient's ability to produce a tone was disturbed grossly, whereas speech remained unaffected. In fact, most of the tunes were sung in a monotone fashion with incorrect pitch expression. One finding of these Wada tests was that the rhythm of each tune remained intact, suggesting the possibility of some limited left-hemisphere processing of musical stimuli (Bogen & Gordon, 1971; Gordon & Bogen, 1974).

Current conceptualizations of the locus for the musical disturbance rely on a more bihemispheric involvement, with the right hemisphere handling spatial properties (e.g., comprehension of the overall composition) and the left side handling analytic features (e.g., temporal ordering and sequencing of the individual notes). As Benton (1977) and Brust (1980) further observed, aphasia and amusia sometimes can occur together as part of a more magnified picture of impairments in both linguistic and musical processing (see the section on affective aphasia earlier in this chapter). Similar to aphasia and prosody, amusia also can be differentiated in terms of receptive (comprehension) and expressive (production) dysfunctions. However, the findings still remain inconclusive as to whether the same cortical regions, posterior and anterior, respectively, can be associated with these subtypes. One can conclude that right-musical processing has much more in common with left-linguistic processing than previously speculated.

In very severe cases of visual object agnosia, where the patient can draw or describe an object but cannot identify it or say what it is, bilateral damage also is found, specifically within the parietal and occipital lobes of the hemisphere along with some disconnection of interhemispheric pathways feeding from the right's visual processing areas to the left's language centers. Tactile recognition of objects can occur with milder expressions of the disorder, but even this modality demonstrates impairments with more extensive interhemispheric damage (Farah, 1990).

A special case of this agnosia, prosopagnosia (i.e., the inability to recognize familiar faces), tends to have a strong bilateral component. Both Farah (1990) and Benton (1980, 1985) showed that prosopagnosic patients cannot recognize their own faces in a mirror, let alone identify faces of friends whom they know. Yet, these subjects realize they are seeing faces and can verbalize many relevant details of each facial stimulus they encounter (including their own countenance). These researchers argued that although bilateral damage is implicated in the appearance of this disorder, specific injury to the right hemisphere's parietal–occipital lobes also must be present. A second more common type of facial agnosia, the inability to recognize novel or unknown faces, is largely, if not entirely, attributed to unilateral damage in the right hemisphere's posterior (and sometimes anterior) regions.

Based on this accumulated evidence, it has been theorized that the right brain has a specialized mechanism for processing human faces that is independent of and much more powerful than its other visuospatial functions. It also seems probable that the human's unique ability to recognize familiar (as opposed to unknown) faces cannot be disrupted so easily, because both hemispheres are involved, relaying the most salient features and holistic configurations of stimuli that have been apprehended many times in the organism's past.

Current Findings with the Neglect Syndrome

Unlike amusia and prosopagnosia, hemispatial inattention (i.e., the neglect syndrome) is a more unilateral type of disorder traditionally associated with right-brain injury. Most patients' drawings reflect a very pronounced spatial disorganization, with the left-hand parts often remaining unfinished or prominently distorted due to hemispatial neglect of that particular body side (Delis, Robertson, & Efron, 1986; Goodglass & Kaplan, 1979; Heilman & Watson, 1977). However, other reports (Kaplan, 1980; Poizner et al. 1990) pointed to a similar difficulty experienced with left-lesioned patients, namely a neglect of features within the right half of drawn figures. Figure 4.4 illustrates some of these contralateral neglects

FIG. 4.4.   Hemispatial neglect in the drawings of left- and right-lesioned patients. From *What the Hands Reveal About the Brain* (p. 181) by H. Poizner, E. Klima, and U. Bellugi, 1990, Cambridge, MA: MIT Press. Copyright 1990 by MIT Press. Reprinted by permission.

in left- as well as right-hemisphere-damaged subjects. Although left-lesioned patients produce fairly good drawings of models in comparison with their right counterparts, there is still some indication of distortion, especially in their right-hand side of space. For instance, patient P. D. generated some of the worst drawings, with three right-hind legs on his "elephant" and more distorted right parts to his "cross," "cube," and "house." Omission of details on one side appeared to be a function exclusively reserved to the right-hemisphere injuries (Fig. 4.4). It remains to be determined whether left-hemisphere impairments will ever demonstrate the extent of neglect found with the right.

Although right-brain-damaged patients show a much stronger neglect, not all are hemianopic (i.e., blind) to the contralateral field. In certain tachistoscopic tasks, some actually were able to report having seen simple geometric forms flashed to their left side. However, if different forms were flashed simultaneously to both fields, these patients only identified stimuli displayed in the right visual space. Sometimes within the simultaneous field presentations, they guessed under forced choice conditions what was presented to the neglected left side, although they could not acknowledge the form with direct inquiry (Volpe, LeDoux, & Gazzaniga, 1979).

Moreover, if a single, large stimulus pattern that crossed both left and right fields was presented, these subjects identified the complete drawing (such as a safety pin or key). As Fig. 4.5 illustrates, right-field input alone would have been insufficient to produce the number of correct recognitions patients made to the gestalt figures (Deutsch, Tweedy, & Lorinstein, 1980). Apparently, half-blindness is not an adequate explanation for the neglect exhibited in all right-brain impaired subjects.

Volpe et al. (1979), among others (Deutsch et al. 1980; Springer & Deutsch, 1989), attempted to explain these research findings by a stimulus extinction process that presumably occurs with conflicting inputs. When information from the right visual field is registered in the left hemisphere, it overrides left-field input from the damaged right hemisphere. The result is that all stimulation from the left field is wiped clean (or extinguished); hence, patients only can identify forms directly in their right visual space with bilateral presentations. However, if the left hemisphere cannot make sense of the input coming from its contralateral side (as in the case with gestalt figures), it will make use of the information projected to the right brain to interpret the forms meaningfully. Therefore, whether the left spatial side is discriminated or extinguished is determined primarily by how the left brain operates in conjunction with the damaged right. This new view of neglect, although mainly left-hemisphere driven, incorporates bilateral processing within both brains to explain the perceptual phenomenon.

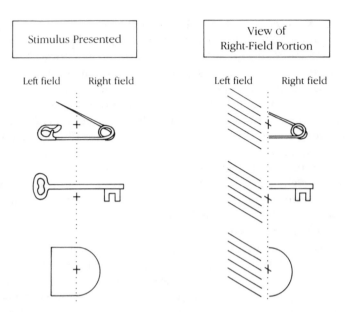

FIG. 4.5.   More neglect patient identifications with gestalt stimuli. Patients identified each configuration, although it has been claimed that they are blind in their left visual field and can only discriminate the right side. From *Left Brain, Right Brain* (p. 195) by Sally P. Springer and Georg Deutsch, 1989, New York: W. H. Freeman. Copyright 1989 by Sally P. Springer and Georg Deutsch. Reprinted by permission.

SUMMARY AND CONCLUSIONS

In the beginning of this chapter, the question was raised, "What do neuropsychological disorders reveal about brain asymmetries?" From the evidence presented, it seems that linguistic disturbances reflect greater lateralization in the left hemisphere and, conversely, visuospatial (and other related) disorders show more lateralization in the right hemisphere. These specializations are more relative than absolute. In other words, both brains can be implicated in most functions, except that one side is more involved than the other in the expression of those relevant behaviors.

To summarize the major points in chapter 4:

1. Historically, left-sided disorders were researched to a greater extent than the right, primarily because many of these disturbances involved very overt language deficits (e.g., Broca's production and Wernicke's comprehension aphasias). Even the Penfield and Wada clinical procedures

were designed to locate the major speech centers in the left hemisphere. However, in the last 50 years, an enormous focus has been directed to the neglected right brain, which has resulted in the identification of a new range of disorders extending from musical deficits (i.e., amusia) to visual agnosias and hemispatial neglect.

2. More recent evidence has indicated that large sections of the left hemisphere (anterior, posterior, and subcortical) are associated with various linguistic disorders. Even the right hemisphere is implicated in the expression of some of these disturbances, such as the affective aphasias, constructional apraxia, and deep dyslexia. Alternately, the left brain displays some involvement in the nonverbal deficits (e.g., amusia, prosopagnosia, and neglect).

These clinical observations demonstrate the complexity underlying brain functioning. Apparently large cortical regions in the anterior and/or posterior lobes are integrated within as well as between the cerebral hemispheres to allow humans to operate effectively, both linguistically and spatially. Should these regions become damaged, some recovery in behavioral functions still can occur via the uninjured hemisphere, whether left or right.

As Ashbrook (1988) contended, the human brain is wondrously made: Each hemisphere grasps a different part of reality. As long as the damage is restricted to one hemisphere, humans still can make sense of that reality and comprehend it through the symbols they employ (whether words or pictures) from the intact brain side.

CHAPTER FIVE

Are Split-Brain Patients Truly Divided in Cognitive Functioning?

Erikson (1940) and other researchers (Van Wagenen & Herren, 1940) were among the first to suggest that epileptic seizures could spread from one cerebral hemisphere to the other via the corpus callosum. However, if this interconnecting band of nerve fibers were damaged, the incidence of the seizures was reduced drastically in some human patients. These early findings paved the way for the commissurotomy operations performed in the 1960s.

THE EFFECTS OF INITIAL COMMISSUROTOMIES IN EPILEPTICS

The Vogel and Bogen Operations

Two neurosurgeons, Vogel and Bogen, considered sectioning the entire corpus callosum, as well as several smaller commissures (i.e., the anterior and hippocampal), in patients suffering from intractable epilepsy. It was reasoned that the convulsions could be limited to the hemisphere of their origin if all interconnecting pathways were disrupted. Two dozen such subjects were operated on, with the result being that many never experienced another convulsion after their commissurotomy. It also appeared that the Vogel and Bogen operations left the patients' personalities, intelligence, and behavior generally intact (Pinel, 1990). More extensive neuropsychological evaluations subsequently executed by Gazzaniga (1967) and Sperry (1964) on these subjects revealed a strikingly different story.

71

The Sperry and Gazzaniga Tests

The Gazzaniga (1967) and Sperry (1964) procedures basically involved delivering stimuli to only one of the patients' hemispheres. Tachistoscopic tasks were suited best to achieve this goal. Although the subjects fixated on a small black dot in the center of a display screen, stimuli were flashed onto either the left or right side for a brief duration (typically 0.1–0.2 seconds). The exposure time was short enough to reduce the confounding effects of patients' saccadic eye movements, yet long enough to allow subjects to perceive the visual stimuli correctly. Using such tachistoscopic procedures enabled subjects to transmit all information shown in their left visual field (LVF) to the contralateral right visual cortex and, alternately, all stimulation presented in their right visual field (RVF) to the respective left cortex. Verbal identifications of these stimuli then were elicited. Further tests examined the tactual and motor skills of these subjects, specifically by allowing them to handle objects under a ledge (located at the bottom of the display screen) and perform cross-modal matches with the recently viewed input.

Results consistently showed that commissurotomy patients were able to report simple words or pictures if they were flashed to their RVF, not their LVF. Yet, they still were able to perform correct recognitions by the right hemisphere (via LVF input) if a nonverbal means of stimulus identification was used. In this case, the subjects' left hand was able to select the appropriate object name from a list of words as well as find the matching stimulus from a wide array of unseen objects.

As Sperry (1964) reported, some of the patients typically experienced confusion across the test trials. Although they were able to verbalize their reply via the left hemisphere, the only way they could make a right-hemisphere identification was through the left hand. Obviously patients knew they had seen something flashed to their LVF, but were limited in how they could express this information and so became quite frustrated as the trials proceeded. Conversely, if patients were asked to name the object placed in their left hand, they were surprised to find that they were unable to do so, again exhibiting a split in responses. Sperry (1964) concluded that the severing of the corpus callosum actually had split the hemispheres into two independent cognitive processing units, with verbal processes being regulated by the left side and nonverbal ones by the right.

More investigations conducted by Gazzaniga and Sperry (1967) confirmed this hypothesized hemispheric split in functions. These patients (now commonly referred to as *split-brain*) were unable to accurately report bilateral inputs shown to both visual fields simultaneously. For instance, if the word *heart* was tachistoscopically flashed before the patients with the "he" portion in the left field and the "art" portion in the right, only "art" could be spoken directly (via the left hemisphere). Yet, subjects could still point to the "he" part with the left hand (or right hemisphere), indicating that both portions had been registered by the brain, but were unable to be integrated satisfactorily into the complete word *heart* (Fig. 5.1).

Similar findings were obtained for bilateral pictorial presentations: Patients only could name the RVF object and only could select the LVF object with the left hand. If the subjects switched hands, the RVF object then could be identified. Apparently, this functional asymmetry was not restricted to verbalizations, but also could be displayed in the patients' hand palpations.

In another tachistoscopic test, Sperry (1968) effectively demonstrated that split-brain subjects express feelings, yet remain unaware of their own reactions to particularly arousing stimuli. Specifically, a nude picture of a human figure was flashed to the patients' LVF, after which a brief description of the stimulus was requested. Although subjects claimed nothing had been presented, they still giggled and blushed whenever this particular input was shown. Sperry (1968) reasoned that the right hemisphere had processed the picture and responded in a typical non-verbal fashion. However, the left hemisphere did not acknowledge what its counterpart had seen and so could not make sense out of the unusual situation (except to say that the experimenter had "some funny machine"). Emotional experiences (e.g., linguistic processes) could be limited to one of the patients' hemispheres as a result of brain bisection.

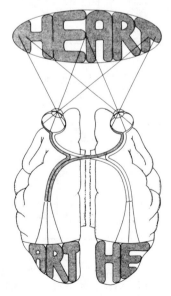

FIG. 5.1. Diagram of word portions tachistoscopically shown to the split-brain patients' visual fields. Note that the "he" part is projected to the right hemisphere and, alternately, "art" to the left hemisphere. From *The Psychology of Consciousness* by Robert E. Ornstein, New York: W. H. Freeman. Copyright 1972 by W. H. Freeman and Company. Reprinted by permission.

One frequently overlooked finding in the Sperry and Gazzaniga investigations was that the ipsilateral hemisphere gradually was able to acquire control over some motor functions. For instance, whereas patients initially were unable to execute with the right hand or foot spatial instructions conveyed to the LVF (or right hemisphere), eventually they were able to follow the simple motor commands. Moreover, under competing dichotic stimulation conditions, the left hand gradually mastered verbal commands presented to the right ear (or left hemisphere). Because most of the *apraxias* disappeared over time, Bradshaw and Nettleton (1983) speculated that either hemisphere of the split-brain patient could acquire control over ipsilateral (i.e., same-sided) motor pathways, as well as the verified contralateral ones.

Bradshaw and Nettleton's (1983) hypothesis has received additional support from Bogen (1969b) and Gazzaniga (1970), who extensively examined the drawing ability of these subjects. Although the patients' right hand (left hemisphere) retained the ability to write, it was unable to reproduce figures very well in comparison with the left hand (Fig. 5.2). However, the right hand's constructional apraxia, similar to the previously mentioned impairments, was of a transient type. Within a few months, better drawings were produced as the right hemisphere obtained

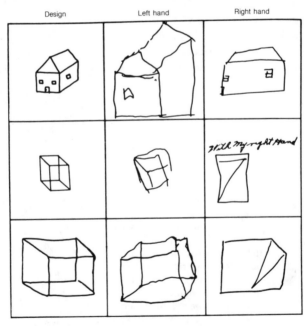

FIG. 5.2. Split-brain patients' drawing reproductions with left and right hands. From *The Bisected Brain* (p. 99) by M. S. Gazzaniga, 1970, New York: Plenum. Copyright 1970 by Plenum. Reprinted by permission.

more effective control over the ipsilateral hand. Block assembly with the right hand also improved with the passage of time. Apparently, split-brain patients compensated for some of their pronounced functional divisions by rerouting information through their ipsilateral motor pathways while still retaining control of the cross-sided ones.

FURTHER RESEARCH WITH SPLIT-BRAIN PATIENTS

Since the Sperry (1967) and Gazzaniga (1970) studies, work has continued at a rapid pace throughout the 1970s and 1980s to determine how far commissurotomized patients were really split in cognitive functioning. A review of the most important research findings is presented.

Visual Completion of Partial Figures

Trevarthen and Kinsbourne (1974) were the first to report that split-brain patients were able to complete figures that only were partially shown to each visual field. For instance, subjects accurately identified squares as well as other geometric forms, even though the left half of each figure projected to one hemisphere (i.e., the right) and the right half projected to the other hemisphere (the left). Verbal sightings of each form and sketchings of the entire figure with the left hand clearly indicated that the patients had completed the partial field inputs, suggesting that their visual perceptions of the world still could be integrated into relevant and meaningful gestalts.

As mentioned in chapter 3, visual completion also has been shown in the processing of chimeric figures. Split-brain subjects typically perceive complete, bilaterally symmetrical faces, even though each of their visual fields only has registered a half face of a distinctly different individual. Levy, Trevarthen, and Sperry (1972) found that subjects almost always verbally selected the completed version of the facial half that was presented to the RVF (or left hemisphere). Conversely, if asked to point to the completed face among a series of alternatives, they usually chose the one that corresponded to the LVF (right hemisphere half). Chimeric pictures of common objects (e.g., a rose and a bee) produced similar field asymmetries (Levy & Trevarthen, 1977).

Levy and his colleagues concluded that each hemisphere of the split-brain patient could exercise its own type of visual completion, seemingly independent of the other cortical side. The response required of the subject—verbal or nonverbal—appeared to be the critical factor in determining which hemispheric completion finally was perceived by the overall brain.

Cognitive Modal Divisions and Integrations

Split-brain patients also exhibit a division between their left-analytic and right-synthetic modes of information processing (Levy, 1974; Sperry, 1985). In one study involving chimeric stimuli adapted from drawings of common objects, subjects were required to point to one of several alternatives that matched the chimeric one on the basis of function or appearance. As predicted, function instructions generally allowed the left hemisphere to operate in its preferred cognitive style, namely the analytic. For example, if "cake" was projected chimerically to the RVF, patients usually chose the "spoon and fork" alternative, which was related functionally to "cake" (Fig. 5.3).

On the other hand, appearance instructions enabled the right hemisphere to operate according to its preferred mode of operation, the holistic. Returning to our example, if "cake" was projected chimerically to the patients' LVF, the alternative, which most structurally resembled "cake," eventually was chosen (in this case, the "hat" in Fig. 5.3). The same pattern of results typically occurred when more ambiguous instructions of matching were administered, further highlighting this split-brain division in information processing (Levy & Trevarthen, 1976). Moreover, differences in hand palpations on form-matching recognition tasks supported the modal preferences of each hemisphere. Specifically, tactile exploration with the left hand (or right hemisphere) was rapid and silent, whereas right-hand (left-hemispheric) performance often was accom-

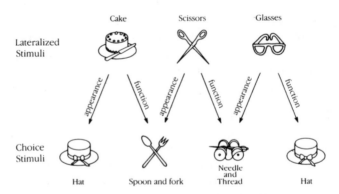

FIG. 5.3.   Function and appearance stimulus matches by split-brain patients. When the left hemisphere views one of the lateralized stimuli, it typically will match by function. Conversely, when the right hemisphere sees the respective stimulus, it usually will match by appearance. From "Metacontrol of Hemispheric Function in Human Split Brain Patients" by J. Levy and C. Trevarthen, 1976, *Journal of Experimental Psychology: Human Perception and Performance, 2,* p. 302. Copyright 1976 by the American Psychological Association, Arlington, VA. Reprinted by permission.

panied with a running verbal commentary of the subjects' actions (Levy, 1969).

Within the chimeric study conducted by Levy and Trevarthen (1976), a number of split-brain patients' responses did not conform to the modal division pattern of left analytic and right synthetic. Sometimes the right hemisphere (on the basis of LVF input) performed a function match; other times the left hemisphere made an appearance match with RVF input.

The researchers reasoned that, on occasion, a particular hemisphere may not process all information in the manner expected of it. Rather, it may choose to adopt a new modal strategy that is not the optimal or preferred one. Thus, left- and right-brain sides can utilize both analytic and synthetic modes of information processing, and still can operate (to a limited extent) with integrated cognitive styles although the major communicative channel (i.e., the corpus callosum) has been disconnected.

Other theorists (Preilowski, 1979; Trevarthen, 1974) complemented these remarks by stating that the ability of split-brain patients to vacillate between cognitive styles, especially within the same hemisphere, allows these subjects to derive more unified experiences and perceptions of their surroundings, similar to the visual completion effects already discussed.

Right-Hemispheric Processing: More Than a Simple Visuospatial Superiority?

As indicated earlier in this chapter, the left hand (right hemisphere) usually demonstrates a superiority to its counterpart in visuospatial tasks, whether they be part-to-whole matching, block assembly, or drawing assignments. In fact, the performance of commissurotomized patients working on these tasks with the right hand (left hemisphere) has been found to be quite similar to subjects who have had lesions lateralized to their right hemisphere (Gazzaniga & LeDoux, 1978; Poizner et al., 1990). Therefore, do these results imply that the split-brain patients' left hemisphere is incapable of executing any visuospatial functions?

LeDoux, Wilson, and Gazzaniga (1977a, 1977b) attempted to address this issue by tachistoscopically presenting block design patterns exclusively to the subjects' RVF. Afterward, patients had to choose, from a series of alternatives, the actual configurations that, in their opinion, resembled the one just viewed. Surprisingly, the commissurotomized left hemisphere performed this simple visuospatial task quite well, although it could not form the overall design by assembling blocks together with the right hand. Therefore, it was argued that the right-hemisphere advantage primarily was due to its superiority in manipulating spatial components within the environment (i.e., a manipulospatial superiority). However, more general types of visuospatial skills not requiring extensive manipulation could be handled adequately by either divided brain side.

More recent findings have suggested that these cerebral asymmetries also reflect mental variations in the way patterns and other configurations are assembled by each hemisphere. When subjects were required to match unseen objects with unassembled, geometric forms presented in free vision by hand, their right hand made a significantly greater number of errors in comparison with the left. As the object contours became less geometric and more free form, right-hand performance drastically deteriorated, whereas the left continued to show the same strong level of response (Franco & Sperry, 1977; Puccetti, 1981a). It might be that the consistent right-hemisphere superiority in visuospatial tasks reflects a cognitive advantage on the subjects' part in visualizing what the viewed figures would look like if they were assembled completely (in this case, folded up), as well as a cognitive realization of which parts to palpate for correct matching to occur. On the other hand, the left hemisphere appears to be incapable of executing these more complex, mental functions.

Right-Hemispheric Processing: The Involvement of Linguistic Components

The Zaidel Technique. Earlier studies investigating the lateralization of spatial and verbal functions in split-brain patients were extremely limited because tachistoscopic presentations rarely exceeded 200 milliseconds. This time restriction prevented subjects from freely scanning the stimuli for whatever period was necessary. Further, the stimuli almost always consisted of simple types of input; therefore, more complex materials (e.g., sentences and spoken instructions) could never be examined effectively with the conventional tachistoscopic procedure. These problems were eliminated by the development of the *Z lens* (termed after its inventor Zaidel) in 1975.

Specifically, split-brain patients were fitted with a contact lens on one of their eyes. The lens contained a small screen that projected stabilized retinal images to only one of the patients' visual fields. Vision through the other field was blocked by having that respective side of the lens opaque to the projected input. The Z lens made it possible for subjects to scan the images freely, as well as manipulate objects in association with the lateralized images presented. Zaidel's (1975) major intent behind this technique was to compare the abilities of the two commissurotomized hemispheres on a variety of verbal tasks that had been employed previously with children and aphasic individuals.

The Linguistic Right Hemisphere: A Case To Be Made. In auditory vocabulary tests involving the Z lens, Zaidel (1978a) required subjects to match spoken words with lateralized pictures of the actual objects as well as their written counterparts. The disconnected right hemisphere was able to demonstrate some linguistic capabilities, especially with high-frequency, concrete words. However, when the items involved abstract referents, the right hemisphere's auditory comprehension significantly deteriorated, suggesting that its verbal memory was not as extensive as the left brain's.

To more effectively determine whether the right hemisphere could understand a number of verbal instructions, Zaidel (1978b) next administered the standardized Token Test to these subjects. In this task, an oral command was first given (e.g., "put the red square under the green circle"). Then the patients were asked to arrange different colored plastic shapes (or tokens) in accordance with the command. Once again, the input was presented through the Z lens, ensuring that only one hemisphere actually viewed the colored tokens. Much to the surprise of his colleagues, Zaidel (1983b) found that the right hemisphere was just as competent as the left in following many of the directions, until they became too complex or lengthy, at which time the left hemisphere exercised its functional superiority.

The more advanced linguistic skills of writing and reading also were examined extensively with the Zaidel (1983b) technique. Consistent with previous findings, the commissurotomized right hemisphere could form upper- and lowercase letters while executing some limited writing with the left hand. Although subjects could grasp simple grammar and syntax, their reading ability was generally poorer than their auditory comprehension, possibly indicating that the right brain's visual vocabulary was much smaller than its acoustic one. To further account for this reading deficiency, Zaidel (1983b) speculated that because the right hemisphere processed information holistically, words were combined more naturally into visual gestalts (i.e., chunks), with the end result being that the overall textual meaning was sacrificed.

Based on the aforementioned results, Zaidel (1985) made a rough estimation as to the right hemisphere's linguistic age, placing its comprehension level somewhere between 3 and 6 years of age and its vocabulary at a slightly higher level (10 years). The right hemisphere's linguistic behavior was compared further to a nominal aphasic's, because it acknowledged an object's use and primary qualities, but was unable to recall the object's specific name. Zaidel (1978b) also discovered that although the disconnected left hemisphere was superior to the right across many language tests, it still evidenced some pronounced deficits such as in vocabulary richness and reading speed. Zaidel (1978b) attributed these impairments to the separation of the linguistic right hemisphere from its counterpart, suggesting that the asymmetrical differences were relative (instead of absolute) ones.

The "Talking" Right Hemisphere: A Case To Be Made.   On the verbal tasks conducted by Zaidel (1978b), the disconnected right hemisphere was found to be almost entirely mute, except for single-word cliches or phrases that it occasionally generated. Zaidel (1978c) and Poizner et al. (1990) concluded that speech production and phonological processing (unlike other language-related functions) were, for the most part, lateralized in the left hemisphere of split-brain patients. However, other evidence seems to indicate that the commissurotomized right hemisphere could recover some expressive speech functions if the left side suffered damage.

This argument was based primarily on the longitudinal research reported by Gazzaniga (1983, 1989). He found that a few of his patients exhibited right-hemisphere speech in their attempts to identify words as well as objects flashed to the LVF, and, further, that early injury to the left hemisphere had occurred in each of the cases. These results tend to complement those already mentioned in chapter 4, where aphasics show language recovery after experiencing left-hemisphere lesions (Cummings et al., 1979). Although the evidence might not be particularly compelling, Zaidel (1983a) noted that recovery of speech by the separated right hemisphere is strongly dependent on the extent of damage to the left brain, with more "takeover" possible as injury becomes more global. However, Zaidel (1983a) still argued with Gazzaniga's (1983, 1989) conclusions on the bias that the right hemisphere is not flexible enough to completely recover all speech functions apparently lost by the left side. Thus, whether the disconnected right hemisphere is able to attain a level of spoken competence equivalent to the left still remains an issue to be researched in more depth by future neuropsychologists.

Cross-Cuing: Indirect Communication Between Hemispheres

Although the hemispheres of the split-brain patient have no direct means of neural communication, sometimes relevant cues can be picked up from the environment that still can make information indirectly available to both sides. This phenomenon, termed *cross-cuing*, was identified originally by Gazzaniga (1967). In his procedure, a red or green light was flashed initially to the patients' LVF (right hemisphere). Subjects then had to report verbally the color that they viewed. As the trials proceeded, performance began to improve above chance level, suggesting that a particular strategy was employed by the patients to obtain the correct responses. Gazzaniga (1967) noted that if the flashed light were red but the patients incorrectly guessed green, a frown immediately appeared on their faces, followed by a shake of the head and the statement, "No . . . it was red." Apparently, the right hemisphere perceived the red light, yet heard the left side making an incorrect response (i.e., green). Acknowledging that the answer was wrong, the right brain eventually cued its cortical neighbor by way of nonverbal reactions (such as frowns and head shakes) so that the left hemisphere could correct its reply.

Sperry's (1968) split-brain study on emotional responses cited earlier certainly could be explained by Gazzaniga's (1967) process of cross-cuing. Although the left brain did not acknowledge emotionally what the right had seen (in this case, a nude photograph flashed to the LVF), it still verbalized that the tachistoscope was conveying funny messages to the viewer, indicating that some input was crossing over indirectly via the right-hemispheric motor cues of blushing and giggling. Other studies performed by Gazzaniga in the early 1970s (Gazzaniga, 1970; Gazzaniga & Hillyard, 1971) continued to verify the existence of deliberate cross-cuing between hemispheres, not only from the right to left side, but vice versa as well.

Nebes (1978) replicated Gazzaniga's results in a more recent study. Some split-brain patients were able to name numbers that were flashed to the LVF, with right-hemispheric reaction time being largely dependent on the magnitude of the digit presented (which extended from 0 to 9). Nebes (1978) hypothesized that the left hemisphere began counting subvocally after the LVF input was shown. In turn, the right hemisphere picked up on these subvocal cues and stopped the counting by way of some bodily movement when the correct number had been reached. This cross-cuing allowed the left hemisphere to identify the digit and call out that particular number.

Nebes' (1978) hypothesis appeared to be a valid one, especially because greater LVF reaction times occurred when the digit was a larger number. Obviously in this situation, the left hemisphere had to generate subvocally a longer list of numbers before arriving at the correct one. On the other hand, RVF (left-hemispheric) response times were quite prompt to all the numbers, highlighting that cross-cuing involved a period of time to move the information from one hemisphere to the other (as opposed to the more direct RVF verbal route).

The cross-cuing phenomenon also was identified in the Zaidel (1978a) ocular scanning tests. When subjects were required to write down with their left hand the names of particular objects they had just viewed, the left hemisphere began to assume control halfway through the task, incorrectly completing the word as well as verbally supplying its guess.

It seems that the right-hemispheric hand movements cued the left, but in such a way that only a limited amount of information could be transferred to that respective brain side (Zaidel, 1978a).

Additional research executed by Sperry, Zaidel, and Zaidel (1979) indicated that the emotional reactions of split-brain patients were able to cross quite rapidly from the right side to the left. In their study, the right hemisphere was capable of locating affectively charged pictures of themselves, their relatives, friends, pets, and even belongings from a wide assortment of photographs presented to the LVF. The right brain's nonverbal reactions (e.g., nodding, shaking of the head, or spelling out answers with cutouts supplied to the left hand) triggered the appropriate left-hemispheric verbalizations. In fact, in more than one instance, the right hemisphere deliberately cued the left by specifically using the left hand to trace the letters of the correct item onto the back of the right hand. Obviously affective information could diffuse to the left brain via intact brain stem connections so that important categorical distinctions (e.g., friend vs. relative) could be verbalized. However, these subjects could not describe accurately the identity of particular people and the visual details of scenes. These findings suggest that cross-cuing is restricted to particular types of input, especially connotative (not denotative) ones. It remains to be determined what subcortical routes are employed to transfer these inputs interhemispherically.

MISCONCEPTIONS AND THEORIES INVOLVING SPLIT-BRAINS

This final section examines some of the more common misconceptions and popularized accounts associated with split-brain behavior, with particular attention paid to the view that cognitive processing capacity is not only increased, but doubled, as a result of commissurotomy. Some of the more recent models of callosal functioning also are presented to achieve a better understanding of this clinical syndrome.

Behavior After Surgery: Fact and Fiction

Incidents of bizarre split behavior immediately following commissurotomy have been reported occasionally in the literature. For instance, one patient could not put his trousers on because his left hand continually struggled with the right. When angered by his wife, the same patient wanted to reach out with his left hand to strike her, but the right hand prevented the gesture from ever occurring (Gazzaniga, 1970). Other patients have shown these dramatic, "Dr. Strangelovianesque" hand movements years after the surgery (Ferguson, Rayport, & Corrie, 1985). However, most observations reveal more subtle deficits in split-brain performance following the callosal sectioning. Consider the more realistic symptomatology of these patients.

One difficulty experienced by several split-brain subjects is the inability to associate names of people with their faces. Although they eventually learn the associations, it seems that the disconnecting of the verbal left hemisphere with the nonverbal right hemisphere primarily accounts for this short-term deficiency (Levy et al., 1972). Some patients also have trouble performing geometrical tasks, especially ones involving the matching of two- and three-dimensional forms on the basis of common features. Left-hemispheric deficits generally are found on these tasks, again because the verbal naming functions of this respective side have been separated from the spatial abilities of the corresponding right side (Franco & Sperry, 1977).

Although dreaming does not appear to be impaired significantly as a result of the surgery (Greenwood et al., 1977), memory performance scores are typically lower in a number of split-brainers, compared with control groups of epileptics not given the commisurotomy (Zaidel & Sperry, 1974). Chronic verbal memory and sequencing deficits have been shown in a few patients more than 3 years after callosal sectioning (Ferguson et al., 1985). However, these cognitive impairments usually are not expressed in the majority of split-brain cases. In fact, most of the difficulties already mentioned do not persist more than a few weeks, or months, in duration.

If anything, only an *acute disconnection syndrome* has been identified consistently in patients immediately following surgery. The symptoms often include a period of mutism, the inability to control the left side of the body for a time, and short-lived competitive hand movements (Springer & Deutsch, 1989). Based on this evidence, one could argue that (a) any initial split-brain impairments are due most likely to the surgical trauma involved in separating the hemispheres, and (b) any interpretation regarding split-brain hemispheric functions will be dependent on when patients are examined postoperatively. With respect to the latter factor, recovery in cerebral functions takes time (more for some subjects, less for others), yet it does occur. Thus, in this author's opinion, a wait-and-see period probably will yield more factual and objective accounts about the true capabilities of the two commissurotomized hemispheres. Pinel (1990) and Zaidel (1985) further supported this position by warning readers not to distort significantly or overpopularize the slight hemispheric differences found in the aforementioned studies. Otherwise, the facts will get so buried by the widely accepted fictions of our age concerning asymmetries that any accurate assessment of split-brain functions never will be achieved realistically.

Two Brains, Double the Capacity?

For a number of years, it was thought that commissural sectioning created two entirely independent streams of consciousness, or completely separate minds. Sperry (1968) and Selnes (1974) argued that the split-brain was able to carry out two distinctly different hemispheric tasks simultaneously; therefore its potential processing capacity could be increased, perhaps even doubled, by the surgery. Evidence for this view came from studies where postoperative patients were able to execute separate discrimination tasks in each visual field much faster than normal subjects (Ellenberg & Sperry, 1980; Gazzaniga & Sperry, 1966). One patient of LeDoux et al. (1977a) even showed that each hemisphere could answer questions asked of it in a different manner from its neighbor. For instance, when asked to select the career of choice, the right brain arranged "Scrabble" letters to spell out the words *automobile racing*, whereas the left side contradictorily asserted its preference of craftsmanship. Further, in some recent postoperative cases, memory functions have been found to actually improve instead of worsen (Sass, Novelly, Spencer, & Spencer, 1988). According to this approach, commissurotomy actually allows the two hemispheres to function as independent processing systems, whereby even more input can be registered and appropriately handled in contrast to the more limited effectiveness of the intact brain.

However, many researchers would not make this claim based on their observations of split-brain patients within these same tasks. Although subjects could discriminate colors in the RVF with the right hand and brightness levels in the LVF with the left hand, the functions required of the two hemispheres were relatively simple ones. As task-level complexity increased, the patients' reaction times lengthened, suggesting that the split-brain (overall) was not more efficient than the unified one (Sperry, Gazzaniga, & Bogen, 1969). Trevarthen (1974a) even added that the patients' allocation of attention to each hemisphere was impaired significantly as a result of commissurotomy. Therefore, unilateral mental sets could not be formed to help subjects solve the more difficult discriminations.

Based on these reports, the general conclusion is that split-brain patients possess a relative duality of consciousness, without actually doubling their cognitive capacity. If anything, some reduction in hemispheric processing could occur after the surgery (particularly with respect to the attentional component) so that cognitive styles could not be used most effectively.

Functions of the Corpus Callosum

Models of Callosal Functioning.   As expressed in chapter 1, the traditional views associated with callosal functioning have been to regard the series of interconnecting fibers as either: (a) duplicating information between the hemispheres in a carbon copy fashion; or (b) suppressing one hemisphere's activity so that the other, more suitable one can process the information according to its preferred mode. Unfortunately, neither view provides reasons why most split-brain patients show excellent recovery after surgery (Levy, 1985), nor why one of their disconnected hemispheres, at times, selects the complementary processing strategy that is not the most appropriate one to display (Levy & Trevarthen, 1977).

More recent models of callosal functioning posit an inhibitory transfer of information between the two hemispheres so that the same activity does not occur in each brain side. Cook (1984a) proposed that the callosum topographically inhibits the input from being registered by the same grouping of cells. However, adjacent neurons subsequently are excited and carry a slightly different message from the originally transmitted one. Woodward (1988) provided a slightly different account for callosal inhibition. Although cortical circuitry is functionally similar in each hemisphere, callosal signals suppress the dominant type of circuit (specifically vertically arranged, nonoverlapping connections) so that the more recessive type (horizontal intersecting circuits) is employed to a greater extent.

Regardless of which model is supported, the end result of callosal inhibition is to generate a two-brained perspective on the exact same input. It has been remarked that the intact brain closely resembles the split one in that it ordinarily possesses two relatively independent streams of consciousness (presumably generated by callosal inhibition). Commissurotomy intrusively makes this preexisting duality more apparent. Thus, humans are predisposed to think with two minds, not one (Puccetti, 1981b). Whether the reader accepts this extreme position or not, the idea that there are more similarities than differences between normal and commissurotomized subjects is a fascinating one to consider.

Agenesis of the Corpus Callosum.   Few people are born without a callosum. This condition, commonly referred to as *callosal agenesis* (or *prenatal commissurotomy*), gives the researcher the opportunity to determine the extent to which the callosum mediates communication between the two brain sides. Across a wide variety of behavioral tests designed to examine visual field and ear superiorities, congenital acallosals typically have been found to resemble normal subjects, demonstrating the same right-sided advantages for verbal materials. Other intact abilities include cross-modal matching of items presented visuotactually, reading words spanning the visual-field midline, verbally identifying objects by name as they are palpated with the left hand (or right hemisphere), and retrieving with either hand objects whose pictures are projected to either visual field (Milner & Jeeves, 1979).

Chiarello (1980) attempted to explain these maintained skills by suggesting that other interhemispheric pathways (e.g., the anterior commissure) are spared, although greatly enlarged to compensate for the missing callosum. Moreover, the deployment of particular cross-cuing strategies and the greater reliance on ipsilateral auditory, somatosensory, and motor pathways have been implicated in the recovery process. However, even with these structural substitutions, acallosal patients still experience some performance deficits like their split-brain counterparts. These impairments are examined in more detail.

Although tactile cross-modal matching is unaffected, inferior bimanual manipulation and coordination occasionally have been reported in congenital acallosals, along with difficulties in the interhemispheric transfer of kinesthetic inputs (Jeeves, 1965). Further, these subjects never experience total perceptual completion; often they can detect the midline join in chimeric stimuli, noting the incompleteness of such pictures as well as words (Bradshaw & Nettleton, 1983). This symptom rarely is seen in commissurotomized patients.

The most consistent problem identified in acallosals is that their intelligence often is below average, with marked discrepancies evidenced between their verbal and performance IQs (Field, Ashton, & White, 1978; Weber & Bradshaw, 1981). One explanation offered for this intellectual disturbance is that speech might have developed bilaterally at an early age, similar to other major brain pathologies. The argument goes that bilateral speech produces a "cognitive crowding" (i.e., functional competition), particularly for spatial skills in the right hemisphere. As a result, nonverbal performance IQ levels are impaired dramatically (Smith & Sugar, 1975; Sperry et al., 1969).

Some of these difficulties associated with the acallosal syndrome usually disappear with the passage of time (Bogen, 1985). It seems that patients, whether acallosal or split-brain, show recovery in most of their basic behavioral and cognitive functions. Although noncallosal channels are utilized to a greater extent in both groups, the corpus callosum should still be regarded as an important inhibitory mechanism for effective functioning to occur between the cerebral hemispheres. In the case of acallosal subjects, the development of language in the right hemisphere cannot be inhibited properly; therefore subsequent intellectual problems soon develop. Thus, for complete interhemispheric functioning, an intact callosum still is required.

SUMMARY AND CONCLUSIONS

This chapter took an intensive look at the split-brain syndrome in the hopes of answering the question "Are such patients significantly divided in cognitive functions?" Some overall conclusions are provided.

1. Although Vogel and Bogen regarded commissurotomy as a relatively safe procedure, leaving the patients' personality generally intact (Pinel, 1990), the subsequent investigations undertaken by Gazzaniga (1967; Gazzaniga & Sperry, 1967; Sperry, 1964, 1968) revealed some striking hemispheric divisions. The most prominent ones were in verbal identifications to stimuli presented in the RVF (or left hemisphere), and left-hand recognitions to LVF (right hemisphere) input. However, many of these separated functions gradually were acquired by the ipsilateral hemisphere. In addition, the cross-cuing phenomenon was operative in some instances, especially with emotionally arousing stimuli.

2. More current research findings on this syndrome have suggested that the patients' split-brain is a relatively divided one. Subjects still could complete figures partially shown to each visual field or split at the midline (e.g., chimeric faces). Each hemisphere could use either cognitive style, depending on whether it thought it could process effectively the input that particular way. At times, the left hemisphere could perform simple visuospatial functions and the right could evidence some limited linguistic abilities (apart from speech production). Moreover, as techniques became more advanced with respect to stimulus administration (e.g., the Zaidel presentations), cross-cuing was seen as a much more common transfer process occurring between brain sides.

3. It appears that any pronounced deficits experienced in split-brain patients were, for the most part, acute ones that disappeared in a few months. This recovery was attributed primarily to other interhemispheric pathways that apparently were spared from the callosal separation. Intact channels include such structures as the colliculi and brain stem.

As Springer and Deutsch (1989) indicated, although the callosum harmonizes the hemispheres, often in an inhibitory manner, each brain side is not removed totally from the other. Thus, a relative (rather than an absolute) duality of consciousness is present in the split-brain. Whether the same relative split in cognitive functions is evidenced in the intact brain remains a relevant inquiry for future scholars.

Is There Convincing Evidence for Cerebral Asymmetries in the Clinical Pathologies and Developmental Disabilities?

Part II concludes with an examination of cerebral asymmetries in dysfunctional groups, such as the psychoses and developmental disorders (in particular, dyslexia). Investigations into these pathologies have shown that left brain–right brain differences play an extremely important role in their expression.

ASYMMETRY'S LINK WITH THE MENTAL DISORDERS

The Psychoses

Schizophrenia: The Flor-Henry Hypothesis. Psychiatrist Flor-Henry (1969a, 1969b) was one of the first to associate *schizophrenia* with a left-hemispheric disturbance. Fifty patients who suffered from temporal lobe epilepsy and showed signs of psychosis were found to have greater neurological damage to their left brain, compared with a control group of epileptics without the psychotic symptoms. Further analysis of the psychotic cases indicated that left-hemisphere damage was more common with the schizophrenias, whereas right-hemisphere injury was associated more frequently with the affective disorders, especially unipolar depression. (More is said about these specific disorders at a later point in this chapter.)

Earlier reports that studied the effects of soldiers' head wounds obtained during World War II tended to confirm Flor-Henry's (1969a, 1969b) findings. Those injured who were classified as schizophrenic typically experienced some type of linguistic disturbance, as opposed to those who were not psychotic (Qalker & Jablon, 1961). As Gruzelier and Flor-Henry (1979) later formulated, the schizophrenic disorder could be associated with lesions restricted to the left hemisphere, which coincidentally was also the site where language mainly was lateralized.

More current research would support Flor-Henry's (1969a, 1969b) left-hemisphere malfunction hypothesis. Many of the cognitive deficits associated with schizophrenia resembled those found in left-hemisphere lesioned patients. Besides the prominent aphasia, the common symptomatology included inability to draw logical inferences, failure to use abstractions, and impairments in conceptualization (Gur, 1979). Moreover, morphological differences have been identified in the left hemisphere of schizophrenics; the normally wider left occipital lobe was not as readily apparent (Naeser, Levine, Benson, Stuss, & Weir, 1981), whereas electroencephalogram (EEG) waves were abnormally high in the left temporal lobe (Hollandsworth, 1990). It even has been proposed that because schizophrenics have these temporal disturbances, especially within the left limbic system, they often display emotional problems such as blunted affect and catatonia (Flor-Henry, 1976).

One interesting physiological difference was that some chronic schizophrenics exhibited a significant increase in the size of their corpus callosum, compared with normals who were examined upon postmortem. Some researchers have speculated that the callosal increase was required to compensate for the defective transfer of information, which presumably occurred from the impaired left side to the more intact right and back again (Beaumont & Dimond, 1972). Based on these results, it appears that schizophrenia is characterized, to a large extent, by particular abnormalities in the structure and functions of the left hemisphere, as Flor-Henry (1976) claimed.

Schizophrenia: The Behavioral Tests.

A wide variety of tests designed to measure the relative strength of the schizophrenic asymmetries also has yielded some interesting findings. Skin conductance to mild electrical currents and other electrodermal responses examined by Gruzelier and Hammond (1976, 1979) revealed that the schizophrenic's left hand was not very reactive to repeated auditory stimulation or input which was emotionally significant. These experimenters concluded that the ipsilateral hemisphere, which controlled left-hand responsiveness, was disturbed on that respective side; therefore, normal reactions could not be expressed properly, in contrast to the right side. Apparently a dulling of affect (as well as related emotional disturbances) could be produced in schizophrenic patients if the left brain were activated continually within these tasks.

Evidence for *greater* left-hemispheric involvement in schizophrenics comes from a variety of sources. Krynicki and Nahas (1979) indicated that the number of schizophrenics who were left-handed (as well as ambidextrous) exceeded chance level. It should be recalled that the ipsilateral left hemisphere exerts some control over this particular hand. Therefore, if this side is used more frequently across a wide range of manual tasks, presumably the psychotic left brain is being called on to a greater extent than the right. In addition, a number of studies have shown consistently that schizophrenic patients tend to display more right-sided lateral eye movements (or LEM) in response to spatial and verbal types of questions (Schweitzer, Becker, & Welsh, 1978; Tomer, Mintz, Levi, & Myslobodsky, 1979). In fact, the only inquiries that did not generate more right LEMs were ones having to do with a combined spatial–emotional component.

Most experimenters reasoned that if LEMs truly reflected cerebral activation, then the schizophrenic left hemisphere was being employed more frequently than the right to process many kinds of inputs, some of which were not necessarily appropriate to this side (e.g., the spatial questions). The left brain's failure to discriminate among the various inputs could be contributing to the major deficits identified in schizophrenia.

Before continuing, a brief word should be mentioned about some of the schizophrenic patients' eye movement dysfunctions (EMD). In a recent review, Clementz and Sweeney (1990) listed a number of eye problems in these subjects that included less frequent smooth pursuit movements to track certain objects, as well as more inappropriate saccadic movements during both fixation and tracking, compared with control subjects. As Holzman (1985) and Iacono (1988) discussed extensively, these EMDs can serve as important biological markers for the detection of schizophrenia. Investigations should continue in this area to establish a link between these dysfunctions and the right LEMs typically displayed in schizophrenics. Perhaps the patients' frontal lobes should be examined more thoroughly, especially because voluntary control of eye movements (including some saccadic) is initiated in this region (Levin, 1984).

Using a different behavioral approach, Beaumont and Dimond (1972) effectively showed that the schizophrenic condition was related to a much wider callosal impairment than just the left hemisphere. When stimulus pairs were presented tachistoscopically to either visual field, patients' judgments in discriminating whether the elements were the same or different were directly comparable to control subjects'.

However, when each member of the pair was projected to a different hemisphere, performance subsequently deteriorated, indicating that the interhemispheric callosal channel was operating in a defective manner (Fig. 6.1). This more general deficit possibly could account for other

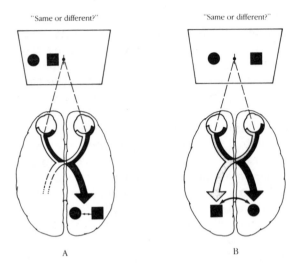

FIG. 6.1.   Within hemisphere versus between hemisphere: "same" and "different" judgments. A. When stimuli are projected unilaterally to the same hemisphere, schizophrenics perform just as well as controls. B. When stimuli are projected bilaterally to both hemispheres, schizophrenic performance deteriorates compared with controls. From *Left Brain, Right Brain* (p. 281) by Sally P. Springer and Georg Deutsch, New York: W. H. Freeman. Copyright 1989 by Sally P. Springer and Georg Deutsch. Reprinted by permission.

difficulties experienced in schizophrenics, such as right–left body side confusions as well as poor right- and left-hand tactile sensitivities (Krynicki & Nahas, 1979).

Based on this evidence, one might conclude that the left-hemispheric disturbance in schizophrenic patients is more reflective of an overall callosal malfunction between hemispheres, as Blau (1977), Claridge (1985), and Hollandsworth (1990) have remarked. Only time and continued study will truly reveal to what extent this psychotic malfunction incapacitates these subjects.

The Affective Disorders.   If schizophrenia has more left-hemispheric involvement (or damage), then the affective psychoses would seem to have the complementary sided asymmetry. Flor-Henry (1969b) noted this hemispheric reversal when he examined the site of epilepsy in his patients. Since then, studies have suggested that the right hemisphere is implicated in the *affective disorders*, especially unipolar depression. To summarize the major findings: (a) skin conductance response amplitudes were significantly lower in the depressed patients' right hands (Gruzelier & Hammond, 1976); (b) their EEG waves displayed a fluctuating activity, with more power in the right brain during the illness and upon posttreatment less, particularly in the respective right posterior region (Davidson, Chapman, & Chapman, 1987; Henriques & Davidson, 1990); and (c) a greater correlation of self-reported negative emotions has been found with right-hemispheric frontal lobe activity (Davidson, Schwartz, Saron, Bennett, & Galeman, 1979; Silberman & Weingartner, 1986).

One area that definitely has stimulated clinical interest has been the effects of unilateral electroconvulsive shock (ECS) on these affective disorders. In general, right-sided ECS has reduced effectively more of the debilitating consequences of the intrusive brain treatment, in comparison with the left-sided applications. Depressed patients consistently have experienced less memory loss, linguistic impairment, and verbal memory disruption following ECS administration to their right hemisphere (Annett, Hudson, & Turner, 1974; Warrington & Pratt, 1973). The ECS research appears to be one of the most convincing pieces of evidence to date for lateralization of the affective psychoses.

A possible explanation as to why schizophrenia and the affective disorders have complementary hemispheric disturbances has to do with their biochemical precursors. Schizophrenia has been associated with an overactivity of the dopamine receptors, whereas unipolar depression has been correlated with underactivity at the noradrenergic or norepinephric) synapses (Carlson, 1991; Lee & Seeman, 1980; Pinel, 1990; Snyder, 1986). As proposed in chapter 2, right-brain lateralization possibly proceeded from the left, in much the same way that norepinephrine was derived from dopamine.

Therefore, it can be reasoned that the affective psychoses developed from the schizophrenic, and eventually came to be housed in the emotional right hemisphere as the left side functionally set itself apart to regulate those linguistic components mainly associated with schizophrenia. Whether this view remains a valid one is for future neuropsychologists to decide.

Autism

A disorder related to schizophrenia is *childhood autism*, in which linguistic impairment and social withdrawal are the primary symptoms. Curiously, autistic children are able to demonstrate exceptional right-hemispheric abilities (e.g., in art or music), although their speech skills are depressed. These discrepancies have led researchers to consider the likelihood of hemispheric asymmetries in this particular group of abnormal subjects.

The most consistent finding reported in the literature is that autistics have a higher rate of nonright-handedness than normal controls (Boucher,

1977; Fein, Humes, Kaplan, Lucci, & Waterhouse, 1984). Pathological left-handedness (PLH) typically has been correlated with a shift in speech lateralization from the left to the right brain (Satz, Orsini, Saslow, & Henry, 1985a, 1985b), as well as an increased potential to develop a learning disorder or other related behavioral impairments (Geschwind & Galaburda, 1987). Brain damage, particularly to the left hemisphere, has been linked most often with PLH in autistic children. It even has been claimed by some that if the left-hemispheric injury occurs in early childhood (by approximately age 5), the visuospatial skills of the right hemisphere will remain unaffected, whereas the left's linguistic functions never will recover fully, thus accounting for many of the major symptoms displayed in autism (Lansdell, 1969).

Compatible with these previous hypotheses, Dawson, Warrenburg, and Fuller's (1982) *EEG* study showed that autistic children generated a "reverse" brain wave pattern compared with controls, with the right hemisphere dominant over the left on linguistic-type tasks. Further research with dichotic listening assignments revealed that the typical right-ear advantage (REA) for verbal materials was not especially strong in autistics. In fact, opposite ear superiority or no ear advantage were the more common patterns (Fein et al., 1984), providing additional support for the left-hemispheric dysfunction and reversed lateralization theories proposed earlier.

As Prior and Bradshaw (1979) have advised, more testing and clinical observations need to be performed on this syndrome before one advocates the position that left-sided brain damage is the identifying characteristic of most (if not all) autistic subjects. Nonetheless, a similar asymmetrical hypothesis has been advanced in the literature for both schizophrenia and childhood autism. Perhaps this left-hemispheric lateralization difficulty explains why the two abnormal disorders share a common symptomatology, but perhaps not. Work continues to proceed on the etiology of these two clinical pathologies.

Alcoholism and Other Age-Related Disorders

According to a number of recent reports, specific hemispheric impairments have been linked to a number of age-related disorders. *Alcoholism* has been studied the most extensively, with neurodegenerative alterations speculated to occur more frequently in the right hemisphere of chronic cases (Jenkins & Parsons, 1981; Miglioli, Buchtel, Campanini, & DeRisio, 1979). The strongest evidence for this theory comes from tests assessing alcoholics' visuospatial abilities. For the most part, severe cases do poorly on the Performance scale of the Wechsler Adult Intelligence

Test, with particular deficits noted on the Block Design and Object Assembly subscales (O'Leary, Donovan, Chaney, Walker, & Schau, 1979). Left visual-field problems in identifying nonverbal targets also are evidenced within tachistoscopic tasks; typically, long-term alcoholics' search times are slower in this field, with response accuracy generally lower than control subjects' and those who have more short-term drinking difficulties (Oscar-Berman & Bonner, 1985; Oscar-Berman, Goodglass, & Cherlow, 1973).

A reevaluation of the right-hemisphere dysfunction hypothesis would seem to be in order, however, because verbal problems have been uncovered gradually in this particular group of subjects. More severe (i.e., late-stage) alcoholics tend to show language impairments in the following areas: verbal learning and memory (Ryan, 1980; Ryan & Butters, 1986), word fluency (Bolter & Hannon, 1986), and word list generation, as well as syntactic comprehension (Rada, Porch, Dillingham, Kellner, & Porec, 1977). Further, Golden et al. (1981) and Gebhardt (1981) obtained convincing physiological evidence that cerebral atrophy was present to a greater extent in the left (not right) hemisphere of alcoholic brains, with enlarged ventricles and wider sulci generally displayed on that side.

These findings suggest that chronic alcoholism is a neuropsychological disorder associated with widespread cerebral decline, affecting both right and left brains, perhaps to equivalent degrees. As Ellis and Oscar-Berman (1989), Parsons (1987), and Tarter (1976) have argued, this more diffuse cortical damage model might replace the asymmetrical one, given sufficient empirical data. For the moment, it can be posited that the cognitive disabilities in long-term alcoholics can be associated with right- and, to a lesser extent, left-hemispheric dysfunctions.

Presenile Alzheimer's disease and the closely related *senile dementia of the Alzheimer's type* (SDAT or late-onset Alzheimer's) are age-related disorders characterized by progressive loss of memory and other mental functions. The cognitive deficit usually involves the most recent events; therefore the afflicted subjects typically experience an anterograde amnesia, which worsens over time. Eventually, people become bedridden and completely helpless as they succumb to the disease (Terry & Davies, 1980; Wurtman, 1985). The presenile as well as the senile form have been known to produce a severe organic degeneration of the hippocampus and neocortex, especially in the frontal and temporal lobes. On autopsy, slices of these brain areas reveal abnormally shaped neurons, with neurofibrillary tangles and other foreign structures present in the cell bodies. Decreased acetylcholine (ACh) activity also is associated with these regions (Carlson, 1991; Summers, Majovski, Marsh, Tachiki, & Kling, 1986).

Hemispheric asymmetries have been also identified with these types of Alzheimer's disease. Seltzer and Sherwin (1983) compared patients who had either type and discovered that fluent aphasia and left-handedness were much more common with the presenile form. As implied earlier, PLH has been correlated with left-hemisphere degeneration. Because aphasia was a particularly striking manifestation of the early onset type, Seltzer and Sherwin (1983) concluded that the speech regions, especially in the left posterior area, subsequently were affected by Alzheimer's.

Later reports have confirmed these findings; specifically, presenile patients repeatedly have shown problems with spontaneous speech, word fluency, and object naming (Nebes, 1989; Nicholas, Obler, Albert, & Helm-Estabrooks, 1985). Recently, Geschwind and Galaburda (1987) claimed that Alzheimer's patients experience delayed development of the left linguistic areas very early on in life (perhaps even as far back as the fetal stage). Therefore these subjects are much more susceptible to contract this disorder at a later point. Support for this position comes from the developmental disability research, which has demonstrated convincingly that left-sided epileptic seizures often are identified in the young brains of dyslexic, autistic, stuttering, and other language-impaired children (Stefan, Milea, & Magureanu, 1981). Whether other intellectual disorders have the same maldeveloped left cortex is a question that only neuropsychology can unravel.

ASYMMETRY'S CONNECTION TO THE DEVELOPMENTAL DISABILITIES

I will now direct the focus to developmental disorders to determine the extent to which hemispheric asymmetries exert an influence over their expression. Particular attention is paid to *developmental dyslexia*, which has generated a considerable amount of experimental research over the past decade.

Developmental Dyslexia

Definition for Dyslexia: A Unitary Disorder? Developmental dyslexia traditionally has been defined as a reading disability with some accompanying form of central nervous system dysfunction (Harris & Hodges, 1981). This childhood disorder usually is presumed to occur in the presence of normal intelligence and is not directly attributable to sociocultural background, mental retardation, emotional difficulty, or other handicapping condition (Gaddes, 1985; Hynd & Semrud-Clikeman, 1989). Estimates of this disorder's incidence vary substantially, from conservatively 1 in 500 to more precisely 6 in 100 (Hynd & Cohen, 1983; Pirozzolo, 1979). Generally, dyslexia is more common in boys than girls (a

4:1 ratio), because the bilateral representation of language functions in females more effectively insulates them from displaying this impairment. Moreover hereditary components have been implicated, with a higher dyslexic concordance rate typically shown in monozygotic twins compared with dizygotic pairs (Bakwin, 1973).

A survey of the literature shows that dyslexia is not a unitary disorder, but is composed of a number of subtypes. Vernon (1979), Aaron (1978), Keefe and Swinney (1979), and Naidoo (1972) argued that dyslexics either show an auditory–linguistic deficit or a visuospatial impairment. Put in the cognitive style classification, dyslexics either experience a left-analytic or right-holistic hemisphere disturbance. As Pirozzolo (1979) further described, the most common subtype involves problems with phonology; specifically, subjects read words as entire visual gestalts and subsequently are unable to decode these huge groupings into phonetically distinct units. Thus, an auditory–linguistic (or left-hemisphere) deficit generally occurs in the majority of dyslexic cases. Deep dyslexia is another name given to the aforementioned disorder (refer to chapter 4 for more details on this condition). In the less frequent subtype, referred to as visual–spatial (or right-hemisphere) dyslexia, subjects demonstrate the reverse impairment; namely, they cannot process words into visual gestalts and so must sound out the individual letters of each word.

Because the two types are so distinctive (and hemisphere specific), there is much confusion and disagreement in the literature regarding the dyslexic symptomatology. Empirical findings have varied (and will continue to vary), depending on the subgroup that is examined. The following is a historical look at the way brain lateralization and this reading disability were correlated originally.

Orton's Mirror-Image Lateralization Hypothesis. According to Orton's (1925, 1928) initial observations, childhood dyslexics tended to confuse mirror-reversed letters (e.g., *b* and *d*, *p* and *q*) and often reversed letter sequences in their reading (i.e., they interpreted *saw* as *was*). Yet, these same subjects displayed some rather unusual abilities. They could read better if the input was presented via a mirror, and they could write in mirror-image form exactly as was shown in the glass. Orton (1925, 1928) attempted to explain his findings by suggesting that there was a poorly established cerebral dominance in dyslexics, based on this group's fluctuating hand preferences from the normal right-handed pattern. This pathological handedness apparently was reflective of a weaker lateralization of linguistic functions in the left hemisphere. As already indicated, PLH has been associated with behavioral disorders as well as underlying asymmetrical shifts in hemispheric functions. So far, Orton's (1925, 1928) approach has been quite consistent with other current conceptualizations relating handedness variations to overall brain pathology.

However, Orton (1966) then speculated on a theory of cerebral dominance that stated, in essence, that because the brain had a symmetrical organization around the midline, the two hemispheres represented inputs in opposing left–right orientations. Elaborating on Orton's (1966) model further, the dominant hemisphere in the normal brain (i.e., the left) typically registered events in their correct orientation, but the right recorded the very same events in the reverse, mirror-image form (Fig. 6.2). Generally, problems would not be experienced with these complementary perspectives because normal subjects relied on their left hemisphere to process many types of inputs in their correct orientation. But in the dyslexic condition where cerebral dominance failed to develop properly, confusion in the subjects' reading and writing ensued as a direct result of these normal and reverse orientations competing with each other for control of behaviors (a condition known as *strephosymbolia*). Thus, the right hemisphere's mirror-image perspective was not able to be suppressed or elided by the left's correct one, and so mirror-reversal responses and associated problems became salient characteristics of this disorder.

A Critique of the Orton Model.   Corballis and Beale (1976, 1983) were one of the first research teams that pointed out that the hemispheres would not respond to stimuli in mirror-opposite ways, as long as both eyes and both visual fields transmitted information to the brain. Therefore, it seems unlikely that representations are laid down in a mirror-image fashion, as Orton (1966) speculated. A more plausible, physiological explanation for mirror reading (and writing) in dyslexics is that the reverse orientation would stimulate information flow from the RVF to the LVF, and subsequently would facilitate greater processing of messages by the unimpaired reading-related areas of the right hemisphere. In the normal

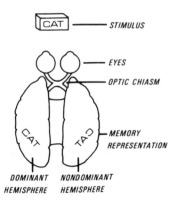

FIG. 6.2. Diagram of Orton's (1966) mirror-image lateralization theory. The visual stimulus cat is represented in opposing orientations within the two hemispheres, with a left–right reversal reflected in the right brain. From *The Ambivalent Mind: The Neuropsychology of Left and Right* (p. 212) by M. Corballis and I. L. Beale, Chicago: Nelson-Hall. Copyright 1983 by Nelson-Hall. Reprinted by permission.

reading of English from left to right, the very next words to be read would lie in the RVF; therefore the input would be correspondingly relayed to the disabled left hemisphere, which could not process the received messages effectively (let alone transmit them to the undisturbed right side).

The more recently formulated hypothesis by Geschwind and Galaburda (1987), although definitely superior to the Orton (1966) model, still needs to be put to the test. One way is to compare dyslexic performance across several languages, some of which are in the reverse orientation (e.g., Hebrew), to determine if different degrees of impairment exist in reading skills. The prediction is that those dyslexics who could read English easily in mirror fashion might not show the dyslexia when learning to read other, "reversed" languages, such as Hebrew. One other point should be considered before accepting this current theory. Not every dyslexic child demonstrates these left–right reversals. It still remains debatable whether the spatial confusions mentioned by Orton (1966) are any more common in developmental dyslexics than among beginning readers (Fisher, Liberman, & Shankweiler, 1978; Ginsberg & Hartwick, 1971).

Nonetheless, Orton (1966) should be credited with making the first link between reading disability and hemispheric asymmetry. Also, his finding that there was a raised incidence of sinistrality in developmental dyslexics is, for many, an uncontestable observation even to this day. The latest studies by Geschwind and Behan (1982, 1984), among others (Hier, LeMay, Rosenberger, & Perlo, 1978; LeMay, 1981; Parkins, Roberts, Reinarz, & Varney, 1987; Rosenberger & Hier, 1980; Zangwill, 1978), revealed that there was an elevated frequency of personal and familial left-handedness in dyslexics over the expected rate in the normal population. In fact, in one of their studies, Geschwind and Behan (1984) discovered that the rate of dyslexia was 15 times as high in their dominant left-handed group as in the strongly right-handed counterpart. As these researchers have cautioned, the greater incidence of nonright-handedness does not imply that the cause of the dyslexic condition has been identified, only that sinistrality should be considered an important marker of a possible alteration in the normal pattern of hemispheric dominance. To further confirm Orton's (1966) claim, Porac and Coren (1981) remarked that although some neuropsychologists deny this fairly noticeable increase of left-handedness in the dyslexic population, not a single study has shown the reverse trend, namely a deficiency of nonright-handedness.

One other aspect of Orton's (1937, 1966) theory, which requires examination, was that the incomplete cerebral dominance of dyslexics usually is reflected in their mixed, or crossed, body lateralizations (i.e., left-handedness with right-eye dominance or vice versa). A number of investigators has supported Orton's (1937, 1966) position, finding higher incidences of crossed hand-eye dominance in their dyslexic groups (Bryden, 1970; Dunlop, Dunlop, & Fenelon, 1973). However, Pavlidis (1981), as well as Stein and Fowler (1981), noticed that erratic eye movements occurred in dyslexics when they were engaged in both verbal and visual tasks. In addition, they observed that some occluded one eye when attempting to read particular texts. Based on this more recent evidence, it has been concluded that a stable ocular dominance has not been established fully in dyslexia. This accounts for the poor oculomotor control across tasks, as well as the intentional occlusions on the part of the subjects to stabilize this eye impairment. Apparently an oculomotor instability lies at the root of this disturbance rather than a crossed dominance problem, as posited by Orton (1937, 1966) and his followers.

Behavioral-Brain Asymmetries in Dyslexia. With respect to auditory laterality effects, a number of studies have failed to find significant differences between dyslexics and normal subjects. In fact, both groups have shown the typical REAs across trials within the dichotic listening tasks (Hynd, Obrzut, Weed, & Hynd, 1979; Naylor, 1980). However, a weak (although insignificant) LEA sometimes has been observed in the dyslexic population (Thomson, 1976; Witelson & Rabinovich, 1972). Moreover, under certain conditions, dyslexic subjects have generated a bimodal laterality distribution involving the dichotic responses, with some displaying the usual REA and others the complementary LEA. As Keefe and Swinney (1979) suggested, these differences might be explained by dyslexia being composed of different subtypes, with the LEA group possibly experiencing a left-hemisphere deficit and the REA group an associated right-hemisphere disturbance. Therefore, the dyslexic type that is selected and subsequently tested might have a direct influence on whether dichotic ear asymmetries are evidenced.

Another factor exerting an effect on dyslexic performance in dichotic listening appears to be attentional demands. When poorer readers were directed to focus their attention onto one ear side, a reversed ear advantage (LEA) was observed under the left-focus condition. On the other hand, normal readers continued to show the REA regardless of instructions (Obrzut, Hynd, Obrzut, & Pirozzolo, 1981). Apparently, the reading-impaired group was not able to suppress information from the non-dominant left ear if attention was directed to that particular ear side. As Bryden (1986) explained, one needs to consider the influence of attentional bias when interpreting the asymmetrical outcomes within the dichotic tasks. Further investigation with this variable potentially can help scientists distinguish the varying information-processing skills exhibited by different subjects (including normal as well as learning-impaired subjects).

In tachistoscopic studies, the same reduced (or absent) right-sided advantages for verbal materials sometimes are evidenced in dyslexics, in comparison with normal readers (Kershner, 1977; McKeever & Van Deventer, 1975; Young & Ellis, 1981). Even a reversed LVF superiority has been reported by some experimenters, resembling the LEA found within the dichotic tasks (Bakker, 1973; Bakker, Smink, & Reitsma, 1973). Because dyslexia is not a unitary disorder, it can be reasoned that a variety of subtypes, each with its own unique hemispheric disturbance, had been tested across these procedures. Another possibility raised by Naylor (1980) is that not all of the target groups examined were true dyslexics; some simply had poorer reading abilities than their respective controls, further accounting for the variable asymmetrical results.

Other arguments for the visual field differences in dyslexic subjects have been advanced over the years. Young and Ellis (1981) posited that because dyslexics have more oculomotor irregularities, including poorer fixational control, they demonstrate fluctuating and changeable field preferences. Another theory has to do with developmental changes in the cortical processing of verbal inputs presented visually. In normal children, a shift from a LVF to RVF superiority typically is shown as reading skills are acquired. Presumably, the right hemisphere initially is called on to process the unfamiliar words. With repeated exposure to these stimulus patterns, the left hemisphere takes over those right functions to derive meaningful interpretations from the verbal units (Carmon, Nachshon, & Starinsky, 1976; Silverberg, Gordon, Pollack, & Bentin, 1980). Obviously the inability of dyslexic children to develop a more stable RVF advantage might explain why these subjects experience overall reading difficulties. They are overrelying on the right brain's holistic style to process words rather than the more conducive analytic style of the left brain (Satz & Sparrow, 1970; Witelson, 1977b). With intensive practice (especially in left–right discriminations), dyslexics can achieve satisfactory reading skills as they learn to effectively use the nonpreferred left-hemispheric style (Corballis & Beale, 1983).

Morphological Asymmetries in Dyslexia. Some anatomical differences also have been identified in the brains of dyslexics. Wider right parietal and occipital lobes have been shown, with the variations more pronounced in sinistral subjects (Hier et al., 1978). Further, the left temporal planum was just as large as the right in a majority of cases. The bilateral dimensions of the symmetrical plana also tended to be greater than those of normal brains (Corballis & Beale, 1983; Galaburda, Sherman, Rosen, Aboitiz, & Geschwind, 1985). Presumably, the size variation in plana was accounted for by some mechanism (perhaps hormonal) that allowed cortical cells to grow, migrate, and survive in several sublayers of the brain, particularly the white matter of the left hemisphere, where they typically did not belong. According to Geschwind (1984) and Geschwind and Galaburda (1987), these cellular deviations had an effect on the human immune system, making the dyslexic group more at risk for the disorder. Disruptions in the normal rate of cell migration also have produced thalamic disturbances in both hemispheres, as well as subsequent aphasic and correlated reading problems in dyslexics (Galaburda & Eidelberg, 1982). The evidence to date appears to indicate that some meaningful correlation exists between handedness, autoimmune disease, and atypical morphological patterns for this developmental disorder.

Stuttering

Orton (1925, 1937) was the first to observe that an increased rate of *stuttering* accompanied dyslexia. Therefore, it was quite natural for him to assume that a weaker cerebral dominance was present for both stuttering and dyslexia. Orton (1925, 1937) proposed that both right and left hemispheres competed for the control of speech (rather than the left exclusively), with the end result that articulation problems usually were expressed in these children. One predisposing agent in stuttering also was advanced at this time, namely shifted-handedness. According to the theory, forcing youngsters who showed a natural preference for the left hand to use the complementary right had potentially serious consequences on their overall development, including an increased risk for stuttering. As recently reported by Corballis and Beale (1983), some cases of stuttering began only after children were induced by their parents to change their writing preference from the left to right hand. Apparently this hand shift (estimated to be as high as 70% in some studies) created the corresponding cortical change from unilateral to bilateral representation for speech, as originally formulated by Orton (1925). Retraining children to use their left hand might be one way to correct very serious stuttering difficulties.

Because stuttering has been correlated with handedness, particularly left-handedness, the true incidence of this dominance has been a matter of investigation (and debate) over the past few years. Although some older studies have found no differences in the distribution of handedness in the general population of stutterers (Andrews, Quinn, & Sorby, 1973; Sheenan, 1970; Van Riper, 1971), more current research has suggested that there are large preference asymmetries, with higher rates of sinistrality typically replicated across studies (Bishop, 1987). Similar to dyslexia, strong familial left-handedness has been confirmed in a subgroup of stutterers who displayed the hypothesized bilateral control of speech upon Wada testing (Jones, 1966). Although PLH might be associated with this disorder, one certainly should not generalize the aforementioned results to all stutterers, at least not until more specific subtypes are identified and put through more rigorous testing.

Besides atypical hand dominance, dyslexia and stuttering share another characteristic, namely the preponderance of males suffering from either affliction. Other gender differences have been noted consistently in the literature as well. A higher proportion of men than women are (a) left-handed (Loo & Schneider, 1979; Oldfield, 1971), (b) men are more prone to birth stressors such as oxygen deprivation (Bakan, 1975; Bakan, Dibb, & Reed, 1973), and (c) men often lag behind women in the development of speech lateralization in comparison with more visuospatial skills (Denckla, Rudel, & Broman, 1980; Hier & Kaplan, 1980). These conditions certainly would predispose the male gender to developmental disorders involving more language-related functions (i.e., speech, reading, and writing). On the other hand, females would be considerably less at risk, because their bilateral mechanism for speech representation develops much earlier and more naturally, often before puberty. Thus, women do not have to contend with the environmental pressures associated with making left-to-right hand (and brain) shifts as men obviously had to do.

One final similarity between dyslexia and stuttering should be mentioned. Behavioral-brain studies often have reported reversed or reduced functional asymmetries in stutterers, resembling those of particular dyslexic subtypes. In dichotic listening tasks, most stutterers either have shown very pronounced LEAs or significantly smaller ear differences compared with normal controls (Brady & Berson, 1975; Quinn, 1972; Sommers, Brady, & Moore, 1975). All of these experiments directly examined the perception of speech sounds by stutterers, not the production of speech per se. Sussman and MacNeilage (1975a, 1975b) subsequently developed a dichotic procedure that would assess more effectively whether stutterers were less lateralized for vocalizations, as Orton (1966) claimed.

In the Sussman and MacNeilage (1975a, 1975b) design, subjects heard a target tone that was varied randomly in frequency within one of their ears. At the same time, a cursor tone was played in the other ear. Subjects were required to match the frequency of the cursor with the varying target tone; they only could achieve this by moving their jaws a certain way, which would align the pitch of the cursor with the target appropriately. Sussman and MacNeilage (1975a, 1975b) found that although normal controls tracked the target more accurately when the cursor was presented to the right ear, the stutterers failed to demonstrate these laterality differences. Because the stutterers' jaw movements resembled those implicated with speech, the inability of this group to display the normal REA presumably reflected a bilateral representation for vocalizations.

Although lateralization of visual perception was not directly relevant to the etiology of stuttering, quite surprisingly LVF advantages have been demonstrated by stutterers in tachistoscopic studies involving word presentations (Moore, 1976). Another measure to test linguistic bilateralization has been employed with stutterers as well: brain wave recordings when subjects read textual material aloud. Alpha waves (generally associated with rest and relaxation) were more diminished in incidence across the right hemisphere of stutterers, implying that this brain side was processing the verbal input to a greater extent than the left (Moore & Lang, 1977).

These reversals in functional asymmetry definitely provide convincing evidence that anomalies of cerebral lateralization exist in stutterers, as with dyslexics. Nearly all of the subjects who showed reversals were right-handed ones. However, they could have been forced to change their hand dominance to this side at a very early age, as Orton (1966) formulated. Although the behavioral studies lend credence to the Orton theory, it still remains to be determined whether the unswitched, left-handed stutterers exhibit the same reversals as their switched, right-handed peers.

Dyscalculia and Other Right-Hemisphere Syndromes

This discussion has been limited to left-hemispheric learning dysfunctions, because these have generated the most intensive experimentation and study. But this chapter would not be complete without focusing on the complementary disabilities attributed to right-brain malfunctioning. *Dyscalculia* is one such disorder that has been tied directly to deficiencies in visual–spatial organization and nonverbal integration.

Children with dyscalculia usually cannot differentiate objects on the basis of size, shape, amount, or length. Although their auditory skills and word reading abilities show no particular impairments, most of the childrens' drawings lack elaborate detail and organization. Disturbances in body image and spatial relations are observed further (Johnson & Myklebust, 1971). Perhaps the most salient deficiency lies in the dyscalculics' inability to perform basic arithmetic and geometric operations (Landsdown, 1978). Early damage to areas within the right hemisphere, including the thalamus and medial posterior lobe, appears to contribute significantly to these mathematical difficulties, along with associated problems in map drawing and other graphic skills (Ojemann, 1974; Querishi & Dimond, 1979; Semrud-Clikeman & Hynd, 1990). Social–emotional impairments also may be reflective of the right-hemisphere injury because these underachievers in arithmetic are, for the most part, less well adjusted and sociable than the respective controls (Badian, 1983b; Kirby & Asman, 1984).

Another disorder related to right-hemispheric dysfunctions is the *non-verbal perceptual-organization-output disability* (commonly referred to as NPOOD). Rourke and Finlayson (1978) claimed that NPOOD children displayed above average reading and spelling skills, but major weaknesses were evidenced in visuospatial abilities and, to a lesser extent, arithmetic operations. In one such task, NPOOD children could not match nonverbal cues (i.e., facial expressions and gestures) with the appropriate verbal content (Ozols & Rourke, 1985). A flat affect, combined with monotonous speech patterns, also was noticed by several research teams (Rourke, 1982; Strang & Rourke, 1985). In fact, clinical depression, severe anxiety, and social withdrawal all are considered to be part of the typical psychopathological profile of the NPOOD child. Depression in some of these youngsters is very consistent with aforementioned theories that emphasize the right hemisphere's involvement with sadness and other negatively affective states (Davidson et al., 1979; Lavadas, Nicoletti, Umilta, & Rizzolatti, 1984). In further support of this hypothesis, NPOOD subjects showed greater brain wave activity in the right frontal and temporal lobe regions (Ternes, Woody, & Livingston, 1987).

One final characteristic of the NPOOD syndrome is the differential incidences between the genders. Rourke (1982) discovered that this learning disability affected females to a greater extent than males, with at least a 50% estimated incidence for the former gender. It might be that the females' bilateralization of linguistic functions placed them at a potentially greater risk for one of the nonverbal learning disorders, especially because the right hemisphere was not lateralized primarily to handle spatial skills in a competent fashion. Thus, Rourke (1982) logically reasoned that females experienced a "cortical trade-off": Language representation in both hemispheres saved them from dyslexia and other verbal types of disorders, whereas at the same time created a higher vulnerability for the complementary nonverbal impairments. The stronger asymmetrical pattern evidenced in males apparently produced the opposite risk, with significantly higher incidences of dyslexia and stuttering generally reported for this gender. As Semrud-Clikeman and Hynd (1990) advised, this gender difference needs to be addressed properly in future learning disability (LD) studies to see whether early deviations in cortical development are correlated strongly to gender.

Two other right-hemisphere disabilities should be discussed briefly: *Asperger's syndrome* and the *left hemisyndrome*. Unlike typical autistics, children with Asperger's syndrome show early speech and good grammar. However, visual–spatial and motor skills often are delayed, and nonverbal aspects of communication can be extremely limited, particularly in facial expressions and gestures (Asperger, 1979; Wing, 1985). Similar to NPOOD, dyscalculia is a frequently noted characteristic of Asperger's syndrome (Baron, 1987; Isaev & Kagan, 1974). Although the social withdrawal resembles the autistic type, the significant deterioration in right-hemisphere abilities clearly differentiates this disorder from traditional autism (Wolff & Barlow, 1979).

With respect to the left hemisyndrome, motor system impairments in reflexes, muscle tone, coordination, eye tracking, and eye fixation commonly are identified. Again dyscalculia is shown, along with geographical disabilities and difficulties in processing gestures, vocal intonations, and associated facial expressions. Although there appear to be mild delays in speech and reading, these reach a satisfactory level of competency over time. Interestingly, the acquisition of normal verbal skills becomes one of the most salient markers of the left hemisyndrome. Based on the deficits in arithmetic and social perception abilities, Denckla (1978) and Voeller (1986) localized this dysfunction primarily in the right hemisphere, as had been done previously with NPOOD and Asperger's syndrome.

It appears that in all of these right-hemispheric learning disabilities, a set of common symptoms can be listed, which includes: dyscalculia, visuospatial difficulties, social withdrawal, weaker performance abilities (and higher complementary verbal ones), and deficient social skills. For this reason, some experimenters would classify these disabilities as extending along a possible continuum. Asperger's syndrome represents the most severe type of disorder, and subsequently is positioned at the more involved end of the speculated scale (Semrud-Clikeman & Hynd, 1990). Refinements undoubtedly will continue to be made in the diagnostic schema as more studies relate morphological deviations of the right brain with certain neuropsychological outcomes.

SUMMARY AND CONCLUSIONS

Chapter 6 addressed the issue of whether there was convincing evidence for brain lateralization in clinical subjects as well as children with developmental disabilities. The results tended to show that the strongest asymmetries were in the learning disorders, followed by some clinical impairments (i.e., autism, Alzheimer's disease, and unipolar depression). The key points of this chapter include:

1. Pertaining to the psychoses, the schizophrenic condition has been correlated with a left hemisphere dysfunction, whereas, alternately, unipolar depression has been associated with the complementary malfunction. However, the asymmetrical findings for schizophrenia in particular have not been consistent always, let alone conclusive. In fact,

Hollandsworth (1990) and others argued that it is extremely difficult to know what part of the schizophrenics' cortical system is dysfunctional. Therefore they would rather speculate that both brain sides do not function in a coordinated manner.

2. With respect to the other clinical disorders, autism and presenile Alzheimer's disease have been linked to delayed lateralization of speech in the left hemisphere as well as higher incidences of pathological left-handedness (PLH). On the other hand, chronic alcoholism seems to demonstrate widespread cortical declines in both hemispheres (similar to the schizophrenic psychosis).

3. Two developmental disabilities of the left hemisphere—dyslexia and stuttering—have shown some rather extreme variations from the typical behavioral asymmetries obtained in dichotic and tachistoscopic tasks, signifying that anomalies in cerebral lateralization exist in these affected children. The greater proportion of left-handed males (relative to females) further confirms this argument. Finally, right-hemispheric learning disorders (e.g., dyscalculia, NPOOD, and Asperger's syndrome) were discussed at some length to generate a fairly distinctive profile on these at-risk children. Common characteristics included: visuospatial difficulties, socialization problems, and weaker performance abilities relative to verbal skills.

To date, it has been accepted widely that if lateralization differences have been reported in these various populations, they would appear to be related most directly to specific subtypes (e.g., auditory–linguistic dyslexia with left-hemisphere deficit, and visual–spatial dyslexia with right-hemisphere impairment). Obviously, more observations are required before one can answer satisfactorily the inquiry posed at the beginning of this chapter.

The encouraging piece of evidence to help solve this puzzle is that if asymmetrical differences have been identified in specific clinical and/or developmental groups, a stronger case can be made for hypothesized hemispheric variations in particular subgroups of the normal population (e.g., one gender or hand-dominant group). But, one should keep in mind that the brain differences obtained, no matter how pronounced, are still relativistic ones. As Bradshaw and Nettleton (1983) postulated, any skill can potentially implicate both left- and right-brain components. Therefore, disturbances in any ability (e.g., dyscalculia) will be reflective of a two-sided malfunction, not just one exclusively.

With this in mind, I now direct attention to the studies involving more normal subjects to see if a similar asymmetrical pattern holds for some of these members. Part III focuses on the types of tests used to assess normal brain laterality, and then examines the performance of specialized groups on these tests.

PART THREE

EVIDENCE FOR CEREBRAL ASYMMETRIES IN NORMAL SUBJECTS

Now that I have identified clinical brain asymmetries in neuropsychological, split-brain, and other pathological populations, the question remains as to whether the normal brain displays the same lateralized arrangement between hemispheres. This overall inquiry is answered by first looking at the standardized procedures used to study normal brain asymmetries (chapter 7), and then focusing on lateralization differences within specific groups of the normal population: males and females (chapter 8), dextrals and sinistrals (chapter 9), as well as younger versus older subjects (chapter 10). The direction and magnitude of each of these group differences is provided, along with a theoretical explanation as to why such asymmetries are observed in these particular subjects.

CHAPTER SEVEN

How Are Asymmetries
Studied in the Normal Brain?

Fortunately, most people have two intact hemispheres that are connected via a normally functioning corpus callosum. Yet, although these subjects possess a neurologically sound brain organization, laterality differences that surprisingly complement those of commissurotomized and other clinical patients still can be evidenced. This chapter reviews the standard procedures that have been employed with normal subjects in the hopes of uncovering further information about cortical asymmetries. Some of the techniques discussed resemble ones already in use in clinical populations (i.e., tachistoscopic and dichotic presentations), whereas others focus more extensively on changes in normal brain activity within particular tasks (e.g., EEG, CLEM, blood flow, and PET scan indices). The chapter begins with an investigation of the visual and auditory asymmetries.

TACHISTOSCOPIC AND DICHOTIC TASKS

Visual Field Asymmetries

Visual studies with normal subjects typically have used tachistoscopic stimulation projected to a specific field, with exposure times averaging approximately 150 milliseconds or less to ensure that the information is relayed to only one hemisphere at a time (Young, 1981). Although the commissures allow for effective communication between the two hemispheres, there is still some apparent loss in the transfer of information from one cortical side to the other. Thus, asymmetrical advantages can be obtained in normal subjects, although the field differences are generally smaller than those found in commissurotomized patients. Testing large groups of people over many trials tends to make this less pronounced tachistoscopic effect more reliable and, hence, more measurable (Corballis & Beale, 1983).

With accuracy of recall as the dependent measure, a number of visual studies has demonstrated the following results consistently: RVF (left-hemispheric) advantages and shorter vocal-naming latencies under this respective field for unilateral single-letter (Bryden, 1965, 1966; Zurif & Bryden, 1969), digit (Geffen, Bradshaw, & Wallace, 1971; Rizzolatti, Umilta, & Berlucchi, 1971), as well as word presentations (Bradshaw & Gates, 1978; Bradshaw, Nettleton, & Taylor, 1981; Leiber, 1976); and, alternately, LVF (right-hemispheric) superiorities for simple nonverbal stimuli ranging from dot detections and localizations (Bryden, 1976; Davidoff, 1977; Umilta et al., 1979) to photographed faces and cartoon line drawings of people expressing strong emotions (Berlucchi, Brizzolara, Marzi, Rizzolatti, & Umilta, 1974; Hilliard, 1973; Ley & Bryden, 1977, 1979; Suberi & McKeever, 1977). In addition, significantly larger RVF advantages have been obtained when letters and words were presented bilaterally (in comparison with the standard unilateral procedure), suggesting that the left hemisphere was a more efficient processor of the competitive verbal stimulation being directed to both visual fields simultaneously (Hines, 1972; McKeever, 1971; McKeever & Hurling, 1971). However, whether stronger LVF superiorities can be found for most types of bilateral, nonverbal inputs has yet to be determined (Bradshaw & Nettleton, 1983).

Unlike split-brain patients, normal subjects can vocalize words and other verbal materials flashed to their LVF. This is mainly because the right hemisphere still can communicate with the left's speech centers via the interconnecting callosum. Hence, any LVF advantages that typically are displayed are clearly more relative ones than those of commissurotomized subjects.

Differential Trends in Field Asymmetries.   It seems that the nature of the tachistoscopic stimuli presented has a bearing on which field processes the input more effectively. Although a strong RVF superiority generally is shown for letter and word stimuli, sometimes the alternate advantage might emerge. For instance, if the verbal materials were handwritten instead of in the standard typescript, LVF identifications were accurate more often than right field (Brooks, 1973). Further, if the typeface was more complex (i.e., unusual, florid, or Gothic style), the right hemisphere once again was invoked to a greater extent, presumably due to the spatial nature of these particular patterns (Bryden & Allard, 1978; Gordon & Carmon, 1976). RVF superiorities also have been reduced, and even reversed, when mirror-oriented letters and digits were viewed (Bradshaw et al., 1976; Cohen, 1975). Possibly subjects overrelied on the right hemisphere to transform the mirrored stimuli to their proper orientation so that correct recognitions subsequently could occur in the respective left field. On the other hand, the left hemisphere probably could not mediate these spatial transformations and so was at a loss to identify these particular stimuli except in their original orientation. Similar to the mirror-reversal inputs, languages in which reading naturally proceeds from the right to left (e.g., Hebrew and Yiddish) sometimes can be processed more accurately by the LVF, but the effect is not always found to be reliable (Barton, Goodglass, & Shai, 1965; Mishkin & Forgays, 1952).

Some studies have reported an RVF (instead of an LVF) superiority for familiar types of faces with nonverbal types of stimuli (Marzi & Berlucchi, 1977; Marzi, Brizzolara, Rizzolatti, Umilta, & Berlucchi, 1974). However, this appears to be a function of a hemispheric processing shift taking place over time, with the left hemisphere gradually acquiring the ability to handle the forms as they became less novel and, hence, more commonplace (Umilta, Brizzolara, Tabossi, & Fairweather, 1978). One of the most striking effects is that an RVF advantage can be evidenced when nontarget schematic faces are compared to targets, where the discrimination is based solely on the discernment of a single, differing feature in each nontarget (Patterson & Bradshaw, 1975). Classification of faces by gender also has produced a similar field advantage (Jones, 1979). One viable explanation for these latter results is that the left hemisphere may be better at categorizing stimuli (both verbal and nonverbal) as well as analyzing the fine details of objects, in contrast to the right's more holistic style of processing the inputs.

Besides the tachistoscopic materials, the task requirements have been known to influence which hemisphere displays the relative advantage. In one procedure (Bradshaw & Nettleton, 1983), if subjects were asked to judge pairs of letters "same" or "different" based on their names (e.g., Aa would generate a "same" response), faster RVF judgments occurred. However, if the physical shape of the letter pairs was the determining factor in subjects' judgments (e.g., now Aa would generate a "different" response), LVF advantages were shown. Therefore, letters could elicit either right- or left-hemispheric processing, depending on whether they were to be perceived as shapes or verbal symbols. Other studies (Moscovitch, 1976; Umilta, Frost, & Hyman, 1972) have yielded the same results, namely RVF superiorities for acoustic-matching assignments and, alternately, LVF ones for visual-matching tasks.

Certain cultures have replicated these field differences with their own unique communication systems. The Japanese have two writing structures, *Kana* and *Kanji*, that are sound based (i.e., syllabic) and meaning based (i.e., ideographic), respectively. As might be suspected, the graphic complexity of the Kanji characters is much more detailed and spatially structured, whereas the Kana symbols resemble the letters of the Western alphabet. When nonsense words were devised under both writing systems and then presented tachistoscopically, Japanese subjects consistently showed an RVF superiority in identifying the Westernlike Kana symbols and, conversely, a weaker LVF advantage in identifying the complementary spatial, Kanji characters (Hatta, 1977, 1978; Sasanuma, 1980; Sasanuma, Itoh, Mori, & Kobayashi, 1977). Therefore, the type of linguistic processing to be executed (e.g., acoustic or spatial) will, more or less, determine which hemisphere should be primed to register that input. Obviously, this effect can be generated cross culturally across fairly standardized tachistoscopic procedures.

Field Asymmetry Models.   Most asymmetries found in tachistoscopic tasks usually have shown stronger RVF (than LVF) advantages, with more consistent results expressed for verbal stimuli such as words or letters. If left-hemispheric advantages are more pronounced than right ones, the question "Why do these hemispheric differences occur?" can be posed. Two models of brain asymmetry recently have been proposed by Springer and Deutsch (1989) to address this issue.

The *direct access model* posits that the first hemisphere to receive the tachistoscopic input is the one to process the information. To provide an example, if RVF verbal material was received subsequently by the left hemisphere, that particular side of the brain would handle the input (and, in this case, a superiority would emerge because the left brain was specialized to deal with that type of information). However, if LVF verbal material were registered by the right hemisphere, this side would process the input, although it was not equipped to handle it. In the latter scenario, an LVF advantage would not be displayed because the respective hemisphere was not specialized (or primed) for that type of material.

Conversely, in the *indirect relay model*, information always is processed by the hemisphere that is best suited to deal with that material. If the input reaches the specialized hemisphere directly, clearly a field advantage would be found. However, in the situation where the nonspecialized hemisphere initially registers the input, a crossover between hemispheres via the callosum would be necessary before the information could be processed indirectly by the specialized one. If LVF verbal material is received by the right hemisphere, a disadvantage would be shown (similar to the first model), because the input would have to undergo an interhemispheric transfer to the more specialized left brain. This transfer would not only generate a time delay, but also a loss in informational clarity as the callosal route was followed to its termination point.

Thus, whichever model is subscribed to, the end result is the same: One hemisphere will display a processing advantage over the other, with the cortical asymmetry being dependent on the type of material presented or the task required of subjects to perform. Corballis and Beale (1983) attempted to go one step further. They argued that left-hemispheric functions hold the higher priority, based on the powerful evolutionary need in the human organism to communicate with other members of its species (primarily through language as well as other manipulative movements involving the hands). Therefore, RVF advantages are stronger than LVF ones, because the two hemispheres do not share the same degree of specialization, and have not done so for some fairly lengthy historical period. However, it still remains to be contested by some theorists (Webster, 1977) whether the left brain always should be regarded as the "leading specialist" when it comes to information processing and analysis.

Use of Fixation Controls and Other Techniques.

Experimenters noted that, under bilateral stimulus presentations, subjects on occasion deliberately attended to one field side or the other. A control measure had to be instituted eventually to reduce these directional scanning movements as much as possible so that response biases would not occur. McKeever and Gill (1972) employed a fixation stimulus (e.g., a digit or letter) located in the center of the tachistoscopic screen to which subjects could attend. The subjects then were tested directly on what they had seen at the fixation point either immediately before or after the lateralized materials were presented.

Results with the *fixation control technique* certainly have been less than encouraging. Significant RVF superiorities still have been obtained even with the inclusion of the control stimulus, indicating that subjects continued to display preference scans to that particular field side (Hines, 1972). Also, the nature of the fixation stimulus appeared to have an effect on tachistoscopic performance. If a geometric shape were displayed at the fixation point, an LVF advantage subsequently was shown, whereas a fixation letter or digit generated the opposite RVF superiority (Kershner, Thomae, & Callaway, 1977). As argued by several researchers (Hellige & Cox, 1976; Mancuso, Lawrence, Hintze, & White, 1979), apparently the control stimulus established an attentional set in subjects to process field inputs on the right or left side, depending on whether the item to be fixated on was a verbal or nonverbal stimulus, respectively. However, other studies (Duda & Kirby, 1980; Hines, 1978), have found no significant effect with the type of fixation stimulus employed.

Because the findings have been somewhat inconsistent, it probably is best to adhere to the advice of Bradshaw and Nettleton (1983), who warned readers against using the technique, primarily because it might be contributing its own confounding bias to any tachistoscopic field advantage obtained across trials. (I return to the attentional set variable at a later point within the chapter when I discuss more current experimental procedures used in the assessment of cerebral asymmetries.)

Variations of the standard tachistoscopic technique also have been tried, in which lengthier scanning times are provided to subjects so they can process the field inputs more effectively. However, most of these attempts rarely have been successful. For instance, the Zaidel contact lens (or *Z lens* described in chapter 5) is costly to implement, because each subject requires a different prescription. Further, the lens often produces slippage problems as well as uncomfortable sensations, especially in those who have never worn contacts before. Dimond and Farrington's (1977) opaque lens did not fare much better in the field. Although the small slit within the contact can channel input to either cortical hemisphere for extended periods, subjects again experience too much visual discomfort to apply this technique practically on any broad experimental scale. It seems that despite the limitations of tachistoscopic scanning, researchers will continue to use this standardized procedure until these other methodological problems can be resolved satisfactorily.

Auditory Asymmetries

In another perceptual task designed to assess cerebral asymmetries, different paired materials are presented to each ear simultaneously. The materials have to be aligned temporally between the two ear sides and matched in intensity levels, otherwise one ear will be more inclined to show an advantage at the outset of the study. For example, if the ear inputs are separated for even 500 milliseconds, the later materials will be perceived much better, presumably because they mask the earlier stimulation. Further, baseline intensities from 50 to 80 decibels in both inputs typically are recommended; differences of 5 or more decibels from these standard levels also will produce a favored ear side (Berlin, 1977).

To align materials for simultaneity of onset as well as amplitude, dichotic recordings generally are made on separate channels of audiotape.

Subjects then listen to both channels through stereo headphones for a fixed number of trials. After each of the trials, subjects are tested on their recall by generating as many of the sounds they heard, in any order (Kimura, 1961). The overall number of correct responses for each ear side is tabulated across trials, and then comparisons are performed, usually by computing an ear difference score (i.e., subtracting the percentage of correct left-ear responses from the percentage of corresponding right-ear ones, or vice versa). The percentage of error responses for each ear side also can be used as an alternative measure of auditory laterality (Marshall, Caplan, & Holmes, 1975).

Ear Advantages in Dichotic Tasks.   REAs are reported most often for dichotically presented verbal materials, including words (Dirks, 1964), nonsense words (Zurif & Mendelsohn, 1972; Zurif & Sait, 1969), digits (Kimura, 1961, 1967), consonant–vowel (CV) syllables such as "pa" and "da" (Shankweiler & Studdert-Kennedy, 1967; Studdert-Kennedy & Shankweiler, 1970), and even speech played backward (Kimura & Folb, 1968). See Krashen's (1976, 1977) reviews for more details on these REAs. Conversely, LEAs commonly are identified when competing nonverbal materials are employed, such as melodies (Goodglass & Calderon, 1977; Johnson, 1977; Spellacy, 1970), musical chords and notes (Cutting, 1974; Kallman & Corballis, 1975), piano tones (Sidtis & Bryden, 1978), nonspeech vocalizations such as laughing and crying (Carmon & Nachshon, 1973), emotional components of speech and associated intonational patterns (Blumstein & Cooper, 1974; Haggard & Parkinson, 1971), as well as common types of environmental sounds (Knox & Kimura, 1970). Although the nonverbal LEAs are generally weaker than the complementary verbal REAs, they can be comparable in magnitude if more complex tones are introduced (Sidtis, 1980, 1981).

Although dichotic presentations have generated a number of significant ear asymmetries, monaural stimulation can produce its own impressive reaction-time differences, with faster REAs shown for verbal inputs and, correspondingly, quicker LEAs for nonverbal stimuli (Bever, Hurtig, & Handel, 1976; Fry, 1974; Kallman, 1977, 1978). It remains to be determined whether these monaural effects can be elicited as reliably in normal subjects as in dichotic ones (Bradshaw, Farrelly, & Taylor, 1981; Teng, 1980).

Kimura's Ear Asymmetry Model.   Because the two ears consistently demonstrated opposing superiorities for verbal and nonverbal materials, Kimura (1967, 1985) advanced an explanation for the dichotic findings. In addition to the already posited hemispheric specialization for particular inputs, she argued that the contralateral (or crossed) auditory pathways leading to the brain were much stronger than the ipsilateral (or uncrossed) projections, primarily because the latter pathways were suppressed whenever the contralateral ones were activated. Thus, right ear–left hemispheric projections were better suited to process verbal inputs, and, likewise, left ear–right-hemispheric tracts were the more appropriate ones to handle nonverbal types of stimuli.

Similar to the relay model already discussed with field asymmetries, Kimura's (1967, 1985) ideas reflected the view that information would be in a degraded form if it were transmitted initially to the nonspecialized hemisphere. Apparently, callosal transfer to the specialized side resulted in additional deterioration of the signal's strength along the traveled route. Figure 7.1 provides an illustration of the basic principles within the Kimura (1967, 1985) model. In a typical dichotic presentation involving a pair of CV syllables, "ba" (heard in the left ear) would be relayed contralaterally to the right hemisphere, whereas "ga" (heard in the right ear) would be transmitted more appropriately to the left hemisphere. (Remember that the ipsilateral pathways would be inhibited whenever these contralateral ones were stimulated.) Because the left brain was the more specialized one to process the syllables, "ga" would be reported more often than "ba," which obviously lost some of its clarity in the transfer from the right to left side.

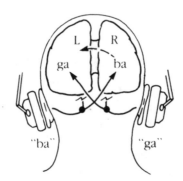

FIG. 7.1. Kimura's (1967, 1985) ear asymmetry model. In the dichotic "ba–ga" presentation, "ba" is relayed contralaterally to the right hemisphere and "ga" to the specialized left. An REA subsequently will be shown to "ga," especially because "ba" needs to cross over to the left side to be processed effectively. Note the suppression of the ipsilateral pathways under dichotic stimulation. From *Left Brain, Right Brain* (p. 81) by Sally P. Springer and Georg Deutsch, 1989, New York: W. H. Freeman. Copyright 1989 by Sally P. Springer and Georg Deutsch. Reprinted by permission.

There seems to be some compelling neurophysiological evidence to support Kimura's (1967, 1985) claims. Not only do the contralateral auditory pathways have more fibers, but they also generate more cortical activity than ipsilateral tracts (Hall & Goldstein, 1968; Majkowski, Bochenek, Bochenek, Knapik-Fijalkowska, & Kopec, 1971). Further, those subjects found to have left-hemispheric speech centers upon Wada testing with sodium amytal generally show the predicted, contralateral REAs, whereas those with the less common right-hemispheric speech areas display more contralateral LEAs (Geffen & Caudrey, 1981). However, under ordinary conditions, without competing dichotic stimulation, ipsilateral fibers can function just as effectively as the contralateral. This might explain why ear differences can be obtained even with monaural presentations: The ipsilateral paths now are able to effectively relay inputs directly to the specialized side (i.e., left ear to left hemisphere for verbal types of materials and right ear to right hemisphere for nonverbal types).

A Brief Look at Tactile Asymmetries

Tactile analogues of dichotic listening procedures also have demonstrated handedness asymmetries that resemble the auditory ones. Left-handed advantages (i.e., LHAs) occurred whenever subjects had to match different nonsense shapes originally explored simultaneously in each hand with those subsequently presented in a visual array (Nilsson, Glencross, & Geffen, 1980; Witelson, 1974, 1976). These effects were not evidenced with monohaptic (or one-handed) exploration (Webster & Thurber, 1978). Oscar-Berman, Rehbein, Porfert, and Goodglass (1978) extended the dichaptic (or competing two-handed) technique to a wide variety of stimuli, including line orientations and digits, as well as three-dimensional block letters. Results indicated an LHA for the lines and the complementary RHA for the letters (with no difference found for the digits). Tactile asymmetries also were displayed under different stimulus presentation procedures (Nachshon & Carmon, 1975), with sequential tasks yielding right-handed superiorities and simultaneous matchings yielding left-handed advantages. This confirmed the respective analytic–holistic cognitive style dichotomy elaborated in chapter 3.

Moreover, studies with blind and sighted subjects consistently have shown over the decades that Braille may be read more easily by the left hand (Harris, 1980; Hermelin & O'Connor, 1971a, 1971b). Perhaps the Braille characters (involving specific patterns of dots) are more spatially complex in nature than ordinary letters, thus explaining the right-hemisphere superiority; or it could be that the Braille language is more difficult to recognize, let alone read, than the standard text. Whatever the case, approximately three quarters of blind readers are more proficient in reading Braille with the left hand than the right, suggesting very strong right-hemispheric involvement associated with this tactile perception.

Manipulating Attentional Bias in the Standard Procedures

Kinsbourne's Attentional Bias Model.   Kinsbourne (1973, 1974) was one of the first researchers to posit that in normal everyday situations, the cerebral hemispheres were balanced reciprocally in activity levels. However, when "eccentric stimulation" was provided (e.g., dichotic or tachistoscopic), one of the hemispheres was invoked to a greater extent than the other, thus disturbing this balanced equilibrium. For instance, experimentally produced verbal materials predominantly would activate the left hemisphere; therefore attention would be biased toward the RVF and/or right ear. Alternatively, visuospatial inputs mainly would activate the right hemisphere; therefore attention would be biased in the opposite direction (in this case, the LVF and/or left ear). In effect, Kinsbourne's (1973, 1974) theory basically stated that the subjects' attentional space is shifted to the body side contralateral to the hemisphere that has been activated, primarily for the express purpose of processing specific types of inputs most effectively.

Evidence for the Kinsbourne Model.   A number of studies has tended to support Kinsbourne's (1973, 1974) major assumption of *attentional set*. Spellacy and Blumstein (1970) only obtained an REA in their dichotic verbal task when subjects were expecting speech (or a language set of materials); otherwise, an LEA predominated. As previously indicated, Kershner et al. (1977) found that verbal types of fixation control stimuli produced (nonsignificant) RVF superiorities in young children, whereas nonverbal stimuli produced complementary (and also nonsignificant) LVF advantages. Moreover, Klein, Moscovitch, and Vigna (1976) demonstrated that LVF superiorities could be elicited in a facial-recognition processing task if it was not preceded immediately by a word-processing assignment; likewise, RVF advantages could be obtained if verbal (as opposed to nonverbal) materials consistently were employed throughout various tachistoscopic procedures (Honda, 1978).

Similar results have been reported in dichotic tasks where ear advantages appeared to be a function of the particular stimulus context in which subjects participated. For instance, LEAs could be evidenced if melody recognitions preceded syllabic pairs. In this case, the musical context predisposed subjects' attentional sets toward the left ear (and right hemisphere), which apparently persisted even after verbal inputs were introduced (Morais & Landercy, 1977). In a more recent dichotic study by Hiscock and Hiscock (1988), visual precuing of the targets was found to help subjects process and identify those items mainly within the right, as opposed to left, ear.

Although the aforementioned studies verified Kinsbourne's (1973, 1974) claim that the particular stimulus context "primes" one hemisphere over the other (as well as the respective contralateral pathways), there is a fair amount of research that does not support the model (Guiard, 1980; Hansch & Pirozzolo, 1980; Kirsner, 1980; Wexler & Heninger, 1980). Nevertheless, as many scientists believe, attentional influences probably do contribute to the laterality effects observed in many of the standard procedures.

Bryden's Assessment of Subject Strategies. Bryden (1978, 1979) continued to apply Kinsbourne's (1973, 1974) attentional set model to lateralized perceptual tasks, in particular dichotic listening procedures. He especially noted that most subjects chose to report as many items as possible from the right ear before focusing on identifications within the left ear. As Bryden (1978, 1979), Inglis (1962), and Inglis and Sykes (1967) attempted to explain, the right-ear items might have occupied a favored position in short-term memory, at the expense of continued storage of the left-ear items. REAs were reduced—but not completely eliminated—when subjects were cued experimentally to initially report items from the left (or unfavored) ear (Bryden, 1963, 1965). Thus, whether subjects intentionally focused on one channel or the other did have a bearing on which asymmetrical results were obtained, as well as their overall strength.

Based on these findings, Bryden (1978, 1979) emphasized the need to control (as much as possible) the information-processing strategies that subjects constantly employed in these tasks. Otherwise, subjects would be left to their own initiative in how to deploy their attentional resources, with some presumably adopting a focused ear-side strategy and others opting for a less favored, attentional division between the two ears (with the end result that no ear advantages would be evidenced). According to Bryden (1978), if strategic effects were ignored by methodologists, unwanted intersubject variability was more likely to be produced, making any assessment of cerebral asymmetries difficult, if not impossible, to achieve.

In his basic experimental procedures, Bryden (1979, 1980) specifically instructed subjects to monitor CV syllables coming through one ear only, and then allowed them to report only those items on the attended side. Subjects then were required to shift their attention to the ignored ear on alternating blocks of trials to improve their accuracy on that respective side. In this way, Bryden (1979, 1980) attempted to exert the type of experimental control necessary to handle the variable strategies subjects possibly could deploy within these dichotic tasks. Counterbalancing the attentional monitoring from one ear side to the other further ensured that practice effects would be reduced effectively, if not totally eliminated. For comparison purposes, control subjects were given the standardized instructions to divide their attention between both ears and report as many items as they could on either side, in any order. Bryden's methodology is summarized in Table 7.1 to provide further clarification.

Bryden's (1982, 1986) results clearly indicated a more striking and stabilized REA for individuals in the focused attention group, in contrast to control subjects. This attentional effect also has been consistently observed in the groups that were tested over the years (Iaccino & Sowa, 1989, 1990). REAs were shown with right-sided focus instructions, and weaker (yet still significant) LEAs were shown with the respective left-sided instructions. In addition, both ear advantages appeared to be dependent on the number of focused ear trials presented, with stronger effects occurring over more trials (Iaccino & Houran, 1989, 1991). Bryden's (1982, 1986) major hypothesis of attentional strategies having a direct influence on asymmetric outcomes was confirmed across the various dichotic studies.

Tachistoscopic Results with the Bryden Methodology.   Although Bryden's (1982, 1986) work was mainly in the dichotic listening area, some researchers have attempted to apply his methodology to tachisto-

TABLE 7.1
Bryden's Methodology

Blocks	Groups	
	Attentional Focus	*Divided Attention*
1	Left ear—recall left	
2	Right ear—recall right	Recall as many
3	Left ear—recall left	items on either
4	Right ear—recall right	side across blocks

scopic presentations. In Hardyck, Chiarello, Dronkers, and Simpson's (1985) series of studies, subjects were instructed to attend strictly to one visual field and report whether the items displayed on that side were actual words by pressing the appropriate button. Similar to the dichotic procedures, subjects then were required to shift their fixation to the unattended field side on alternating blocks of trials. Throughout the Hardyck et al. (1985) experiments, a consistent pattern emerged: the predicted RVF superiorities were obtained for word recognitions, but, surprisingly, instructions to bias subjects' attention to the right side did not improve the overall accuracy of these identifications.

Although Hardyck et al. (1985) concluded that visual field differences in lexical decision tasks were not affected by attentional biases, I subsequently conducted a number of tachistoscopic experiments (Iaccino, 1990) in which simpler materials resembling Bryden's dichotic syllables had to be identified. More specifically, after subjects were precued to attend to the appropriate side, consonants were presented in four-by-four matrices unilaterally flashed to either the subjects' left or right visual field. Subjects then were required to recall as many of the letters as possible that were shown on each trial, as well as identify the position that these letters occupied by placing Xs in the corresponding cells of a blank matrix figure (which resembled the original in dimensions). Analyses revealed that RVF advantages typically were displayed in the letter recall (or left-hemispheric) phase, whereas much weaker LVF advantages were seen in the letter position (right-hemispheric) portion. Based on the consistently expressed results, I recommended that subjects can adopt attentional sets for at least fairly simple tachistoscopic stimuli, just like the dichotic materials. Moreover, these sets can be controlled by directed, precuing instructions administered before each tachistoscopic trial, as Bryden originally formulated for his dichotic designs.

The Iaccino Model: Attentional Variability as an Indicator of Cortical Asymmetry. In light of the conflicting findings on attentional bias, I have advanced the following assumptions to clarify some of the inconsistencies identified within the dichotic and tachistoscopic literature:

1. Attentional set is a by-product of cerebral functioning, not an independent process. Bryden vigorously discussed the possibility of isolating strategic effects from true biological differences in cerebral organization. However, if one adheres to this view, a puzzling question remains: From where did the subjects' attentional sets originate? Following the more logical Kinsbourne presupposition, attentional reallocation can be

explained more easily as an outcome of activation by one of the cerebral hemispheres more specialized to handle a particular input than as a process existing independently of cortical functioning. I do not wish to entertain Bryden's notion for long, because it seems analogous to a "body working without a head"; although the possibility is theoretically intriguing, it does not appear to be practically sound. With respect to attentional biases, subjects need to receive their "marching orders" from a higher command (i.e., a cortical hemisphere) if they are to deploy the appropriate focusing strategies as well as contralateral orienting responses within lateralized tasks.

2. Attentional variation may be the norm in many dichotic/tachistoscopic assignments. Although Bryden used a methodology that more effectively controlled for subject monitoring of inputs relayed to one body side, not all attentional strategies can be manipulated in this rather simplistic fashion. Even Bryden (1980) admitted that not every subject approaches a lateralized task with the same information-processing strategy. Some might be physiologically or cognitively predisposed to express certain body preferences; others already might have allocated their attentional resources to a designated side; still others might have their own linguistic set that will allow them to interpret the experimental directions according to their own unique cognitive style. If these subject differences exist (and I think they do), then precuing instructions might not produce the predicted ear and/or field advantages in every experimental instance. It might be just as desirable to monitor these variations as to control them. By observing the more naturalistic ways of information processing and then providing a follow-up strategic inquiry session with each subject, researchers might better assess the numerous strategies that continuously are employed and perhaps capitalize on the strongest ones in well-thought out and much improved methodologies.

3. Attentional variation is a reflection of organizational differences between the two hemispheres. As previously hypothesized, if subjects demonstrate a high level of attentional set variability overall, then one should not expect to find significant (nor consistent) effects every time this variable is manipulated. Likewise, one cannot assume that the two hemispheres have the same functional arrangement for every examinee tested (i.e., mainly verbal for left brain, mainly spatial for right). For instance, Levy (1972, 1976), Harris (1978), and Hicks and Kinsbourne (1978) postulated that some females and sinistrals represent language bilaterally, at the expense of proper localization of spatial skills within the right hemisphere. The way these subjects approach a particular task and interpret the requirements therein will definitely vary from others, primarily because they already have the cortical predisposition

to process inputs according to a certain style (presumably the verbal–analytic). This style of processing also will interact with the attentional component by-products so that reduced or even reversed body-side advantages subsequently will occur, especially for linguistic types of materials. Thus, whether functional asymmetries are evidenced in lateralized assignments is strongly dependent on the inherent cortical organization one group possesses, which in turn influences how and in what manner the attentional resources are deployed most effectively and efficiently.

4. At this point in time, definitive conclusions cannot be reached with respect to cerebral asymmetries. Previous assumptions have indicated that there is a good deal of intersubject variability present within dichotic and tachistoscopic tasks, which can be attributed mainly to cortical and derived attentional differences. Because of these variations, which can become quite pronounced in certain instances, researchers cannot expect consistent and reliable results unless the same procedure is utilized time and time again and the same subjects continually are examined across the multiple replications. Even under these conditions, controlling for individual differences in processing style needs to be incorporated in the major design. However, even with this manipulation, one is not assured that one has reduced effectively intersubject variability to a tolerable level. Realistically, the most that can be hoped for is that some common behavioral pattern can be identified with these procedures. If this cannot be accomplished, researchers should not abandon their endeavors nor erroneously conclude that cerebral differences do not exist in particular population pools. Currently, the resources to verify such hastily conceived generalizations are not available.

Returning to the major line of inquiry, if attentional effects are not found within a single study or series of studies, any number of multiple explanations can be provided—from subjects not having the proper mental set to understand the experimental instructions of monitoring only one body side, to subjects not following directions because the instructions are basically incompatible with their dominant hemispheric style (e.g., right-side attendance vs. right-holistic style or left-side attendance vs. left-analytic style). As Fairweather (1982) advised, standardizing the procedures and materials can be an effective step in the right direction if future conclusions on cerebral asymmetries are going to be reached by a consensus of scientists. I wholeheartedly agree with these sentiments and would like to apply this advice to the conflicting reports on attentional bias, which presently populate the asymmetrical literature.

OTHER CORTICAL ACTIVATION MEASURES

The other performance measures most commonly associated with cerebral lateralization of function in normal subjects are examined next. The first of these to be discussed is conjugate lateral eye movements (or CLEMs).

CLEM Indices

Bakan (1969) originally hypothesized that subjects' eye movements were, in fact, correlated to hemispheric asymmetries. Using an adaptation of the Kinsbourne and Trevarthen models, Bakan (1969) claimed that CLEMs were orienting responses produced by cognitive activity localized within the contralateral hemisphere. Thus, subjects who looked more to the left were right-hemisphere dominant individuals, whereas those who looked more to the right were left-hemisphere oriented. According to Bakan (1969), Day (1964), and Trevarthen (1972), the direction of the eye movements was also indicative of the subjects' preferred cognitive style, whether left-analytic or right-holistic, and reflected particularly strong personality characteristics.

Further research on the types of questions used to elicit CLEMs has shown some support for Bakan's (1969) position over the years. Inquiries dealing with word spellings, definitions, and simple arithmetic problems produced more right (or left-hemispheric) CLEMs and the typical head-turning responses in that direction, whereas those questions involving spatial skills, musical recognitions, and visualization strategies produced more left (or right-hemispheric) CLEMs and the respective head movements to that body side (Galin & Ornstein, 1974; Kinsbourne, 1972; Kocel et al., 1972). Moreover, emotional inquiries (e.g., "what feeling do you tend to associate with your mother?") elicited more eye movements to the left side, suggesting that the right hemisphere was involved more actively in the analysis of affective inputs (Schwartz, Davidson, & Maer, 1975). However, many researchers have been unable to replicate these CLEM effects to date, especially with more lateralized groups such as dextrals (Ehrlichman & Weinberger, 1978; Hiscock, 1977; Shevrin et al., 1979; Takeda & Yoshimura, 1979). Corballis and Beale (1983) attempted to explain these inconsistencies by noting that a number of methodological problems have clouded this area of investigation, not the least of which is the subjects' own habitual tendency to look to the left or right side regardless of the nature of the question.

As advised in chapter 3, one should exercise caution before reaching any conclusion concerning the link between CLEMs and brain asymmetry. Returning to the variability model, it assumes that subjects will be vacillating back and forth constantly in their attentional biases, making it difficult (if not impossible) to obtain stable and consistent CLEMs. Based on my theoretical view, CLEMs might be reflective of hemispheric differences, but the effect may not be pronounced under every experimental methodology utilized. Therefore, one should adopt a wait-and-see attitude while work continues to proceed with this measure.

The Cerebral Blood Flow Index

Changes in cortical activity appear to influence the amount of blood flow relayed to those respective regions of the brain. One technique that has been developed successfully to measure regional cerebral bloodflow (i.e., rCBF) is the *Xenon-clearance method*. In this procedure, a rather harmless radioactive isotope (Xenon-13) either is injected directly into a cerebral artery (Lassen & Ingvar, 1972; Lassen, Ingvar, & Skinhoj, 1978) or inhaled via a special air mixture (Knopman, Rubens, Klassen, Meyer, & Niccum, 1980; Wood, 1980). The isotope's flow through the brain subsequently is monitored by sodium iodide crystal-emission detectors placed on or near the subject's head. The Xenon typically is cleared out of the bloodstream in approximately 15–20 minutes (Gur & Gur, 1980).

Results with this technique clearly have shown differential rCBF responses between the two hemispheres under simple task conditions. On the average, verbal analogies tests produced greater blood flow in the left hemisphere, whereas more perceptual tasks (e.g., picture-completion, line orientation, and mental rotation) generated more blood flow in the complementary right hemisphere (Deutsch, Bourbon, Papanicolaou, & Eisenberg, 1988; Gur & Reivich, 1980; Risberg, Halsey, Wills, & Wilson, 1975). Hand movements on these tasks also produced contralateral activity in the respective hemisphere, with left-hand activity increasing rCBF in the right hemisphere's motor region and right-hand motions slightly elevating rCBF in the left hemisphere's associated area (Halsey et al., 1979).

However, in more complex cognitive tasks (involving speech and/or memory), both hemispheres demonstrated corresponding changes in rCBF, implying that the functional distinction between the two brain sides was a more relative (than absolute) one (Shakhnovich, Serbinenko, Razumousky, Rodionov, & Oskolok, 1980). In addition, variations have been detected in the rate of blood flow to certain hemispheric areas when more attention-demanding assignments were administered, with greater rCBF amounts located in the frontal lobes and lesser concentrations in the posterior regions (Deutsch et al., 1987). The right hemisphere displayed a higher frontal lobe blood flow in these tasks compared with the left, with this effect operating independently of the stimulus materials employed, whether verbal or spatial. It seems that in more complex procedures, hemispheric involvement can extend to both sides with a greater amount of activity relayed to much wider regions (e.g., the larger problem-solving frontal lobes), compared with the more localized brain site functioning for simpler sensorimotor tests. This conclusion seems to correlate quite well with Prohovnik, Hakansson, and Risberg's (1980) research showing the dependency of blood flow activity on subjects' expected levels of mental processing, with higher levels demanding more global changes in blood flow to accommodate those active areas.

Metabolic Scanning Indices

Although the rCBF index reflects a somewhat accurate portrayal of brain activity, it is limited to readings near the cortical surface, not regions deeper down. Another disadvantage attributed to the blood flow measure is that it is frequently unresponsive to the more rapid changes occurring in brain activity, and most often presents the more prolonged or cumulative variations. For these reasons, a cerebral metabolic scanning technique performed at the microscopic level was devised in the early 1970s and eventually implemented with normal healthy subjects. Termed the *PET scan*, it currently is used by over 40 centers in the United States for both research and diagnostic purposes. In recent years, it has enabled scientists to map more effectively the sites for particular brain functions such as language use and its production.

In positron emission tomography (PET), either blood or glucose is irradiated and then intravenously sent directly to both hemispheres of the brain. The streams of gamma rays that these radiated substances emit at the cortical level are detected by the PET ring, which executes sweeps around the subject's head. Within a matter of minutes, computer programs reconstruct the radiated patterns into a three-dimensional image of the brain. The colored image shows how much of the substance has been metabolized effectively within certain cortical areas, with brighter hues corresponding to higher metabolic rates and deeper ones representing lower rates. Typically, the first image highlights those areas of the brain that are most active before experimental stimulation is introduced. Once input is presented to subjects (usually via a computer monitor directly above their faces), other PET scan readings are executed subsequently. By subtracting out similarly colored areas across successive images, scientists can more accurately pinpoint which parts of the brain specifically are implicated in given functions, as reflected by the different hued areas that remain after the comparison deletions (Montgomery, 1989; Raichle, 1987).

PET scans have revealed the predicted patterns for simple auditory and visual stimulation. When monaural input was directed to one ear side, the contralateral hemisphere was activated, with metabolic increases being displayed throughout the respective temporal cortex. Likewise, under visual hemifield conditions, the opposite striate cortex was stimulated, as evidenced by higher metabolic rates in that particular hemisphere (Reivich & Gur, 1985).

More recent studies have focused on specific language functions with repeated PET scan analysis. Similar to the rCBF results, vocalizations of nouns produced metabolic changes bilaterally in the sensorimotor projection areas as well as several frontal lobe regions (Fox, Petersen, Posner, & Raichle, 1987; Petersen, Fox, Posner, Mintun, & Raichle, 1988). Asymmetrical increases also have been reported with various linguistic tasks: Just looking at words stimulated the association areas of the left hemisphere, whereas semantic association tests in which subjects had to give specific uses for presented nouns elicited more activity in the inferior and medial regions of the left frontal lobe, as well as in the cerebellum of the right hemisphere (Petersen, Fox, Mintun, Posner, & Raichle, 1989). It has been theorized that with higher level language activities, such as those required in the semantic assignment, right areas serve to inhibit inappropriate responses, whereas left ones alternatively are allowed to select the correct answers (Montgomery, 1989). This idea is not a new one to the asymmetrical field. One need only recall that, via callosal functioning, neural circuitry can be inhibited in one hemisphere and effectively stimulated in the other (Cook, 1984a, 1984b; Woodward, 1988).

Finally, work with PET scans has enabled scientists to revise linguistic theories in light of the new information provided on the three-dimensional images. More specifically, Broca's area has been shown to be more than just a language production center localized within the left hemisphere. Apparently it can be viewed as a generalized motor center involved with the coordination of many movements, some of which are not restricted necessarily to speech. This area "lit up" with activity whenever subjects were asked to repeat certain words, as well as when they were requested to move their tongues, hands, and, quite interestingly, even when told to imagine movements of their hands. According to Fox (personal communication, 1989), "we use this general motor-programming area . . . even when we are not making actual body movements," suggesting that the Broca region is implicated with many more functions than just linguistic expression.

Reading is another activity looked at quite closely with the PET technique. It has been found to be a much more complex process than previously speculated. If the text is a difficult passage, the left brain's auditory cortex displays the appropriate metabolic changes. However, if the material is easily comprehensible, this phonological area is curiously silent.

Raichle (personal communication, 1989) suggested that as one becomes a more proficient reader, words do not always have to be "sounded out," therefore this pathway can be bypassed easily. Clearly, more surprises await scientists in the coming century as PET scans continue to disclose their pictures of that hidden organ called the brain. Perhaps PET indices also will shed more light on the right hemisphere's covert language capabilities in future decades.

Electroencephalographic Indices

EEG Measures.   Electroencephalographic (EEG) studies have been (and continue to be) based on the premise that differential brain activity in the two hemispheres reflects differential degrees of cortical functioning. EEG recordings basically are produced by placing macroelectrodes on the subject's forehead and various other locations (e.g., the scalp or behind the ears). These electrodes relay the neuronal activity emitted throughout the brain to an amplifier, which, in essence, boosts the very weak 5 to 50 millivolt signal so that a graphic printout of the electrical output eventually can be analyzed to determine the most dominant brain wave patterns. Although this procedure has remained basically intact since its inception by Hans Berger in the 1920s, it was not until the early 1970s that it was discovered that cortical activity was not identical on both brain sides, but that it varied as a function of the type of task subjects had to perform.

Galin and Ornstein (1972) found that more *alpha wave* activity (usually associated with restful and relaxed states) was generated in the right hemisphere when subjects executed writing assignments, and, conversely, that the alpha dominance shifted to the left hemisphere when subjects arranged blocks to correspond to fairly specific spatial patterns. A preponderance of the alpha rhythm across one hemisphere meant that this brain side was "being turned off" or more appropriately "put in idle," whereas the more capable complement took over to handle the special requirements of each task. Since the initial observations of Galin and Ornstein (1972), evidence has accumulated for this hemispheric dissociation phenomenon, with greater alpha blocking over the left hemisphere during verbal tasks and more alpha suppression over the right during spatial tests (Goodman, Beatty, & Mulholland, 1980; Marsh, 1978; Rebert, 1978). Weaker alpha wave asymmetries also have been shown for less lateralized groups such as sinistrals, further confirming the usefulness of this index (Butler & Glass, 1976; Donchin, McCarthy, & Kutas, 1977).

However, deficiencies still can be noted with the EEG measure. First, standardization of procedures (e.g., consistent placement of electrodes on head, use of same stimulus materials) has not been controlled well across designs. Second, the EEG generally reflects the overall pattern of brain arousal, not activity specific to singly presented stimuli per se (Carlson, 1991). Taking into account this latter difficulty, experimenters soon developed a more precise electrical index based on the EEG record, referred to as the *event-related potential* (ERP).

Event-Related Potentials. Any cortical EEG reading following the presentation of a stimulus has two basic components: the weaker response phase to the given stimulus (i.e., the ERP) and the stronger nonspecific background activity (or noise) being generated by an incredibly large number of neurons throughout the brain. The noise of this background is so loud that the ERP almost always is completely masked. A procedure to magnify the ERP consists of a computer-averaging technique, in which the EEG noise eventually is phased out so that the electrical activity specific to the stimulus will emerge as the more dominant potential.

For example, an auditory click is introduced. The subject's responses to the click are recorded over many trials, perhaps 100. A computer is used to identify the precise point on the EEG record at which the click first was presented and correspondingly calculates the average of these 100 responses while factoring out the random noise at the same time. Next, the computer finds the averages for specified intervals (usually milliseconds) extending from the derived stimulus onset time and finally plots the entire set of means for subsequent analysis. As seen in Fig. 7.2, the background noise on the EEG is eliminated effectively, leaving in its place the much more discernible stimulus-specific potential (Pinel, 1990).

The ERP generally can be described as a sequence of positive and negative electrical changes (i.e., the rises and falls displayed in Fig. 7.2) that tend to persist until well after the stimulus is removed. The very obvious pattern of the ERP has been looked at quite extensively with respect to hemispheric activity to determine if there are any electrical variations between the two brain sides as different stimuli are introduced successively. As predicted from earlier EEG studies, materials of a verbal or nonverbal nature have affected the amplitude (i.e., intensity) differentially as well as the latency of ERPs in the functionalized hemispheres. Verbal stimuli consisting of nonsense syllables (Buschbaum & Fedio, 1970), CVs (Papanicolaou, Levin, Eisenberg, & Moore, 1983), words and other speech-related items (Molfese, Freeman, & Palermo, 1975), and arithmetic problems (Papanicolaou, Schmidt, Moore, & Eisenberg, 1983) consistently have generated larger amplitude–shorter latency ERPs over the left hemisphere. On the other hand, nonverbal tasks involving block assembly (Galin & Ellis, 1975), figure completion (Papanicolaou et al., 1983), nonspeech discriminations (Molfese et al., 1975), and emotional-tone judgments (Papanicolaou et al., 1983) more often have produced greater

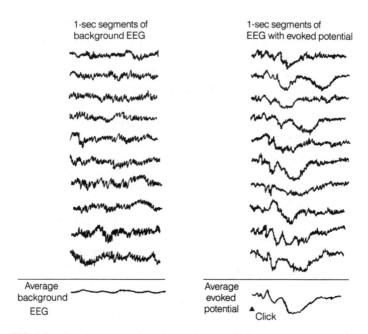

FIG. 7.2.   Computer averaging of an auditory event-related potential. Note that when the background EEG activity is computer averaged across a series of 1-second intervals, a more discriminable ERP is obtained to the auditory click stimulus. From *Biopsychology* (p. 135) by John P. J. Pinel, 1990, Needham, MA: Allyn & Bacon. Copyright 1990 by Allyn & Bacon. Reprinted by permission.

amplitude ERPs across the right hemisphere, although these effects have not always been as strong as the left-sided ones.

More current research on ERPs has revealed some discrepancies from the traditional verbal–nonverbal hemispheric distinction. Molfese (1978, 1980) found that when CVs were presented to subjects, the right brain was more capable than the left in differentiating the vocal onset time of these stimuli (with much larger ERPs being displayed on that respective side), whereas the left continued to maintain its articulation superiority if it was anticipated that these syllables had to be identified verbally. However, when verbal responding was eliminated, greater amplitude ERPs were generated in the right hemisphere throughout the entire procedure, suggesting that this brain side might be more competent in the perception of speech-related stimuli than previously supposed (Segalowitz & Cohen, 1989). Perhaps the most basic level of language is housed in the right hemisphere, whereas the motor capacities for its fullest expression are lateralized in the left hemisphere, specifically in Broca's area (Milberg, Whitman, Rourke, & Glaros, 1981; Ogiela, 1990, 1991). Continued analysis of the ERP index under nonresponse conditions might reflect the level of competence the right hemisphere holds for human speech sounds and perhaps even language.

Contingent Negative Variations. As indicated with ERPs, the expectation of a verbal response apparently biased the subjects' attentional sets to the left hemisphere. When this expectation was removed, their sets then switched completely to the opposite side. An electrophysiological measure has been found to correlate directly to these subject expectations. Termed the *contingent negative variation* (CNV), it is a slowly developing negative potential extracted from the EEG that occurs immediately prior to the onset of an anticipated event. Many researchers (Donchin, Kutas, & McCarthy, 1977; Donchin et al., 1977) have identified rather pronounced asymmetries with the CNV index before the occurrence of various stimuli. When verbal material was expected, larger CNVs typically appeared throughout the left hemisphere. In contrast, when nonverbal material was anticipated, stronger CNVs usually were reported in the right hemisphere. These findings have not been replicated across studies (Levy, 1977). However, this should not discourage researchers from continuing their investigations with this measure, because my attentional variation model predicts such inconsistent outcomes (similar to those obtained with CLEMs). Scientists might have identified a very promising index to assess the variable cognitive states in that complex organism called the human.

To conclude this section on cortical activation, two other indices are examined briefly: electrodermal responses and facial expressions. Although these measures are not employed as frequently as the metabolic or electroencephalographic, they still have yielded some rather fascinating asymmetrical patterns in body side functioning, and, ultimately, in hemispheric activity.

The Electrodermal Index

The *electrodermal response* basically is defined as the subject's cutaneous orienting reaction to specific stimulation. When the stimulus is introduced, skin resistance on the hands to a mild electrical current diminishes, implying that cutaneous sensitivity is heightened to the new input. Over repeated presentations with the same stimulus, this skin conductance response declines rather sharply (i.e., habituates). It already has been pointed out in chapter 6 that for schizophrenic patients, electrodermal activity was virtually nonexistent in the left hand to verbal types of stimulation, suggesting that there was a hemispheric dysfunction presumably located within the ipsilateral (left) cortex. The reverse claim has been postulated for depressed subjects, based on abnormal skin conductance responses with the right hand (Gruzelier & Hammond, 1976; Gruzelier & Venables, 1973; Schneider, 1983).

In contrast, more normal dextrals have shown the usual habituating amplitudes in the hand contralateral to the activated hemisphere in tasks of a verbal as well as nonverbal nature. Further, these asymmetries have not been replicated in sinistrals, as predicted from other indices with this less lateralized group (Lacroix & Comper, 1979; Myslobodsky & Rattok, 1975, 1977). Given these findings, it might be that particular psychological disorders and other clinical disabilities can be diagnosed effectively in the future with such sensitive measures as the electrodermal.

Facial Expression Indices

Experimental and naturalistic observations have supported the hypothesis that the right hemisphere plays a major role in the perception of emotion. Sackheim and Gur (1978) and Sackheim, Gur, and Saucy (1978) were among the first to discover that the left side of the face typically displays a more intense emotional expression. Their methods involved cutting down the midline photographs of people who were posing particular emotions so that right and left halves could be obtained respectively. Mirror images of these halves then were prepared and pasted together. Subjects judged the derived composites by their degree of facial expressiveness. Since the work of Sackheim and Gur (1978) and Sackheim et al. (1978), other investigations consistently have demonstrated the same results (i.e., stronger emotional expressions contained within the left-sided [right-hemispheric] composites; Borod & Caron, 1980; Campbell, 1978; Rubin & Rubin, 1980). Yet, the most problematic feature of these studies was that posed rather than spontaneous facial expressions were employed; therefore affective states within the subjects may not have been assessed accurately by such established procedures.

Thus, other designs like the naturalistic (Borod, Koff, & White, 1983; Moscovitch & Olds, 1982) were instituted effectively, in which subjects' facial reactions in everyday types of environments (e.g., restaurants and parks) were observed. Once again, it was found that the left halves of the subjects' faces expressed more intense emotions than the right, confirming the previous results. In more recent experimental self-assessment procedures (Schiff & Lamon, 1989), subjects were instructed to lift one corner of their mouths and then describe the emotion(s) they were experiencing upon relaxation of those facial muscles. Asymmetrical states commonly were identified, with more negative feelings of sadness and depression being correlated to left-sided (right-hemispheric) contractions and more positive feelings of happiness and general contentment being

FIG. 7.3.   The Schiff and Lamon (1989) unilateral facial contraction procedure. Subjects were told to pull back and lift one corner of their mouths
on the left and right sides, respectively. Each unilateral contraction lasted
approximately 1 minute, during which time subjects had to pay attention
to any affections they were experiencing. These feelings subsequently were
reported to the experimenter. This particular facial movement was chos-
en because those muscles in the lower face were innervated completely
by the contralateral hemisphere. From "Inducing Emotion by Unilateral
Contraction of Facial Muscles" by B. B. Schiff and M. Lamon, 1989, Neuropsychologia, 27(7), p. 927. Copyright 1989 by Pergamon Press. Reprinted
by permission.

associated with right-sided (left-hemispheric) contractions (Fig. 7.3). Other
studies also have linked right-hemisphere activation to negative emotional
states (Davidson & Schwartz, 1976; Davidson et al., 1979; Tucker, Stenslie, Roth, & Shearer, 1981) and even abnormal affections such as unipolar depression (Davidson, Shaffer, & Saron, 1985; Perris & Monakhou,
1979; Silberman & Weingartner, 1986).

Although the right brain is involved strongly in emotional expression,
the left brain still is implicated with feelings to some extent (particularly
the more positive experiences). Future research on facial expressions
should find new techniques that will measure more accurately the precise emotional states subjects are experiencing. CLEM indices might be
appropriate to this area, because left eye movements have been shown
to be correlated with sad states (Ahern & Schwartz, 1979) as well as
depressed psychopathologies (Myslobodsky & Horesh, 1978; Schweitzer,
1979). More complete and detailed criteria also should be provided to
differentiate negative facial expressions clearly from the more positive
or even neutral types.

SUMMARY AND CONCLUSIONS

This chapter presented an extensive and highly detailed account of the
most commonly used methodologies designed to assess cortical asymmetries in normal subjects. Although the list of procedures was not com-

pletely exhaustive, those that were described should have acquainted the reader sufficiently with the most basic techniques and should have provided some definite direction for those who have the desire to conduct original studies in this area. As you may have inferred from the chapter, measures that probably will show the most promise for revealing interesting patterns of brain lateralization include: attentional bias manipulations, PET scans, ERPs, CNVs, and even the occasionally ignored CLEMs. Only the future will disclose whether science will adopt new indices or refine those currently under our direct manipulation and scrutiny.

The major points of chapter 7 follow:

1. Standard dichotic and tachistoscopic procedures have shown the predicted REAs and RVF advantages for most verbal materials and, to a less pronounced (although sometimes still significant) extent, LEAs and LVF advantages for many nonverbal inputs. Direct access and indirect relay models have attempted to explain these asymmetrical results as a function of the information-processing route leading to the specialized hemisphere (i.e., left path for verbal stimuli, right for spatial). Current theories have examined the role that attentional and cognitive factors play more effectively with respect to body side preferences in these tasks. Kinsbourne's attentional set hypothesis, Bryden's attentional strategy approach, and even my individual variation model all are posited on the common premise that subjects have some voluntary control over the strategies they will select to process the given input (with some change in strategies anticipated based on task requirements and subjects' expectations).

2. Measures specifically designed to assess the amount of cortical activation in each hemisphere were looked at subsequently. They included body side movements (CLEMs and facial expressions), metabolic indices (rCBF and PET scans), and various brain wave potentials (EEGs, ERPs, and CNVs). Results with many of these measures tend to indicate that the traditional verbal–nonverbal distinction between hemispheres should be abandoned and that a more relative, flexible dichotomy should be adopted. In confirmation of this conclusion, recent findings with PET scans and ERPs have indicated that the right hemisphere plays a very important role in the perception of speech-related stimuli. My attentional variation model also proved to be quite helpful when interpreting inconsistent or nonreplicable outcomes involving some of the other indices (e.g., CLEMs and CNVs).

Now that the groundwork has been established for studying asymmetries in normal subjects, one logically can begin a discussion of differences in information-processing strategies identified within various subgroups of this population. The first subgroup comparison to be focused on is between male and female subjects in chapter 8.

CHAPTER EIGHT

Are There Gender Differences in Brain Lateralization?

And the Lord God formed man
　of the slime of the earth,
And breathed into his face
　the breath of life,
And man became a living soul. . . .

And the Lord God said:
　It is not good for man to be alone.
　Let us make him a help
　like unto himself. . . .

Then the Lord God cast a
　deep sleep upon Adam,
And when he was fast asleep,
　He took one of his ribs,
　and filled up flesh for it.

And the Lord God built the rib
　which he took from Adam into a woman,
　and brought her to Adam.

And Adam said,
　This now is bone of my bones,
　and flesh of my flesh,
　She shall be called woman,
　because she was taken out of man. . . .
　　　　　　　—Genesis 2:7, 18, 21–23

This passage from *Genesis* of the Holy Bible depicts the story of human creation, of how both man and woman were formed so that each could play a functional role in keeping the other company. More than that, it illustrates the differences as well as similarities between the two genders. Woman is part of man, of his flesh and substance; yet, she is also a separate entity, with an identity apart from man's. By having her own individual qualities, woman can be rightly called "not man." However, it is these very qualities that can complete man, rounding out his development and making him the best creature that he can be.

Man, in essence, needs the feminine qualities if he is ever going to perfect himself. So the *Genesis* passage highlights the importance of differentiating between the two genders. It is in this very differentiation that one can understand most fully what it means to be a fulfilled human being living on this planet.

Therefore, the goal behind this chapter is to focus on these gender differences from a number of theoretical perspectives and to present some compelling experimental evidence to support some of these claims. More specifically, the first part examines two differentiation views: the genetic and the biochemical (hormonal). The latter half approaches the issue of differentiation from another perspective, namely experimental research. The methods already described in chapter 7 are employed to assess the extent to which the two genders differ in brain lateralization. As always, general remarks and concluding comments are provided at the end to properly orient the reader to the massive literature base that has been consulted in addressing the differentiation topic.

THEORIES RELATING TO GENDER DIFFERENCES

The Genetic View

Verbal Versus Spatial Superiority Differences. In tests of general intelligence, gender differences consistently have been observed with respect to specific abilities. Girls tend to score higher on tests emphasizing linguistic skills, such as speed of articulation, fluency, grammar, and verbal production (Burstein, Bank, & Jarvik, 1980; McGee, 1980; McGlone, 1980). As already referenced in chapter 6, females also are less susceptible to learning disorders that are language related (e.g., developmental dyslexia, stuttering, and early infantile autism), further highlighting their verbal advantage over males (Benton, 1975; Hier & Kaplan, 1980). On the other hand, boys exhibit a definite superiority on measures of spatial abilities, including mathematics, maze performance, mechanical skills, mental rotation, picture assembly, block design, point localization, and chess (Harris, 1978; McGee, 1979). These spatial differences are most striking when one considers how many more boys than girls have a greater aptitude for such skills (Adelson, 1985; Benbow & Stanley, 1983).

Although there has been considerable discussion as to when these advantages first appear, with some researchers advocating the strongest superiorities after puberty (Meece, Parsons, Kaczala, Goff, & Futterman, 1982), I (along with others) believe there is an even earlier, perhaps genetically induced, onset to the gender variations (Johnson & Meade, 1987; Newcombe, 1982). McGee (1979) and Burstein et al. (1980) noticed that spatial visualization and orientation skills are very much apparent in boy infants; they demonstrate a natural inclination to explore their environment and select toys and games that capitalize on these capabilities. Conversely, girls are more likely to engage in choral activities, speak sooner and more fluently, develop much larger vocabularies, master more complex syntactic forms of language, articulate more quickly and precisely, and become better readers (Harris, 1977, 1978).

One of the most convincing arguments for the genetic model of predisposed superiorities recently has been made by Johnson and Meade (1987). When they adapted standardized spatial tests to the appropriate grade level of the child, male advantages clearly were shown much earlier than the hypothesized adolescent point. By age 10 (i.e., fourth grade), boys reliably outperformed girls, with the magnitude of this superiority remaining relatively constant through age 18. Additional analyses revealed that the verbal precocity of younger girls (from kindergarten to the third grade) might have masked the male spatial advantage at these earlier ages.

I do not want to rule out environmental factors and influences when considering these gender differences in abilities. Some evidence has been collected that indicates that spatial skills in girls can be improved by selective training procedures as well as intensive practice within tasks (Benbow & Stanley, 1980; Koslow, 1987). However, one must also acknowledge that males manifest a natural ability to do well on these assignments even before such training commences, lending credence to the view that biological factors might be the overriding elements responsible for the identified variations between the genders (Bock & Kolakowski, 1973).

Cortical Organization: Female Bilateralization Versus Male Asymmetry.

Because of this highly significant gender by abilities interaction (with females doing better than males verbally and males outperforming females spatially), theories suggest that the two genders possess different cortical organizations. Two of the more prominent approaches are mentioned here: Buffery and Gray's (1972) *female lateralization* theory and Levy's (1972) *female bilateralization* argument.

Buffery and Gray (1972) claimed that females are more lateralized for speech than males, thus providing an explanation for why this gender displays a faster language development as well as an earlier competency in verbal abilities. The basic premise should be quite apparent: greater lateralization for a given function (e.g., the verbal) results in superior performance for that function. Curiously, a major flaw is inherent in Buffery and Gray's (1972) argument, because males are assumed to have a bilateral (rather than lateralized) representation for the abilities they excel in, namely the spatial.

Levy (1972) adopted a more sound perspective for explaining gender advantages in particular skills. Although she stated that males have an asymmetrical cortical arrangement with the right hemisphere being more equipped to handle spatial functions, she postulated that females are less lateralized for speech in their left hemisphere and alternatively speculated that they represent language in both hemispheres (i.e., bilaterally). Levy (1976) further maintained that this symmetrical organization for language will impair spatial skills, because the right hemisphere has become as verbally proficient as the left side. This cortical trade-off in abilities, with better verbal and poorer spatial, is a very convincing reason that females are not as adept as males when it comes to nonverbal discrimination tests.

Levy (1978) also considered the evolutionary pressures that originally forced men and women to acquire different cortical organizations. Historically speaking, if females were more inclined to be involved in child-rearing practices, they would have needed a fairly well-developed communication system to raise their young. Perhaps verbal bilateralization was the only way they could have performed the rearing task successfully. On the other hand, males did not require this hemispheric arrangement, because they were involved most often in the hunting and collecting of food as well as leading the tribe to new locations where food and other natural resources were abundant. It was necessary for this gender to have a high level of visuospatial skills clearly offset from the verbal to ensure the survival of the group; therefore lateralization of this respective function to the right hemisphere became the dominant organization in males. Other theorists have joined Levy's (1978) band wagon, maintaining that a bilateral spatial representation probably would have caused confusion in left–right directions, resulting in very pronounced disorientations for males who especially depended on strong spatial skills (Corballis & Beale, 1983; Webster, 1977).

Therefore, based on physiological necessity, distinctly different hemispheric arrangements had to develop accordingly in each gender. Perhaps the need no longer remains, but successive generations of males and females continue to be blessed (or cursed, depending on your viewpoint) with these inherited organizations. As is seen in an upcoming section, experimental research has favored Levy's position that women exhibit a lesser degree of cerebral lateralization than men (Bryden, 1979; McGlone, 1978).

Maturational Differences Between the Genders. Waber (1976) offered another approach to why there are gender differences in laterality: The variations are more attributable to the rates at which males and females mature than to the specific gender per se. Waber (1976) noticed that girls gained physical maturity much earlier than boys (with an approximate 2-year advantage over the male gender; thus she reasoned that differences in cortical organization would arise from these maturational changes. Assuming that language is one of the first skills to be acquired, she predicted that the early maturers, typically females, would demonstrate superior verbal abilities, whereas late maturers (i.e., males) would display better spatial abilities.

Also integrating Levy's (1978) views on lateralization into her theory, Waber (1976) believed that early maturers would be more likely to show functional plasticity between the hemispheres and so could represent the linguistic functions more bilaterally than late maturers. In fact, Waber (1976) found that verbal-spatial differences were influenced heavily by the maturation rate and, further, that late maturers evidenced larger asymmetries for vocal inputs than earlier maturers. As anticipated, differences due to gender alone were not significant.

Waber's (1976) argument received additional empirical support over the years (Benderly, 1987; Denckla et al., 1980; Witelson, 1977b). Strong visuospatial skills have been found in "language laggers" as well as developmental dyslexics (both of which have been predominantly male). As Hier and Kaplan (1980) remarked, the greater degree of spatial lateralization places these subjects at a greater risk for one of the language disorders, especially because they rely more on right- and left-hemispheric processing. To date, more researchers have accepted Waber's (1976) approach that differences between male and female brains are more gender related than, as Levy (1978) claimed, gender specific.

Although not discounting this opinion, it still is fascinating that one gender matures somewhat differently from the other. Perhaps the neuronal wiring potential is present at birth for each gender, with more bilateral "plastic" circuits to be established eventually for females. The necessary ingredient that activates this differential wiring is simply maturational readiness on the part of each subject. In light of these comments, it needs to be ascertained whether there are any morphological variations between the male and female brains that can be related to these maturational differences.

Morphological Differences Between the Genders.   Gender appears to play a significant role in morphological asymmetries between the hemispheres. As early as 1800, it was reported that hemispheric weight differences were significantly smaller in female subjects than male subjects (McGlone, 1980). Current anatomical research tends to confirm these earlier gender differences, with more symmetrical sylvian fissures and temporal planums being found in female brains (Wada et al., 1975), and greater left–right asymmetries commonly seen in the male temporal gyri (Kopp, Michel, Carrier, Biron, & Duvillard, 1977). It should be recalled from chapter 1 that these cortical areas have been implicated in important verbal functions. Therefore, if fewer morphological asymmetries have been identified in these regions for women, this would provide further support for Levy's (1978) argument that females are less lateralized for language than males. The much larger corpus callosum also identified in the female brain lends further credence to Levy's (1978) view that this gender's functional organization is more generalized to both cortical sides (Moir, 1991).

Other evidence for gender dimorphism of the brain comes from the study of other species, particularly the white rat. As already indicated in chapter 2, male rats typically show significantly thicker corti (i.e., outer layers) of the right hemisphere, whereas female rats have nonsignificantly thicker left corti at most ages examined (Diamond, 1984; Diamond et al., 1981). One forebrain structure in particular, the *medial preoptic area* (MPA), reveals very pronounced size asymmetries between the genders, with the nuclei of the MPA being three to seven times larger in the male rat brains (Gorski, Gordon, Shryne, & Southam, 1978). The MPA is one of the critical sites involved in the expression of male sexual behavior. Therefore, several scientists have reasoned that sex hormones, especially the male androgens, regulate the size of this brain area (Gorski, 1980). I shall return to this biochemical approach for gender differences shortly.

Although these morphological variations have not been substantiated fully in humans yet, there is no reason to believe that similar differences are not present in human female and male brains at birth or postnatally. As strongly advocated by Kolb and Whishaw (1985), the asymmetries in humans probably follow the same general pattern, although to a lesser degree than in lower level species, making it much harder to detect any significant sexual dimorphisms in human hemispheres.

The Biochemical View

I direct attention to the way sex hormones shape the anatomical structure of the brain as well as influence certain gender-related behaviors displayed throughout most of the lifespan of the organism.

The Effects of Hormones on Brain Circuitry. At conception, male and female human embryos are exactly alike. Previous to the seventh week of development, the gonads are relatively undifferentiated in both genders. But by the second month, the gonads start to develop into the more distinctive female ovaries or male testes. What starts this differentiation process is the presence (or absence) of the masculine androgens within the embryo (Benderly, 1987). One androgen in particular, *testosterone*, stimulates the development of the male sex organs, thus producing a masculinizing effect on the embryo. Without testosterone, the female system normally proceeds on course. It would seem that "Nature's plan is to create a female," because the precursors of the female system are present in both sexes at the earliest stages of gonadal development (Carlson, 1991; Konner, 1983). Therefore, if fetal androgens were not present originally, the human race would have been a unisexual, female-oriented species, with its members perhaps possessing only one dominant cortical organization (i.e., bilateralization of the linguistic functions).

Pertaining to the effects of hormones on the establishment of brain circuitry, rats have been the most convenient subjects to study, because they are born just 22 days after conception, a time when androgens are just beginning to exert an influence on their brain development. Current research strongly suggests that the gender differentiation of the rat brain, like the sex organs, is directed mainly by the presence (or absence) of the male androgens. Diamond (1984) found that if males were castrated at birth, the normal pattern of cortical asymmetries was not evidenced; rather, thicker left (than right) corti were observed by 90 days of age. Moreover, newborn females who had their ovaries removed showed the typical male asymmetries of significantly thicker right corti. These results clearly indicate that testicular hormones do regulate the postnatal development of the hemispheres, especially right-brain lateralization. Apparently these masculinizing effects can even be manifested in female rats once their ovarian hormones are suppressed.

With respect to specific brain structures, dramatic changes have been identified in the MPA under different hormonal manipulations. When male rats were castrated shortly after birth, the nucleus of the MPA (as well as several parts within this cell body) significantly decreased in overall size (Bloch & Gorski, 1988; Gorski et al., 1978). However, the sexually dimorphic pattern could be reinstated if males were given injections of testosterone (Jacobson, Csernus, Shryne, & Gorski, 1981). In newborn females exposed to a single large dose of the androgen before the 15th day, the male asymmetry eventually could be acquired as well (Geschwind & Galaburda, 1987). Based on these studies, one might conclude that the sexual dimorphism of the MPA nucleus is strongly dependent on the early postnatal administration of male androgens.

Considering the effects of female hormones on particular structures, estrogen receptors have been located in the MPA of both male and female rat brains. However, the male region usually has contained a smaller number of these female receptors in comparison to its counterpart. Furthermore, fewer progesterone receptors have been found in the male ventromedial nucleus of the hypothalamus (VMH), a critical site involved in the expression of female sexual behavior. Presumably, androgens exert a defeminizing (as well as masculinizing) influence on developing gender-related areas in the male rat brain (Pfaff & Schwartz-Giblin, 1988; Rainbow, Parsons, & McEwen, 1982).

As this chapter was being written, reports had just been published highlighting the sexual dimorphism of the MPA in the human species. Although fetal brains did not show the hypothesized sexual variations upon autopsy, 4-year-old ones did, with smaller nuclei being evidenced in the female brains. Another interesting finding was that the MPA decreased in size as both males and females matured (Allen, Hines, Shryne, & Gorski, 1989; Swaab & Hofman, 1988). Although more research needs to be conducted in this area, the argument still can be made that it is possible to generalize some of the hormonal results obtained from rat studies to the human species.

Although the data are extremely limited when it comes to studying the influence of testosterone on prenatal brain development, injections of this hormone in the rat fetus can alter cerebral laterality. Rosen, Berrebi, and Yutzey (1983) specifically assessed asymmetries by examining tail postures in newborn rats. Female pups ordinarily position their tails more to the left side, whereas males demonstrate little (if any) lateral preference. But in pups administered the prenatal testosterone, an asymmetrical shift occurred in females to adopt more right-sided postures, suggesting that some changes in brain circuitry had taken place for this gender. Whether the litters were predominantly male or female also played an influential role in tail posture preference, with ones having an excess of males elevating the number of left postures in females. One view that has gained support over the years is that the higher levels of testosterone produced in the male-dominant litters might have lateralized the female brain to a greater extent than in litters where the male–female proportions were distributed more evenly (Glick, 1983). Obviously, future studies should investigate the effects of prenatal hormones on rat cortical structure more thoroughly so that more accurate inferences can be made with respect to cerebral asymmetries in this species (and perhaps even the human).

The Effects of Hormones on Behavior.   Not only do hormones affect the development of brain mechanisms, but they also control particular behavioral patterns in animal and human subjects. The sexual behavior of rats has been studied more extensively than any other laboratory species. As one might expect, the sexual responsiveness of male rodents is strongly dependent on testosterone, because castration totally eliminates this activity (Bermant & Davidson, 1974). The sexual behavior of female rodents also has been correlated with increases in the gonadal hormones, estrogen and progesterone. Elevated estrogen levels actually have been found to prime the release of progesterone just before sexual receptivity occurs on the part of the females (Feder, 1981; Lisk, 1978).

Developmentally speaking, if the rat brain is not exposed to androgens during a critical period shortly after birth, female sexual behavior will predominate in adulthood, provided of course that estrogen and progesterone are administered at this time (Blaustein & Olster, 1989). Refer to the top portion of Fig. 8.1 for more details on the activational effects of these two female hormones on later sexual activity. If the rodent brain is exposed to testosterone postnatally, however, *defeminization* and *masculinization* will be the resultant outcomes: namely, female sexual behavior will be suppressed and, alternatively, male responsiveness will be facilitated in later adulthood (Feder, 1984). Refer to the bottom half of Fig. 8.1.

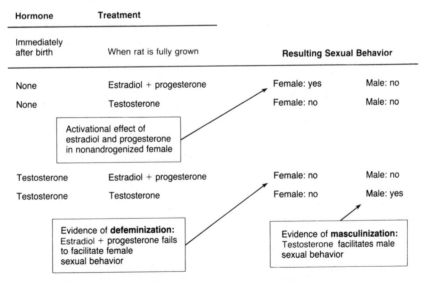

FIG. 8.1. The organizational effects of testosterone on subsequent sexual behavior. If the male androgen, testosterone, is not administered to rats immediately after birth, female sexual behavior automatically results (i.e., "Nature's impulse to create a female will predominate"). However, if androgen is given, male behavior occurs due to the hormone's powerful defeminizing and masculinizing influences. From *Physiology of Behavior*, 4th ed. (p. 326) by Neil R. Carlson, 1991, Needham, MA: Allyn & Bacon. Copyright 1991 by Allyn & Bacon. Reprinted by permission.

Clearly, men and women would not show these behavioral role reversals if their hormonal balances were exchanged. Castrating a normal heterosexual male and then giving him doses of the feminine hormones would not make him assume the female role in sexual activity. Likewise, ovariectomizing a heterosexual female and subsequently giving her testosterone injections would not make her adopt a more masculine interest in members of her same gender. If anything, her heterosexual desires would become even more pronounced (Carlson, 1991). Therefore, one must be careful not to generalize the sexual behavioral outcomes obtained from hormonal manipulations with lower level organisms to humans, because the correlations are weak ones at best.

If men and women do not differ in their sexual behavior per se, they certainly demonstrate wide variations in their sexual orientation (or sexual preference). Some exhibit a homosexual orientation, exclusively preferring partners of the same gender; others show a more heterosexual orientation, only preferring partners of the opposite gender; and still others are of a bisexual orientation, equally preferring members of both genders. In particular, the homosexual orientation appears to be a preference reserved only for the human species (Ehrhardt & Meyer-Balburg, 1981). Investigations into possible determinants of homosexuality have not supported the social factors theory strongly, which emphasizes the deleterious effects of child-rearing practices by domineering mothers or submissive fathers (Bell, Weinberg, & Hammersmith, 1981). Rather, biochemical explanations have been invoked to a greater extent to account for this unique orientation.

The most likely physiological cause for homosexuality apparently involves some abnormal level of male androgens on developing brain structures. Scientific speculations have suggested that the brains of male homosexuals may have received far less exposure to androgens during the early stages of prenatal development, whereas the brains of female homosexuals may have been exposed to a significantly greater concentration of these masculinizing hormones, thus explaining the sexual preferences in both groups.

Recent studies by Gladue, Green, and Hellman (1984) and Anderson, Fleming, Rhees, and Kinghorn (1986) provided some evidence for the hypothesis that male homosexuality may be correlated with androgen-interfering agents. Although no definite conclusions have been reached yet, future research should be directed to discovering the hormonal influences responsible for sexual preferences. One might find that cerebral lateralization is connected to a particularly delicate balance of androgens within the brain. Deviations from this proposed balance might be responsible for the growth of such structures as the anterior commissure reported to be found in the latest autopsies of the homosexual brain (Allen & Gorski, 1992).

Other gender-linked behavior patterns in humans have been associated with certain androgen levels. For instance, spatial performance is especially good for women who have higher than normal levels of the androgen. Curiously, men who have lower concentrations also perform at a very competent level on the spatial assignments (McGee, 1979). These preliminary data tend to support the biochemical model of gender differences. However, better methods of assessing hormonal levels in humans have yet to be achieved, because past estimations mainly have relied on primary and secondary sexual characteristics of the subjects tested (Bradshaw & Nettleton, 1983). Still, most of the variations in spatial ability have been detected at the onset of puberty, a time when male and female hormones generally are secreted in significantly larger doses (Fig. 8.2).

Another gender-related behavior, *social aggression* (sometimes called *intermale aggression*), typically occurs more often between males than females. The most common explanation is that testosterone has both organizational and activational effects on this type of aggression. Prenatally, this androgen not only makes the developing brain more masculine (or more lateralized), but also stimulates the development of androgen-

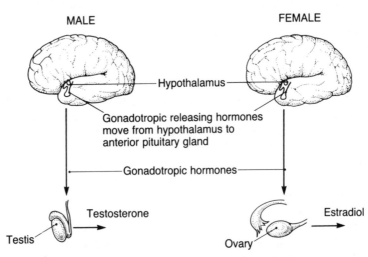

FIG. 8.2. Hormonal effects at puberty. The onset of puberty occurs in men and women when the hypothalamus stimulates the anterior pituitary gland to release its gonadotropic hormones. These substances have a direct effect on the ovaries and testes, causing them to secrete larger amounts of estrogen and testosterone, respectively. In turn, the sexual hormones primarily influence the development of secondary characteristics in each gender. From *Physiology of Behavior*, 4th ed. (p. 320), by Neil R. Carlson, 1991, Needham, MA: Allyn & Bacon. Copyright 1991 by Allyn & Bacon. Reprinted by permission.

sensitive neural circuits. Later on in puberty (or early adulthood), when testosterone levels are increasing significantly, these circuits become activated, allowing the organism to engage more fully in those male patterns of aggressive behavior than at any other developmental period (Edwards, 1969).

The strongest support for this view comes from studies that compared social aggression in rats castrated at birth with ones castrated in adulthood. As predicted from the model, injections of testosterone produced intermale fighting only in those rodents castrated later in life, apparently because these animals already possessed the neurally responsive circuitry for this hormone (Conner & Levine, 1969). Female rats also could be masculinized to display the same aggressive tendencies as males if testosterone were administered immediately after birth and then again in adulthood (Edwards, 1968). The most recent evidence suggests that intermale aggression can be induced in postnatally castrated male rodents if a prolonged series of testosterone injections are given, highlighting that exposure to androgens very early on in life can sensitize the circuitry to control this type of aggression (von Saal, 1983).

Pertaining to human aggression, intermale fighting in boys increases at the time when testosterone levels are high, namely at puberty (Mazur, 1983). Further, androgen-sensitive receptors that have been implicated in social aggression have been found in neurons of the sexually dimorphic MPA nucleus (Bean & Conner, 1978). It seems reasonable to conclude that this brain area directs aggressive behavior in adolescent humans as well as full-grown animals of other species. Castration can decrease the amount of intermale fighting in humans just as it can in other animals. Convicted male sex offenders who have been castrated subsequently usually have reduced sex drives and exhibit fewer displays of heterosexual or homosexual attacks (Laschet, 1973).

Fitting these pieces into the human puzzle of understanding behavioral differences between the genders, it appears that androgens regulate a number of important responses in boys (and men), mainly by exerting their effects on the developing circuitry of the prenatal brain. This is not to say that socialization has little influence on these behaviors, only that the initial control primarily is mediated by the masculinizing hormones and associated neuronal mechanisms.

EXPERIMENTAL TECHNIQUES USED
TO ASSESS MALE–FEMALE ASYMMETRIES

I now direct attention to the experimental research on sexual asymmetries. Although the laboratory is a microcosm of that external social reality, it is fascinating to consider the number of gender differences that still can be identified within such a restricted (and fairly limited) environment. With respect to the male–female variations, the traditional techniques are examined first (i.e., the dichotic and tachistoscopic designs), followed by a review of the other cortical indices (e.g., blood flow, EEG, and facial expression). For a more detailed description of each of these procedures, the reader is directed back to chapter 7.

Findings with the Traditional Dichotic and Tachistoscopic Designs

Dichotic Sexual Asymmetries.   Levy's (1978) female bilateralization argument has received some experimental backing, especially in dichotic listening studies that have employed verbal materials. One of the largest dichotic designs to date, conducted by Lake and Bryden (1976), revealed very pronounced REAs for consonant–vowel stimuli, but only in adult male subjects. Because of these right-ear preferences, the researchers inferred that men were more lateralized for language than women, who apparently processed the CVs to the same degree of accuracy in each ear. Similar male patterns of performance have been identified in a number of dichotic experiments over the years (Harshman, Remington, & Krashen, 1975; Ryan & McNeil, 1974; Thistle, 1975). However, approximately half of the studies has not found these gender differences (Briggs & Nebes, 1976; Carr, 1969; McKeever & Van Deventer, 1977), and a few even have reported a reversed asymmetry, with females demonstrating a greater lateralization for particular verbal materials compared with males (Bryden, 1965; Dorman & Porter, 1975).

The results are more confusing when nonverbal dichotic processing is compared between the genders. If ear asymmetries are obtained on tasks involving the discrimination of melodies and other nonlinguistic sounds, males typically do not display them, but, rather, females do with stronger LEAs being associated with this gender (Piazza, 1980). These conflicting dichotic trends in the literature have yet to be explained. Perhaps Buffery and Gray's (1972) female lateralization hypothesis holds more validity than previously speculated. Obviously, future studies need to replicate this unpredicted behavioral outcome before anything definite can be derived about the degree of gender lateralization for nonverbal types of inputs presented dichotically.

Tachistoscopic Sexual Asymmetries.   The case seems even more compelling for lateralization of functions in male subjects when tachistoscopic studies are considered. The majority of the experiments has indicated an LVF (or right-hemispheric) superiority in males for nonverbal materials, such as photographed faces (Berlucchi, Marzi, Rizzolatti, & Umilta, 1976; Rizzolatti & Buchtel, 1977), dot detection and localization

(Davidoff, 1977; Kimura, 1969; Levy & Reid, 1978), and line orientation (Sasanuma & Kobayashi, 1978; Walter, Bryden, & Allard, 1976). In addition, males have demonstrated very pronounced RVF (left-hemispheric) advantages for various types of verbal materials, extending from single-letter stimuli to actual word units (Bradshaw & Gates, 1978; Hannay & Malone, 1976; Kail & Siegel, 1977). Based on these results, one might arrive at Levy's conclusion that linguistic abilities of females are shared equally by both of their hemispheres, thus creating a symmetrical field preference on their part in many of these laterality tasks.

Of course, like the dichotic, some tachistoscopic designs have failed to find the male asymmetrical advantages (Bryden, 1976, 1982; Leehey, Diamond, & Cahn, 1978; Patterson & Bradshaw, 1975). One theory has been advanced by several researchers to account for the discrepant findings, namely the *gender variability hypothesis*. The basic assumption underlying this hypothesis is that there is a tremendous amount of variability in the way individual members of each gender are lateralized for particular functions. Because of this strong variation, gender differences are that much harder to detect, especially because some males possess less lateralized hemispheric organizations and some females more lateralized ones (Springer & Deutsch, 1989). Offshoots of this theoretical approach are presented to show the reader that the gender asymmetries identified in both dichotic and tachistoscopic assignments might be overgeneralized reports of how an individual male or female subject truly might perform.

Strategic Sexual Asymmetries.   As already described in chapter 7, Bryden (1980) posited that subjects could select any one from a number of information-processing strategies if left to their own attentional resources. By experimentally regulating which strategy was to be employed (usually by administering instructions to focus subjects' attention onto a specified ear or field side), Bryden (1980) claimed that any differences attributed to gender are virtually nonexistent. Although certain studies tend to support this theory (Bryden, 1986; Bryden, Munhall, & Allard, 1983), others have not (Iaccino, 1990; Iaccino & Sowa, 1989), showing instead that males still can express asymmetrical advantages to one body side even when such strategic controls are instituted.

A reinterpretation of the Bryden (1980) approach seems to be in order, based on the more recent (and opposing) findings. My view is that an obvious interaction exists between subject strategies and cortical organizations. Although the female brain circuits might be more bilateralized than the male, modifications still can occur in the processing of various inputs via the type of attentional set adopted by the subject. If the set is more directed to left-hemispheric activation, then right-ear and field advantages might occur in both genders (with the most pronounced effects being displayed in the already lateralized male group). Likewise, if the set is directed more fully to right-hemispheric activation, the complementary left-ear and field advantages might be evidenced, especially in the male subjects tested. Because women already are predisposed to a bilateral cortical arrangement, a lateralized strategy might be particularly hard for them to acquire within the limited block of time provided in the study.

Therefore, if more focused ear trials were administered to females, asymmetries eventually would be obtained that would resemble the male ones. In fact, this happened when more time was given so that both men and women could learn the strategy expected of them, whether it was to distribute more attentional focus onto the right side or, alternately, the left. The REAs for the verbal materials were more powerful than the corresponding LEAs for both genders; the latter advantages were also stronger in men than women under the more directed attentional manipulations (Iaccino & Houran, 1989, 1991). These results clearly confirm my argument that experimental strategies are flexible enough to be acquired by either gender, but that the subject's cortical organization still can exert an influence on the strength of the strategic behavior subsequently expressed. Thus, attentional and cortical variations in men and women possibly could explain the high amount of intersubject variability hypothesized to be present in the aforementioned experiments.

Findings with Other Asymmetrical Indices

Although gender asymmetries have been examined most extensively with the traditional dichotic and tachistoscopic procedures, other indices have been used to assess the degree to which these gender differences can be generalized across a wide variety of designs. The outcomes have not always been consistent ones, but this should not be a source of discouragement, because my attentional/cerebral variation model explains rather satisfactorily that a constant gender effect cannot always be anticipated from one study to the next, let alone one design to another. A discussion of these alternative measures for laterality assessment in both men and women follows by first looking at the regional cerebral blood flow (rCBF) index.

Sexual Asymmetries in Cerebral Blood Flow.   Gur et al. (1982) wanted to determine whether changes in the rCBF pattern would occur when men and women were engaged in certain tasks, primarily of a verbal or spatial nature. They found that during the verbal analogies test, left-hemisphere blood flow significantly increased in both genders. However, when the task involved more spatial components (i.e., line orientation judgments), females exhibited greater increases in right-hemisphere flow compared with males. A more recent study by Linn and Petersen (1985) replicated the latter findings by Gur et al. (1982) of greater right-hemispheric activation in women under similar spatial conditions.

On first inspection, these rCBF results appeared to contradict the previous predictions of weaker laterality in the female gender. But, another explanation has been advanced by some current researchers to account for the apparent gender discrepancies: perhaps cerebral blood flow was really a more accurate measure of the amount of mental effort exerted on a task than the degree of hemispheric laterality per se. Putting this in simpler words, females presumably were having more difficulties processing the spatial inputs because their bilateral verbal blueprint was in direct conflict with that nonverbal function. Nevertheless, they still were trying to use (rather unsuccessfully) a right-sided attentional strategy to handle the information. The end result was that the females had distributed, with a good deal of concentrated effort, most of their attentional resources to a body side that basically was not equipped for spatial processing (Springer & Deutsch, 1989).

In my tachistoscopic experiments (Iaccino, 1990), female subjects more often expressed difficulties in processing positional inputs, relative to their male counterparts. Although this increased mental effort hypothesis effectively integrates the major assumption of attentional variation between the genders, more replications of the female spatial asymmetry need to be obtained before one wholeheartedly accepts this position.

Electroencephalographic Gender Asymmetries. Although a small number of subjects and unequal gender ratios have confounded attempts at deriving an accurate inference on the degree of hemispheric lateralization in each gender (Silberman & Weingartner, 1986), a few electroencephalographic (EEG) studies have shown some curious reversals of past research trends. Either females were processing a wide variety of inputs, verbal and spatial, in exactly the same manner, as evidenced by insignificant alpha wave differences in each hemisphere (Tucker, 1976), or females were better able than males to maintain asymmetrical patterns of alpha activity (Davidson & Schwartz, 1976). Because replications are particularly hard to achieve with such gross brain measures, a wait-and-see attitude probably should be adopted before one claims that previous lateralization theories are wrong or that the direction of the gender asymmetries should be corrected.

Gender Asymmetries in Facial Expression. Another experimental method involved presenting photographs of people who were posing particular emotions in each facial half and then asking subjects to judge their degree of facial expressiveness. Left visual-field (or right-hemispheric) superiorities often have been reported in normal subjects when such emotional recognitions were required (Landis, Assal, & Perret, 1979; Ley & Bryden, 1979). This right-brain lateralization for emotion sometimes seemed to be dependent on the gender of the subject, with males demonstrating the left-sided advantages at times (Graves, Landis, & Goodglass, 1981; Safer, 1981) and females showing the LVF superiorities in other situations (Lavadas, Umilta, & Ricci-Bitti, 1980; McKeever & Dixon, 1981). But, as Silberman and Weingartner (1986) advised, it is still too early to make any definitive statements regarding gender asymmetries in the processing of emotional inputs.

A series of studies on clinically brain-damaged patients revealed some strong laterality effects as a function of gender. Females consistently engaged in pathological crying, whereas males were more prone to bouts of laughter and other mood elevations. These emotions also were found to correlate with damage to a particular hemisphere. The right brain appeared to be specialized for the negative affects, because lesions restricted to this side resulted in more positive expressions. On the other hand, the left brain was specialized for the positive affects, because damage to this hemisphere produced the complementary emotional states (Sackheim et al., 1982). Research on unimpaired subjects has tended to support these findings (Ahern & Schwartz, 1979; Sackheim & Gur, 1978; Schiff & Lamon, 1989), but work still needs to be performed with normal male and female subgroups to see whether the same asymmetrical pattern holds true for these genders.

Gender Asymmetries with PET Scans.   The clinical research that has utilized PET scans and other related metabolic scanning techniques has revealed some fascinating gender differences in brain organization. Depending on the particular function examined, women's brains were shown to be either more or less diffusely organized, in comparison with men's. For instance, speech production and specific hand movements in females were governed by more localized areas, particularly the frontal regions of the left hemisphere. On the other hand, naming words beginning with a specific letter was correlated to more left frontal activation in both men and women's brains. The only language-related skill actually to elicit bilateral activity in the female hemispheres was vocabulary (i.e., the basic ability to define words). However, the comparable skill in males seemed to be organized more focally in the left brain side (Kimura & Harshman, 1984).

Kimura (1985) subsequently reasoned that the female bilateralization argument only was applicable to more abstract verbal functions (e.g., vocabulary), and that a better conceptualization of brain differences in men and women should examine those specific properties of the verbal and spatial dimensions more thoroughly. By such detailed analyses, Kimura (1985) proposed that a more accurate assessment of the types of gender variations could be achieved as well as extended across a wide variety of materials. Perhaps research trends in the future will look more closely at these functional levels, or, at the very least, the information-processing strategies that can be employed within these specific tasks.

SUMMARY AND CONCLUSIONS

Based on the information provided in chapter 8, one easily can state that there are gender differences in brain lateralization. However, one cannot give a reply so easily about the magnitude of the variations, because they seem to fluctuate from one experimental procedure to the next. The best approach to take would be to compare individuals within each of the gender groups to determine which information-processing strategies are utilized most effectively. Through the examination of these individual subject strategies, more accurate inferences possibly can be derived about brain organization and its functioning in respective members of each gender.

The major points that were covered in this chapter are highlighted:

1. Although I do not deny that early child-rearing conditions and other environmental factors contribute to important gender differences, genetic and biochemical variables also play a significant role in shaping the eventual behavior patterns of both men and women. Increased levels of the male androgens, in particular, have been found to influence such responses as interspecies aggression and gender preference, as well as the prenatal circuitry of the brain and associated structures therein (e.g., the MPA and the VMH). Morphological symmetries in language-related areas also have been identified more often in female brains, providing support for the verbal bilateralization theory as originally formulated by Levy.

2. Experimental techniques also have yielded some interesting asymmetries with respect to the subject's gender. The dichotic and tachistoscopic results tend to support Levy's view that ear and field advantages either are reduced or absent in women, especially for more verbal types of materials. However, the findings from other cortical indices (e.g., blood flow and EEG) suggest that generalizations cannot be made so easily with respect to either the male or female hemispheric organizations. My attentional variation model appears to be the most applicable explanation for such inconsistent effects found between the genders.

Obviously, future research should be directed toward deciphering the reasons for these gender discrepancies. Until then, some alternatives to Levy's theory should be supported vigorously, such as Waber's maturational difference hypothesis. I focus next on another variation—handedness differences—to uncover the pattern of cerebral asymmetries associated with this variable.

CHAPTER NINE

Are There Handedness Differences in Brain Lateralization?

But when the Son of Man shall come
  in his majesty
  and all his angels with him,
Then he will sit on the throne of his glory.

And before him will be gathered
  all the nations,
And he will separate them one from another,
As the shepherd separates the sheep
  from the goats;
And he will set the sheep on his right hand,
  But the goats on the left.

Then the king will say to those
  on his right hand,
"Come, blessed of my Father,
Take possession of the kingdom
  prepared for you
  from the foundation of the world . . ."

Then he will say to those
  on his left hand,
"Depart from me, accursed ones,
Into the everlasting fire
  which was prepared for the devil
  and his angels . . ."

> And so those [on his left]
>   will go into everlasting punishment,
> But the just [on his right]
>   into everlasting life.
> —*Matthew* 25:31–34, 41, 46

This passage from the Bible clearly associates the left side with evil and an unredemptive sinisterness. (In fact, according to Springer and Deutsch, 1989, *left-handed* means sinister and underhanded.) As one researcher argued, this particular Vision of Judgment has done more to maintain the prejudice against left-handers than any other pronouncement in history (Barsley, 1979). Perhaps this is an overexaggeration on the author's part, but the fact remains that most Westerners are familiar with the *Matthew* passage, whatever their religious beliefs might be.

Not all evil actions reported in the Bible are connected to left-handed activity, however. When Eve is tempted by Satan in the Garden of Eden, she takes fruit from the forbidden Tree of Knowledge (see Genesis 3:6); yet, the hand that initiates the downfall of man and woman is never revealed. Also, when Cain leads his brother Abel into the fields to kill him (refer to Genesis 4:8), we are not sure which hand actually commits the most serious sin of taking the life of another. Other significant incidents are described just as vaguely in the holy text, suggesting that one should exercise some caution before ascribing all of the world's evils to the left hand.

Returning to Matthew's Vision of Judgment, it is not the left hands of sinners per se that are cursed; rather, it is where those sinners are located with respect to the Son of God (i.e., on the left side) that determines their everlasting fate. Therefore, one must not read into the Bible passages more than what is actually there. To do so places some groups like sinistrals (and females) at a distinct disadvantage and only heightens the discriminations and prejudices already present within the world.

This chapter's format proceeds in the following fashion: First, I concentrate on relevant issues related to handedness (e.g., its origins and assessment); then, I critique particular theories of hand variations to identify the major factors responsible for right- as well as left-handedness; finally, I review the experimental results on hand asymmetries with the aim of supporting one or more of the previously described theories. As has been done in preceding chapters within this part, the magnitude of these asymmetries is focused on so that meaningful inferences can be derived with respect to the cortical organizations of right- and left-handers.

TRACING THE ORIGINS OF HANDEDNESS

Of the American population, approximately 90% is right-handed, whereas about 7–8% is left-handed. Furthermore, this distribution of handedness does not seem to change, whatever culture is examined (Springer & Deutsch, 1989). The basic inquiry that can be posited is whether the universality of right-handedness always has been the norm, historically speaking.

Some authorities have argued that the ancient Hebrews might have been predominantly left-handed, because their writing proceeded from right to left (Erlenmeyer, 1883). Yet, others have countered that the direction of script bears absolutely no relationship to handedness. In fact, speculations have been made that in engraving hieroglyphics within clay or stone, it was only natural to begin on the right side, because that was where the best hand was located (Hewes, 1949). Similar claims of left-handedness have been attributed to the ancient Egyptians, on the basis that most humans and animals were depicted in more of a contralateral right profile (Wile, 1934; Wilson, 1872). However, it also should be considered that a general law of art widely accepted at this time was to present the right sides of figures to the spectator instead of the left, implying, if anything, that the ancient Egyptians were actually a right-handed people (Erman, 1894).

Coren and Porac (1977) attempted to trace the origins of right-handedness by examining works of art (i.e., drawings, paintings, and sculptures) spanning over 50 centuries. Not surprisingly, they found that the depiction of right- and left-handed usage did not change over this lengthy period. Rather, the incidences remained relatively constant from past to present, with the right hand always being the more dominant preference. Although animals apparently demonstrate more symmetrical paw preferences, recent findings have indicated that asymmetries can occur in nonhuman primates if tasks are more cognitively complex, requiring more finely tuned motor responses (Fagot & Vauclair, 1991). Still, the tendency for humans to be a strongly right-handed species appears to be a unique one on the evolutionary scale of development.

Corballis (1983, 1989) proposed that this consistent pattern of human dextrality may extend even further back than the historical limit of Coren and Porac's (1977) research. Most prehistoric tools and weapons look as if they had been made by—and for—the right hand. Human's earliest known ancestor, *Australopithecus*, who lived over 2 million years ago, also seemed to be predominantly dextral. This conclusion was reached after forensic analysis of baboon skulls that littered the sites of Australopithecus' fossilized remains. Examination revealed that most of the baboons had been struck from the front and on the left side, strongly suggesting that Australopithecus used the right hand to kill his prey. Even members of his own species were murdered in this fashion, making a convincing case for the genetic control of human aggression (Dart, 1949).

Annett (1983) tried to account for these lateral preferences displayed throughout the course of human history by explaining that chance factors ultimately decided which hand would be favored. Once the shift toward dextrality was made, humans continued to employ the right hand across a majority of activities, including writing and eating. The bias toward dextrality was enhanced further by societal pressures over the centuries. According to Annett (1983), one of the cortical hemispheres gradually began to acquire control over the dominant right hand. There apparently was some evolutionary advantage in having the left hemisphere mediate right-handed movements; thus this contralateral association has been maintained to this day. In fact, the most recent estimates place approximately 97% of all dextral adults as more left-hemisphere dominant, particularly for speech and other verbal-related functions (Thomas, 1989). As Harris (1986) noted, a dextral association might have contributed to the eventual lateralization of speech by the left hemisphere.

I return to a theoretical discussion of the factors responsible for handedness asymmetries at a later point within the chapter. For now, I say that a biological predisposition exists (and has existed) for dextrality ever since humans evolved as a species distinctly different from their ape relations.

THE ASSESSMENT OF HAND DOMINANCE

Although individuals would classify themselves as either left- or right-handed, questionnaire analyses have revealed that there are *degrees* of handedness. People rarely use one hand exclusively for all manual activities. Rather, one hand is preferred for one type of task and the other hand is preferred for a different type of task. In measuring hand preferences, subjects typically are asked to indicate which hand they use the most for a number of different activities, and then an overall sum of right to left usage is computed based on their responses. The obtained value reflects the direction as well as degree of handedness (whether strong, moderate, or weak) for each subject who is surveyed.

One of the most commonly employed questionnaires to assess hand preference is the *Edinburgh Handedness Inventory*, developed by Oldfield (1971) at Edinburgh University. Subjects specifically are queried about which hand they prefer across 10 different skills, including writing, drawing, throwing, cutting with scissors, brushing teeth, cutting with only a knife, holding a spoon and a broom, striking a match, and raising

	LEFT	RIGHT
1. Writing	☐	☐
2. Drawing	☐	☐
3. Throwing	☐	☐
4. Scissors	☐	☐
5. Toothbrush	☐	☐
6. Knife (without fork)	☐	☐
7. Spoon	☐	☐
8. Broom (upper hand)	☐	☐
9. Striking Match (match)	☐	☐
10. Opening box (lid)	☐	☐

FIG. 9.1. Instructions and items on the Edinburgh Handedness Inventory. The survey consists of 10 activities to which subjects indicate their hand preference. Laterality quotients are found by subtracting the number of left pluses from right ones, and then multiplying by 100. Appendix II from "The Assessment and Analysis of Handedness: The Edinburgh Inventory" by R. C. Oldfield, 1971, *Neuropsychologia, 9,* p. 112. Copyright 1971 by Pergamon Press. Reprinted by permission.

a box lid (Fig. 9.1). A laterality quotient for each subject is obtained subsequently by tabulating the number of right-handed (as opposed to left-handed) preferences and then multiplying by the constant 100. The quotient's limits generally extend from +100 for extreme right-handedness to −100 for extreme left-handedness, with 0 representing ambidextrous activity (i.e., equal use of both hands).

Variations of the Edinburgh Inventory also have been formulated over the decades, yielding similar activity items as well as scoring procedures. For instance, Annett's (1967) 12-item *Hand Preference Survey* tests subjects across a broad range of manual skills (e.g., throwing a ball, writing a letter, and unscrewing a jar). A score of −1 is assigned to every *left* response provided, a score of +1 to every *right* response, and a 0 to every *either* response that occurred. Subjects' hand preferences are then determined within the upper and lower limits of −12 and +12, representing extreme left- and right-handedness, respectively (Nagae, 1983).

Findings have been quite consistent from one survey to the next. People typically have shown either a left- or right-handed preference, with ambidextral activity being a relatively rare outcome. To give an example, on the Edinburgh Inventory, approximately 50% of right-handers had laterality quotients greater than 80, whereas the same percentage of left-handers had quotients less than − 76, revealing that subjects clustered more toward the ends (rather than the middle portion) of the left–right preference continuum (Fig. 9.2). Moreover, preferences were distributed more evenly across the left-handed range than the right (Oldfield, 1971). Because right-handers belonged to the stronger hand dominant group, left-handers appropriately have been labeled *nonright-handers* by some investigators to indicate the diffuse preferences of these subjects (Corballis & Beale, 1983).

Most experimental studies using these preference measures typically have classified people as either left- or right-handed on the basis of their laterality quotients or hand usage sums. However, problems have arisen when determining the placement of those weaker preference subjects. One solution is to select only those with the strongest left or right preferences. In this way, the researcher is not faced with the arbitrary, and often difficult, decision of selecting the boundary limits between the two handedness categories. Within-subject variability can be reduced further by selecting the most hand-dominant individuals. The only disadvantage to this selection process is that strongly dominant left-handed subjects are

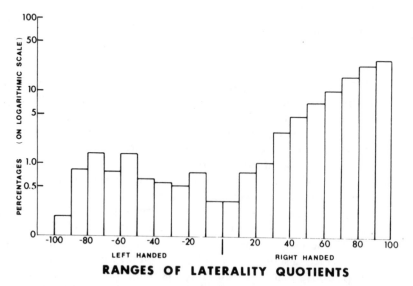

FIG. 9.2.   Ranges of hand preferences on the Edinburgh Handedness Inventory. This graph shows the percentage of surveyed people (*n* = 1128) with different laterality quotients on the Edinburgh Inventory. Note that subjects tended to fall near the extremes of the preference continuum, with left-handers displaying a more evenly distributed range of preferences than their counterparts. From "The Assessment and Analysis of Handedness: The Edinburgh Inventory" by R. C. Oldfield, 1971, *Neuropsychologia, 9,* p. 100. Copyright 1971 by Pergamon Press. Reprinted by permission.

much harder to find in the general population from which the subject pool is derived, making the initial stages of research that much more difficult to conduct. However, until a better subject selection strategy is implemented, one has to deal with these problems to the best of one's capabilities. The major theories of handedness asymmetries are reviewed in more detail next.

THEORIES RELATING TO HAND ASYMMETRIES

The Environmental Explanation

The Right-Sided World Hypothesis. Porac and Coren (1981), Ashton (1982), and Coren and Halpern (1991) pointed out that very powerful cultural pressures are exerted on many natural left-handers to use their right hand. Parents, teachers, and other socializing agents continually enforce the societal norm of dextrality on left-handers. They do so to such an extent that a right-handed shift will occur relatively early on in their development. This theory might explain why there is such a high incidence of dextrality in cultural populations, because some of the proportion is composed of these converted right-handed subjects.

An example of this cultural bias toward dextrality is the following. Left-handed writing in the Western school system, although permissible, still is difficult to execute because the environment emphasizes the right-sided orientation. Spiral notebooks, desk drawers and tops, wall pencil sharpeners, and scissors and rulers are all educational materials designed for the right-handed (not left-handed) student (White, 1986). This favored preference is definitely more problematic in other countries (e.g., Germany, Greece, Asia, and Russia) where left-handed writing is absolutely forbidden (Thomas, 1989). However, the situation is improving in the United States, where a more permissive attitude is being adopted by parents and teachers with respect to left-handed activities, such as writing or eating. In fact, the incidence of sinistrality appears to have risen in the last few decades because of less rigid and authoritarian practices being instituted at home and in the educational institution (Bradshaw & Nettleton, 1983). Still, one cannot deny that the environment is better suited for right- as opposed to left-handed activity.

Expanding on this view, Porac and Coren (1981) referred to the *Right-Sided World Hypothesis* to account for the many overt and covert pressures on individuals to change their handedness from natural left to culturally appropriate right. These researchers argued that lateral asymmetries favoring the right side exist at numerous levels within the population. Most tools and equipment (e.g., power saws and wrenches) are structured for right-handed activity; personal items (e.g., winding stem on wristwatches and lapel buttonholes on jackets) also are biased toward dextral usage; even recreational gear, such as fishing reels and bowling balls, only can be operated by that preferred hand. Given these dextral biases, Porac and Coren (1981) suggested that there is a *nurtural* (rather than natural) selection process occurring in favor of the right hand so that the individual only can function effectively within the society if this particular hand preference is adopted. With the passage of enough time, a number of left-handers gradually can learn to shift to this world-preferred appendage. Recent evidence appears to support the left- to right-handed switch across some of the sinistral population, confirming Porac and Coren's (1981) Right-Sided World Argument (Leiber & Axelrod, 1981; Porac, Coren, & Searleman, 1986).

Environmental Risk Factors.   Because left-handers do not fare very well in this right-sided world, it has been proposed that these subjects are more accident prone than their dextral counterparts (Coren & Halpern, 1991). Left-handers' reputation for clumsiness has been references as far back as the 1930s, where behavioral descriptions abound as to the sinistrals' "shuffling and shambling gait," their "floundering movements [like seals out of water]," their general "awkwardness in the house and in games," and their numerous "fumbling and bungling attempts in whatever they execute" (Burt, 1937, p. 287). It seems that left-handers place themselves at some environmental risk if they either (a) repeatedly use their preferred hand on machinery primarily designed for dextral manipulation or (b) switch to their nonpreferred (or clumsier) hand to operate such equipment. As Bracha, Seitz, Otemaa, and Glick (1987) mentioned, collisions with other individuals and even accidental spills at job settings might be the direct consequence of the left-handed subjects' inability to cope with many of the right-sided world biases.

Until recently, sinistral risk was not seen as an issue worthy of investigation. However, Coren (1989a) changed the research focus when he queried undergraduates as to whether they had experienced any serious accidents requiring medical attention within the last few years, either at home, at work, with tools, while driving, or in sports-related activities. Interestingly, left-handers showed an increased risk of accident-related injuries in comparison with their dextral peers. An important implication that can be derived from Coren's (1989a) study is that such accident-prone behaviors ultimately might reduce the longevity of the sinistral population. The most current survey data tend to support this conclusion. Using death records and next-of-kin reports, Halpern and Coren (1990) found that left-handers were at least five times more likely to die of accident-related injuries than right-handers.

To summarize, the environment not only plays a major role in shaping the hand preferences of its subjects, but it also places certain members at potential risk of injury or death by its emphasis on one type of preference, namely dextral usage. Cultural biases might explain why there is an almost complete absence of left-handedness in older age groups, such as those between 40 and 80 years of age (Fleminger, Dalton, & Standage, 1977; Porac, Coren, & Duncan, 1980b). These subjects, as well as ones more naturally born to this preferred orientation, might not be able to handle the dextral pressures of the world (Fig. 9.3).

The Genetic Explanation

Although the culture in which one is reared impacts on subjects' hand preferences, one must not forget that there is a long historical record of using the right hand for various activities. Obviously, genetic factors contribute to dextral dominance in the human species, and perhaps even indirectly exert their influence over the environment so that it can capitalize on this right-sided predisposition. Some of the genetic models that have been derived with respect to the topic of handedness asymmetries are examined next.

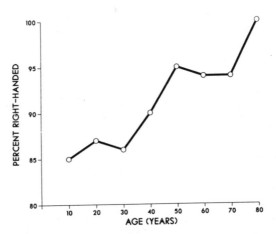

FIG. 9.3. Percentage of the population right-handed as a function of age. Porac and Coren's (1981) lifespan study was based on a sample of 5,147 subjects ranging in ages from 8 to 100 years. Their results show an interesting age trend toward increasing percentages of right-handedness in the older aged groups, with a complete absence of left-handedness by age 80. From "Left-Handedness: A Marker for Decreased Survival Fitness" by S. Coren and D. F. Halpern, 1991, *Psychological Bulletin, 109*, p. 91. Copyright 1991 by the American Psychological Association. Reprinted by permission.

The Simple Genetic Model of Hand Preferences: A Critique.
One of the first genetic models of handedness formulated by Ramaley
(1913), and later by Annett (1964), assumed that hand preference innately
was determined by either a right-dominant (D) or left-recessive (r) gene
pattern. It then was reasoned that those offspring who had inherited the
dominant gene from both parents (DD) would be consistently right-
handed, whereas those who had acquired the recessive gene from both
parents (rr) would be consistently left-handed. Other offspring who inherited a mixture of the genes (one dominant and one recessive, or Dr)
would be generally right-handed, because dextrality was governed by the
dominant gene pattern.

Although this theory is an easily comprehensible one, it does not appear to fit the empirical data on sinistral hand usage. A compilation of
survey studies (Annett, 1978; Corballis, 1980) has revealed that, on average, just over 50% of the children of sinistral relatives are left-handed.
This finding runs contrary to the hypothesized expectation of almost
100% complete sinistral expression. Fluctuation in sinistral percentages
between surveys probably was due to different historical criteria being
used to assess left-handedness. Further investigations have revealed that
left-handed subjects who have no familial history of that particular preference are, paradoxically, the most strongly left-handed (Hardyck &
Petrinovich, 1977; Leiber & Axelrod, 1981). Even Annett's (1973) data
disprove the simple genetic model, because she discovered a staggering
84% of sinistrals had two right-handed parents, whereas approximately
50% of dextrals had two left-handed relatives.

Perhaps the most compelling evidence against the single gene model
for hand determination comes from the monozygotic twin research. If
hand preference actually is governed by a single dominant gene (or lack
of one), one would expect an almost perfect correlation in handedness
between monozygotic twins, especially because they share the same genetic environment for a time (in comparison with dizygotic twins and control nontwin siblings). The results obtained from 13 studies that compared
the handedness concordance rates in monozygotic as well as dizygotic
twins (Coren & Halpern, 1991) showed that the rates were not significantly higher in the monozygotic pairs. In fact, the twin concordance
patterns were not significantly different from the percentage expected
by chance, which was predicted from the distribution of left- and right-
handers in the normal population. Other current findings have replicated these outcomes (McManus, 1985; Springer & Searleman, 1980). Some
even have revealed a 25% discordant rate for handedness in twins,
whatever their zygosity happens to be (Springer & Deutsch, 1989). That
is, one out of every four pairs of twins had a left- *and* a right-handed
member.

The results of familial sinistrality and monozygotic twin concordance rates suggest that if genetic mechanisms are operative, they are not of the simple type, but much more complex (particularly in their transmission of hand preferences to the offspring or other family members). In light of these data, other models have been developed to take into consideration strong species-specific biases toward dextrality as well as associated left-hemisphere dominance.

More Complex Genetic Models Implicating Brain Lateralization. Taking into account the opposing empirical findings, Annett (1972) refined her first model, explaining that individuals probably did not carry a dominant or recessive gene for right- or left-handedness per se. Rather, most of the population inherited a relatively strong genetic component to be oriented toward its right side. Termed the *right shift factor* (or rs +), its expression biased the majority of subjects toward various degrees of dextral usage, with a distribution pattern resembling the bell-shaped curve (Fig. 9.4). Annett (1972) further characterized the right shift group as having language primarily lateralized in the left hemisphere. According to Annett (1972) it was this asymmetrical arrangement that apparently produced the right-shiftedness in the human population (not vice versa, as others have claimed).

However, for a minority of individuals, the right shift factor was missing (rs –), predisposing this group to have a neutral hand preference and an unlateralized cortical organization for language (Fig. 9.4). The resultant outcome was that half of these subjects eventually would become

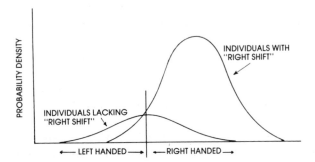

FIG. 9.4. The distributions of individuals who have as well as lack Annet's (1972) right shift factor. Note that the majority of subjects possesses the right shift factor (rs +), and thus there will be a strong bias toward dextrality in the population. The smaller group, which lacks this factor (rs –), will be approximately evenly distributed in right- and left-handed preferences. From *The Ambivalent Mind: The Neuropsychology of Left and Right* (p. 123) by M. Corballis and I. L. Beale, 1983, Chicago, IL: Nelson-Hall. Copyright 1983 by Nelson-Hall. Reprinted by permission.

left-handed (and left-language oriented), whereas the remaining members would become right-handed (and right-language oriented), similar to the 50-50 chance asymmetries obtained in Collins' (1970) experiments with mice.

The absence of this right shift factor neatly explains why only half of the offspring of sinistral parents turns out to be left-handed. Annett's (1972) remodified theory did not attempt to account for the twin or sibling handedness data (Corballis, 1980), but it did provide a reasonable answer to why sinistrals show a more diffuse and inconsistent body-side laterality, even in foot and eye preferences (Friedlander, 1971; Peters & Durding, 1979). Annett's (1972) nonlateralized factor can be applied further to the variable results generated on verbal measures of cognitive aptitude in left-handed subjects (Levander & Levander, 1990; Searleman, Herrmann, & Coventry, 1984).

Perhaps the most sophisticated model of hand asymmetries was proposed by Levy and Nagylaki (1972), in which two genes are presumed to govern the expression of handedness. One of the genes primarily determines which cortical hemisphere will be specialized for language, with an inherited (and dominant) L pattern representing left-hemisphere speech and a recessive r pattern representing right-hemisphere speech. The second gene determines whether that speech hemisphere will control the ipsilateral (i) or contralateral (C) hand for writing and other skilled movements. To provide an example, someone who inherits an LrCi pattern from both parents will have the left-hemisphere speech side executing more contralateral, right-handed movements; on the other hand, the person who inherits the LLii pattern will have the left-hemisphere speech side controlling more ipsilateral, left-handed actions.

Corballis and Morgan (1978) pointed out that the Levy-Nagylaki (1972) model works rather well to explain why few dextrals are right-hemisphere speech oriented, because both genes would have to be transmitted recessively from each parent for this relatively rare occurrence. In addition, some extensions of the model have been made to the writing postures of dextral and sinistral subjects. Levy and Reid (1976, 1978) argued that the way the hand is held in writing reflects which hemisphere is regulating the speech functions of the individual. In the noninverted (or more normal) posture, the hand is held below the line of writing with the tip of the pen or pencil pointing toward the top of the page. Conversely, in the inverted (or hooked) posture, which some sinistrals adopt, the hand is brought above the line of writing with the tip of the pen or pencil pointing toward the bottom of the page.

Levy and Reid (1976, 1978) and Lynes (1987) claimed that noninverted writers have their speech centers more localized in the contralateral hemisphere, whereas inverted writers have their speech areas more ipsilaterally focused. As hypothesized, Levy and Reid's (1976, 1978) tachistoscopic results clearly indicated RVF advantages for syllables and LVF advantages for spatial stimuli in right-handers who used the noninverted hand posture. The reverse superiorities were found for left-handers who employed the same writing posture. In sharp contrast, those sinistrals who wrote with the inverted posture performed similarly to the noninverted dextrals, suggesting that linguistic inputs were being processed more effectively by the ipsilateral left hemisphere (as shown by the RVF advantages for these stimuli). The majority of right-handers examined by Levy and Reid (1976, 1978) chose the noninverted style of writing, strengthening the Levy-Nagylaki (1972) argument that ipsilateral-sided, right-hemisphere language combinations were somewhat unique to this population of subjects.

As Bradshaw and Nettleton (1983) advised, it probably is a good idea to view handwriting postures at least under partial voluntary control, with directional patterns being subject to influences within the specific culture. Left-handers might have been encouraged by outside agents to adopt the inverted posture so that they could see what had just been written. (It was assumed that the noninverted style of writing seriously interfered with the sinistrals' ability to scan previous lines.) The right-sided world bias also might have played a role in left-handers positioning their writing paper the same way as dextral subjects—at a diagonal left-to-right type of orientation instead of vice versa.

Although not denying the genetic determinants of handedness and associated variables such as hand posture, I believe that environmental factors further enhance those inherited differences between dextrals and sinistrals. If ipsilateral motor control exists in left-handers, then the culture might choose the most appropriate mode for its expression, namely by the emphasis on a more inverted style of writing as identified by Levy and Reid (1976, 1978).

Levy's Bilateralization Argument Revisited. Levy's (1972) language bilateralization theory, described in chapter 8, has been applied to sinistral performance in verbal and spatial tasks. Significant deficits have been noted especially in left-handers across procedures that strongly rely on visuospatial skills (e.g., block design, puzzle assembly, picture completion, mental rotation, mathematical reasoning and aptitude, and maze speed), compared with more verbal types of assignments (Burnett, Lane, & Dratt, 1982; Gregory, Alley, & Morris, 1980; Herrman & Van Dyke, 1978). Levy (1972) contended that for sinistrals (like women), some language functions apparently invaded the processing space of the right hemisphere. This double dose of language on both brain sides ultimately produced a cortical trade-off: better verbal ability at the expense of effective spatial processing. Thus, it was this bilateral blueprint that dictated the way hemispheres were to evolve in left-handers down through the generations (Levy, 1972, 1976).

Perhaps the most supportive evidence for Levy's (1972, 1976) theory comes from a limited number of studies that reported rather sizable interactions between gender and handedness (af Klinteberg, Levander, & Schalling, 1987; Sanders, Wilson, & Vandenberg, 1982). In these cases, lower spatial abilities were found in sinistral females (i.e., the most bilateralized subjects), compared with their male peers. However, other research has suggested that sinistral men, not women, actually have the inferior spatial skills (Harshman, Hampson, & Berenbaum, 1983; Yen, 1975). Although more research work clearly is required to uncover the dynamics of both gender and handedness on cognitive performance, one outcome can be established firmly: Overall, spatial processing in left-handers is impaired seriously, and this might be correlated directly to the bilateralization of language hypothesized to be present in the sinistral members.

Morphological Differences Between Hand Groups. The typical torque (i.e., twisted) appearance of the brain, in which the frontal lobe on one side protrudes forward and the occipital lobe on the other side protrudes back, has not been evidenced consistently in left-handers under normal computerized tomographic procedures. This lack of a torque effect has been traced back in subjects as early as one year of age, and even has been correlated with patterns of familial sinistrality (Galaburda, LeMay, Kemper, & Geschwind, 1978; Habib, 1989). But, it should be pointed out that not all studies have yielded these anatomical differences. Brain scans were performed by Chui and Damasio (1980) on a large number of dextrals and an almost equivalent number of sinistrals and ambidextrals, the results of which did not verify the predicted torque symmetries (or even reversed asymmetries) in the nondextral subjects. Although Chui and Damasio (1980) concluded that there was not a morphological base for the handedness variations, replications of their research still need to be executed before such a definitive statement can be supported fully.

Maturational Differences Between Hand Groups. Unlike the anatomical inconsistencies, maturational differences have been noted in hand preferences at a relatively early age. Controlled studies initially conducted by Gesell and Ames in (1947) and more recently by Rice and Plomin (1983) and Seth (1973) indicated that infants 16–20 weeks old show an initial preference for the left, not right, hand. After the first year, the majority of the children curiously switch from this sinistral dominance to an increasingly dextral one, which eventually stabilizes by the period of middle childhood. Struck by the orderly way in which children's hand preferences fluctuated across time, Gesell and Ames (1947) reasoned that handedness was determined by programming within the nervous system, which became activated as the human physically matured.

Further evidence for the maturational explanation comes from the consistent observations that 1-day-old newborns display a striking postural asymmetry, either to the left or right side. Called the *tonic neck reflex*, it involves the newborn turning his or her head to a preferred side, with the arm and leg on that side extended and the appendages on the opposing side flexed. Most children show a right-sided tonic neck reflex, with a minority consistently preferring the left side (Turkewitz, 1977; Turkewitz & Creighton, 1974). As Liederman and Kinsbourne (1980a, 1980b) claimed, there presumably is an innate neural response mechanism that biases movements to that particular postural orientation.

This reflex has been related to hand preference exhibited later on in the child's life. Gesell and Ames (1947) followed up 19 children, 9 of whom had the left tonic neck reflex, 7 with the right, and 3 with no reflex preference (i.e., a bidirectional orientation). They discovered that four of those children with the left-sided reflex eventually became left-handed, whereas the remaining ones were right-handed by 10 years of age, but only after some fluctuating preferences between ambidextrality or sinistrality. Those with the right reflex were exclusively right-handed by age 10, and those with the bidirectional reflex became predominantly right-handed by the same age.

Although the correlation between handedness and the tonic neck reflex was not statistically significant, the data suggest that right-turning preferences are accurate predictors of later hand dominance on that particular side. It might be that right-handedness is part of a maturational process that has its beginnings at birth or shortly afterward. As Corballis and Beale (1983) and Corballis and Morgan (1978) cautioned, judgment still should be reserved as to whether left-handedness follows a similar pattern or, if anything, manifests some apparent delay in maturational development. I return to this topic shortly when I discuss maturational deviations from dextrality.

The Pathological Explanation

A higher than expected incidence of left-handedness has been identified in a wide variety of clinical populations, including mental retardates, epileptics, stutterers, developmental aphasics, and dyslexics (Carter-Saltzman, 1979; Hicks & Kinsbourne, 1978; Springer & Searleman, 1980). This type of *pathological sinistrality* has been explained by the presence of traumatic stressors occurring very early on in the organism's life, the effects of which disrupt the normal functioning of the left hemisphere. The eventual result is that natural right-handed dominance is weakened as left-handed preferences develop in reaction to the trauma. Bakan, Dibb, and Reed (1973), Satz (1973), and Satz et al. (1985b) effectively summarized this position by stating that it is not left-handedness per se that is determined genetically. Rather, it is the tendency to inherit one (or a combination) of these pre- or perinatal stressors. Some of the pathological factors that predispose some sinistrals to particular abnormalities and certain neuropsychological disorders are discussed next.

Birth Stress and Sinistrality.   Pathological sinistrality has been claimed to stem largely from an oxygen deficiency at birth. This perinatal hypoxia apparently produces a dysfunction in the contralateral motor pathways of the "more susceptible" left hemisphere, thus creating a sinistral dominance in the affected subjects (Bakan et al., 1973). Some recent findings have supported the hypoxia theory. Schwartz (1988) reported that left-handedness was correlated directly with lower Apgar scores at birth. (Apgar scores measure the extent to which newborns suffer from severe birth trauma such as hypoxia and other neurological insults.) In a recent article, Bakan (1987) further verified these theoretical observations by noting that offspring of mothers who smoke are more likely to display sinistrality. He explained that maternal smoking during pregnancy more than likely induces a hypoxic state in the fetus, thereby aggravating the susceptibility to pathological left-handedness (PLH).

Other birth stressors besides hypoxia have been implicated with sinistral expression. These have included: RH incompatibility between mother and fetus, prolonged labor, premature birth, multiple births, breech delivery, and low birth weight (Badian, 1983a; Coren & Porac, 1980; Coren, Searleman, & Porac, 1982). Moreover, statistics indicate that left-handed sample groups were almost twice as likely to have been born with a history of birth stress than right-handed groups (van Strien, Bouma, & Bakker, 1987). The importance of finding a direct association between birth stress and handedness is that it implies that sinistrality is a by-product of some form of neurological deviation that moves subjects away from the more normal dextral pattern within the population.

Maturational Delay and Sinistrality.   As previously stated, the typical maturational pattern involves a gradual shift toward right-handedness with increasing age. Corballis (1983) attributed this asymmetry in growth rate to a more rapid development of the left hemisphere, which has its start presumably during the prenatal period, with a continuation in its growth extending well into the childhood years. Researchers have assumed that any disruption or delay in the maturational gradient results in a higher incidence of pathological sinistrality, a condition obviously reflective of the developmental arrest. Complications at birth and other related stressors often are thought to be the primary agents responsible for this altered pattern in hemispheric development (Coren & Halpern, 1991).

Several sources have confirmed this idea of a maturational lag in left-handers. Porac, Coren, and Duncan (1980a) compared hand, foot, eye, and ear preferences in a group of mentally retarded individuals with a sample of appropriate age peers. As speculated, the retardates had significantly more left-sided preferences. The interpretation given to these results was that the slower cognitive development in the retardates had extended to such lateralized behaviors as hand dominance and usage. More involved comparisons showed that the retardate pattern resembled the sinistral one exhibited by more immature preschoolers of the same mental age, further supporting the maturational lag hypothesis. Secondary sexual characteristics and relative body size and weight also appeared to be good indicators of handedness in nonclinical groups, with more delays being evidenced in these physical markers if subjects showed sinistral preferences (Coren, 1989b; Coren, Searleman, & Porac, 1986). Returning to the survival data of handedness groups portrayed in Fig. 9.3, it might be that an atypical or relatively immature system ultimately might decrease the viability of the left-hander, thus contributing to this member's disappearance from the population by the elderly years.

Immune Deficiencies and Sinistrality. Besides birth-related stressors, hormonal factors have been implicated in the expression of PLH. According to Geschwind (1984) and McManus and Bryden (1991), high levels of prenatal testosterone (or progesterone) affect the neural development of the brain, specifically by slowing the rate of growth within the left hemisphere. The end result is that a right-hemisphere dominance, reflected in more left-handed preferences, is present in those subjects who possess such abnormal hormonal concentrations. Because males are exposed to higher levels of testosterone than females, one would expect a correspondingly higher proportion of sinistrality in this particular gender. As predicted, studies have found this gender effect, in support of the Geschwind (1984) hormonal hypothesis (Butler, 1984; Hardyck, Goldman, & Petrinovich, 1975).

Along with increased sinistrality, there seems to be an elevated frequency of *immune disorders* (e.g., atopic diseases as allergies, asthma, and hay fever, as well as autoimmune disturbances in which normal thyroid gland functioning is suppressed) in male subjects. Geschwind and Behan (1982, 1984) discovered that strong left-handers were 2.5 times more likely to suffer from one of these disorders in comparison with equally dominant right-handers. Interestingly, as personal or familial sinistrality increased, so did the number of immune disorders, signifying the direct type of relationship that existed between both variables (Benbow, 1988; Benbow & Stanley, 1983).

Geschwind and Galaburda (1987), McManus and Bryden (1991), Searleman and Fugagli (1987), and Smith (1987) speculated that, in these disorders, the sinistral's own antibody mechanisms are fighting each other to such an extent that immunity to particular stressors is diminished. They have further proposed that as part of the anti-immunity process, abnormal defensive reactions (e.g., full-blown allergic symptoms) begin to occur in response to relatively harmless substances, lowering the sinistral's resistance to physiological assault. Similar to the maturational lag theory, a younger age of death would be anticipated in this pathological subgroup of left-handers, especially because physiological endurance over time would be reduced effectively. However, as Geschwind (1984) noted, it would be erroneous to conclude that all left-handers are generally less healthy than their right-handed peers. In light of these comments, work is proceeding to determine whether sinistrals, in fact, evidence lower incidence rates for contracting other types of disorders.

The Alinormal Syndrome: An Alternative to the Pathological View.   Because of the prejudices directed against left-handers, Coren and Searleman (1985, 1987) took the position that severe pathologies should not be correlated solely with this particular hand preference. Rather, given certain birth stressors, maturational lags, or hormonal imbalances, a more subtle and less abnormally exaggerated alinormal syndrome might develop in which sinistrality is but one of several possible behavioral deviations that occur in combination. Other symptoms cited have included inverted writing postures (Searleman, Porac, & Coren, 1982), sleep difficulties and frequent night awakenings (Coren & Searleman, 1985), variability across tests assessing cognitive abilities (Bradshaw & Bradshaw, 1988; Halpern, 1986; Hicks & Beveridge, 1978), and increased usage of alcohol (Bakan, 1973; London, 1986; Smith & Chyatte, 1983) and tobacco (Harburg, 1981; Harburg, Feldstein, & Papsdorf, 1978).

Therefore, sinistrality should be linked to a complex of minor deviations away from the dextral norm; hence, *alinormal sinistrality* might be the more appropriate label for the behavioral syndrome than the heavily loaded and biased term *pathological sinistrality*. One also must not forget that there are many left-handers who are as normal as their right-handed counterparts, performing their work quite competently and achieving some eminence in their various disciplines (e.g., Leonardo da Vinci and Michelangelo). This observation further questions the usefulness of the pathological descriptor to characterize an entire group (or subgroup) of the sinistral population. Keeping these reflections in mind, I discuss some of the experimental techniques that have been employed to assess sinistral and dextral performance across a wide variety of stimulus materials.

ASSESSING HANDEDNESS ASYMMETRIES EXPERIMENTALLY

The Traditional Procedures: Dichotic and Tachistoscopic

Dichotic Findings. Many reviews have indicated that ear superiorities, REAs for verbal inputs and LEAs for nonverbal types, are much more pronounced for dextral than sinistral subjects (Hardyck, 1977; Hicks & Kinsbourne, 1978). In specific dichotic studies, reversed asymmetries and even symmetrical trends have been observed more often with left-handers (Bryden, 1970; Curry, 1967; Dee, 1971; Satz, Achenbach, Patishall, & Fennell, 1965). McManus (1979) further tabulated the results from 10 large-scale dichotic studies that determined the cerebral speech dominance of the two handedness groups. He found that approximately 81% of the dextrals had the typical left-hemisphere dominance, whereas only 62% of the sinistrals had the same lateralized arrangement. Levy's bilateralization theory can account best for these differences by suggesting that left-handers are able to represent verbal functions in both hemispheres, similar to the cortical organization hypothesized to be present in the female gender (refer to chapter 8 for more information on these male–female asymmetries).

Besides preference, other handedness variables have been investigated over the decades with the dichotic procedures. One, strength of hand dominance, has shown a significant correlation with ear-side advantage: namely, as dextrality increased, so did the magnitude of the REA (Shankweiler & Studdert-Kennedy, 1975). Conversely, strongly sinistral subjects usually displayed the reversed LEA (Demarest & Demarest, 1980). Moderately or weakly dominant dextrals and sinistrals generally did not differ in their processing capabilities between ear sides.

Another factor, familial sinistrality, has been known to exert a direct effect on dichotic outcomes. In one study conducted by Zurif and Bryden (1969), left-handers with sinistrality in the immediate family were found to be less lateralized (i.e., showed no ear advantages) than ones without a family history. However, more recent designs tend to contradict these results, reporting instead that familial sinistrals were the more lateralized subjects. The strongest REAs consistently occurred in left-handers whose parents rather than siblings shared the same hand dominance (Geffen & Traub, 1980; McKeever & Van Deventer, 1977; Nilsson et al., 1980). The bulk of the evidence to date supports the view that nonfamilial sinistrals possess Levy's bilateralized organization to a greater degree than familial sinistrals.

One final variable, handwriting posture, has not fared very well when put to the dichotic test. Quite surprisingly, left-handed subjects with the normal hand posture did not differ in performance from those with the more inverted posture across listening tasks, failing to confirm Levy and Reid's (1976) hypothesis expressed earlier in this chapter (Herron, Galin, Johnstone, & Ornstein, 1979; McKeever & Van Deventer, 1980; Smith & Moscovitch, 1979). As Weber and Bradshaw (1981) recommended (based on their extensive evaluation), hand posture might not be a good predictor of cortical asymmetries, theoretically or empirically speaking. Its usefulness, if any, might be restricted to individual cases instead of group applications, especially with sinistral subjects.

Tachistoscopic Findings.   Under tachistoscopic conditions, sinistrals also appear to be less (or more variably) lateralized, particularly for verbal inputs, in comparison with dextrals. The RVF superiorities reliably evidenced in right-handers were not found in their counterparts, implying a more bilateralized representation of language in the sinistral brain (Bryden, 1973; Hines & Satz, 1971; McKeever, Van Deventer, & Suberti, 1973). Test–retest performance scores on these tachistoscopic tasks also generated a good deal more variability within the left-handed (as opposed to right-handed) groups (Hines, Fennell, Bowers, & Satz, 1980).

When assessing the effects of familial sinistrality on tachistoscopic asymmetries, researchers have come up with a confusing mix of results. Some experimenters have replicated the dichotic findings that nonfamilial sinistrals are more bilateralized (Bradshaw & Taylor, 1979), whereas others have discovered just the reverse pattern, with familial sinistrals displaying less consistent differences between field sides (Schmuller & Goodman, 1979, 1980). Unlike familial sinistrality, handwriting posture is one variable that has yielded similar outcomes across dichotic as well as tachistoscopic procedures. More specifically, in visual-field tasks that employed a variety of verbal stimuli, the hypothesized relationship between cortical lateralization of language and type of hand posture was not confirmed (McKeever, 1979; McKeever & Van Deventer, 1980). Sinistrals who wrote with the inverted posture did not show an RVF superiority like the dextrals who adopted the more noninverted posture, seriously questioning the validity of Levy and Reid's (1976) claim.

Corballis and Beale (1983) interpreted these sinistral symmetries to mean that left-handers have not inherited a factor that predisposes them to display a consistently strong lateralization for language (similar to Annett's [1967] lack of a right shift factor). Estimates as to how many sinistrals lack this lateralization agent range anywhere from 45 to 95%, depending on the population from which the sample is drawn. Although investigators continue to speculate on the differences between sinistrals and dextrals, one fact is clear: The majority of right-handers more often shows this asymmetrical pattern for language-related stimuli (i.e., REAs and RVF superiorities) across laterality tasks.

Effects of Attentional Bias on Hand Lateralities.   According to Bryden (1986), a more stabilized laterality effect could be obtained in dextral samples if instructions were given to focus attention onto a specified ear or field side. Bryden (1986) found stronger REAs in his right-handed subjects under these more focused-attention conditions. I also detected this fairly obvious interaction between subjects' attentional strategies and respective cortical organizations. In a recent series of experiments (Iaccino, 1990; Iaccino & Houran, 1989), dextrals consistently exhibited more pronounced right-ear and right-field advantages to various letter stimuli when more trials were administered to focus attention on those body sides. Even LEAs could result from such directed manipulations (Iaccino & Houran, 1991). On the other hand, sinistrals continued to process inputs to the same degree between sides, regardless of the given focus condition. Apparently, the more lateralized dextral brain benefitted from these experimentally induced attentional sets, whereas the sinistral brain was too bilateralized to adopt one of these fairly focalized sets. As stated in previous chapters, the subject's inherent cortical organization presumably determines the degree to which particular strategic behaviors subsequently are expressed. In this case, sinistral bilaterality appears to be less susceptible to experimental manipulations than dextral laterality; it might even be less flexible than female bilaterality, suggesting that similar brain arrangements might possess subtle variations. More controlled studies definitely need to examine these subtleties between females and left-handers to discover which subject strategies can be employed most effectively to process materials.

Other Indices Assessing Handedness Asymmetries

Alternative measures have looked at handedness asymmetries across a wide range of responses, from eye movements and facial expressions to cerebral blood flow and EEG readings. The outcomes have been quite consistent from one design to the next, highlighting the more bilateralized capabilities of the left-handed subject. The most important findings from each index are reviewed briefly.

Conjugate Lateral Eye Movements. Contralateral orienting responses, consisting of lateralized eye movements and head turns, have been hypothesized to be reflective of the degree of subjects' cerebral lateralization. In agreement with previous theories of handedness variations, dextrals tend to exhibit stronger asymmetries than sinistrals in these orienting responses. In a number of documented studies (Gur & Gur, 1980; Kinsbourne, 1972), right-handers made more right CLEMs and associated head turns to verbal types of questions and, alternately, more left CLEMs and head movements to spatial types of inquiries. Left-handers did not show these directional biases in eye movements or head turns when asked to solve either the verbal or spatial problems. Because the dextrality effect has not been obtained in every experimental situation (Hiscock, 1977), current theories have advanced the view that subjects (whether dextral or sinistral) can exercise some voluntary control over their eye movements, depending on the information-processing strategy that is selected. The end result is that sometimes more directed gazes occur and other times they are less frequent. Therefore, laterality seems to be a more flexible process than previously speculated, not necessarily dependent on a subject's hand preference (Gross, Franko, & Lewin, 1978).

Facial Expressions. As already described in chapter 7, stronger emotional expressions usually are attributed to the left side of facial composites (Borod & Caron, 1980; Sackheim et al., 1978). Not surprisingly, handedness differences have been identified in the processing of these posed facial stimuli, with dextrals displaying more LVF (or right-hemispheric) superiorities in comparison with sinistrals (Heller & Levy, 1981; Rubin & Rubin, 1980). However, one must exercise some caution in interpreting the results, especially because handedness groups have not been examined on their ability to generate their own emotional expressions. Until such studies are executed, any conclusions on dextral asymmetries are limited to the experimental manipulations most commonly cited in the literature.

Electrodermal Responses. Similar to eye movements and facial expressions, electrodermal activity (i.e., skin conductivity) has been reported to be substantially different between the hands of dextral subjects who have been engaged in a variety of stimulus tasks. LaCroix and Comper (1979) found that if a verbal assignment were provided, the skin response amplitude in the right hand (or left hemisphere) was significantly smaller than the left. Conversely, if a visualization test was given, the electrodermal amplitude in the left hand (or right hemisphere) reflected more changes. It was reasoned that the lateralized brain areas of right-handers had strong inhibitory centers that apparently influenced conductivity in the hand contralateral to the activated hemisphere. This asymmetrical pattern was not replicated in left-handers, confirming once again Levy's argument of a more bilateralized organization for sinistral subjects.

Hand Movements, Balancing, and Tapping. Kimura (1976) experimentally verified that dextrals made freer hand movements with the right than the left hand while performing speech-related activities. On the other hand, sinistrals did not show these gestural asymmetries. Based on these results, Kimura (1976) concluded that the simple task of speaking activated (or primed) contralateral hand movements in the more lateralized dextral brains. Further, the contralateral gestures were said to reflect the expressive elements of the dextrals' speech content.

Other procedures have involved subjects balancing rods on either their left or right index finger while repeating sentences aloud. The overall findings from these studies have indicated that verbalization was more likely to interfere with right-handed balancing times (Kinsbourne & Cook, 1971), primarily in dextral subject pools (Hicks, 1975). Obviously, the concurrent assignment of speaking primed the left hemisphere mainly toward expression of that function so that dextrals were unable to both verbalize and balance at the same time. Sinistrals did not experience this handicap, however; therefore their more bilateralized structures enabled them to perform both tasks reasonably well. Right-handed tapping behaviors in dextrals also have been detrimentally affected by such verbal tasks (Bowers, Heilman, Satz, & Altman, 1978; Hiscock & Kinsbourne, 1980), further supporting the assertion that lateralized organizations only can handle particular inputs in a sequential fashion, unlike the more simultaneously oriented sinistral arrangements.

Cerebral Blood Flow. When subjects moved their right hands, rCBF (i.e., regional cerebral blood flow) subsequently was elevated in the left hemisphere's motor region. After the switch was made to their left hands, subjects experienced a reversed rCBF pattern, with very pronounced increases in the right hemisphere's associated area (Halsey et al., 1979). Other experimenters wanted to see whether hand dominance per se influenced hemispheric blood flow. Carmon and Gombos (1970) were among those who specifically measured the amount of blood pressure within the ipsilateral carotid arteries of dextrals as well as sinistrals. (It should be noted that more arterial pressure reflected greater blood flow to the same-sided hemisphere.) Their results revealed a striking correlation between arterial pressure and hand preference, with dextrals showing higher pressure on the right side and sinistrals exhibiting smaller differences between sides. Likewise, in a related study in which rCBF typically was assessed after the intravenous injection of a radioactive substance (Carmon, Harishanu, Lowinger, & Lavy, 1972), it was found that dextrals had greater blood volume once more in the hemisphere ipsilateral to their hand preference—in this case, the right brain. Sinistrals displayed the reverse asymmetry more frequently, with more pressure in their corresponding left hemisphere.

The reason ipsilateral cortex generated more blood flow activity instead of the contralateral side (especially across dextral subjects) has been the focus of discussion among researchers. Some (Linn & Petersen, 1985) adopted the argument that the hemisphere that is less suited to handle a particular task is the one to show more activity, apparently because that brain side exerts more mental effort in the attempt to process the given input. Although this view is still a strictly theoretical one, it appears to be a viable explanation for the discrepant outcomes and has been used to describe rCBF variations between the genders (see chapter 8).

EEG and ERP Recordings.   Brain wave recordings have contributed valuable information about the cortical organizations of both sinistral and dextral subjects. As previously mentioned in chapter 7, greater alpha wave suppression often is identified in the hemisphere more specialized to register a particular stimulus input: namely, more alpha blocking occurs in the left hemisphere during verbal tasks and, conversely, more in the right hemisphere during spatial assignments. Butler and Glass (1976) and Donchin et al. (1977) noted that this typical asymmetrical pattern was absent or in a weakened form when left-handers were examined, as opposed to right-handers.

Cortical event related potentials (ERPs) derived from the basic EEG record also have yielded similar effects between hand groups. Specifically, dextrals showed larger ERPs over the left hemisphere for verbal materials such as CV syllables (Linnville, 1984) and more pronounced ones over the right hemisphere for nonverbal stimuli and associated spatial movements (Kutas & Donchin, 1974). More symmetrical, bilateralized activity generally was found in sinistrals, with fewer large amplitude ERPs displayed to verbal or nonverbal stimuli. Like the other cortical indices, brain wave readings from the sinistral brain seem to suggest that left-handed dominance is radically different from the opposing right, with a weaker lateralized organization being present, especially for verbal types of stimuli. This interpretation is consistent with the Levy and Annett theories, and makes a convincing case for an inherited predisposition to be either left- or right-handed, coupled with a tendency to have either a less or more lateralized brain structure, respectively.

SUMMARY AND CONCLUSIONS

In comparing chapters 8 and 9, it appears that the effects of brain lateralization are much stronger between handedness groups than between the genders. Obviously, genetic factors play a much more powerful role in the formation and subsequent control of hemispheric asymmetries within dextral subjects than within males. Ever since our species' origins, dextrality has been the genetic norm, with less variability being exhibited in its expression compared with sinistrality. It might be that any gender differences noted in cortical organization can be attributed partially to the hand dominance of the subject (or subjects) tested. One should recall that an interaction was found between handedness and gender in a number of experimental studies, with dextral males showing the strongest lateralities and sinistral females the weakest ones, particularly on tasks assessing spatial ability (Levy, 1976; Sanders et al., 1982). This is not to say that environmental factors do not exert an influence on the eventual lateralization of the hemispheres; rather, they might contribute more to the shaping of male (and female) brains than the dextral (and sinistral) ones.

The most salient points of chapter 9 are the following:

1. If dextrality is controlled genetically, it is not governed by a single gene type. Instead, a more complex pattern of genetic activity has been proposed, in which lateralization of language within the left hemisphere is linked with a shift toward dextrality (see Annett's theory cited earlier). Morphological symmetries in the size of the sinistral lobes and associated maturational lags in sinistral development have added their evidence to the genetic approach toward brain lateralization. Given this inherited base, environmental influences have been considered, in terms of their reinforcing the dextral norm within the population as well as their placing sinistral subjects at potential risk by the cultural emphasis on the right-sided world view. The pathological type of sinistrality also was evaluated, with respect to susceptibility to certain environmental stressors (e.g., birth complications) as well as genetic influences (e.g., elevated testosterone levels in males).

2. Moreover, dichotic and tachistoscopic findings have indicated the existence of greater lateralities in right-handers, with pronounced REAs and RVF superiorities for verbal materials as well as LEAs and LVF superiorities for nonverbal inputs. More focused body-side manipulations strengthened these behavioral asymmetries but only in dextrals, lending credence to the inherited lateralization argument for this group of subjects. Other cortical indices (e.g., CLEMs, facial expressions, electrodermal responses, rCBF, EEG and ERP readings) confirmed this hypothesis.

Apparently sinistrals possessed a more bilateralized organization, especially for language and other linguistic-related materials.

Now that I have reviewed both gender and handedness variations with cerebral asymmetries, it is logical to address whether these subjects display lateralized behaviors early on in development, or, as claimed by several theorists, at a much later period in time (e.g., puberty). Chapter 10's inquiry, "Are there developmental differences in brain lateralization?", concludes this particular part of the text.

CHAPTER TEN

Are There Developmental Differences in Brain Lateralization?

The left and right hemispheres
    not only have a physiological equivalency,
But a functional one as well
    in the early years of life.

This equivalency in cognitive functions,
    referred to as an *equipotentiality*,
Allows either hemisphere to assume
    the skills associated with the other,
    upon injury to one cortical side.

As the child starts to acquire language,
    each hemisphere becomes
    more functionally specialized;
And so the resiliency to cerebral insult
    diminishes with the passage of time.

The end result is that by puberty,
    hemispheric "plasticity" is so reduced
    that any deficit on one brain side
    cannot be made up by the cortical twin.

Thus, permanent brain damage
    is more likely to occur,
    after the critical period
    of childhood has elapsed.
        —Rephrased from Lenneberg, 1967

This view, originally posited by Lenneberg in the mid-1960s, has contributed greatly to our current thinking on developmental differences in brain lateralization. Lenneberg's (1967) basic assumption was that lateralization of function in the brain begins at the time of language acquisition (i.e., at approximately age 2), but is not complete until the onset of puberty.

This critical period for lateralization was derived from earlier clinical data collected by Basser (1962), who showed that "in roughly half of the children with brain lesions sustained during the first two years of life, the onset of speech development was somewhat delayed; however, the other half of this population began to speak at the usual time. [Interestingly] This distribution was the same for children with left hemisphere lesions as with right ones" (Lenneberg, 1967, p. 151). Because Lenneberg (1967) could not predict, on the basis of Basser's (1962) results, which intact hemisphere was able to govern language functions following damage to the other during the early years of childhood, he concluded that an equipotentiality existed between the two brain sides.

In further verification of the *critical period hypothesis*, Basser's (1962) teenaged and adult subjects (unlike children) displayed the typical hemispheric asymmetries for language: namely, injury to the left hemisphere resulted in speech disturbances in a majority of cases, whereas injury to the right hemisphere produced these aphasias less frequently. Obviously, Lenneberg (1967) saw that developmental changes in the direction of increasing lateralization (and decreasing equipotentiality) were the behavioral patterns generally expressed by most older members of the population.

In light of Lenneberg's (1967) comments, this chapter takes a critical look at his theory, considering the most recent experimental evidence on the topic of developmental asymmetries. As in previous chapters, the traditional dichotic and tachistoscopic procedures are examined, along with other indices of cortical activation (e.g., electrophysiological measures in combination with facial expressions). It is hoped that the reader will be in a much better position to effectively ascertain when these developmental asymmetries begin to take place, giving the supporting research documentation.

A CRITIQUE OF LENNEBERG'S EQUIPOTENTIALITY MODEL

Advocates of the Lenneberg View

Like Lenneberg (1967), Krashen (1973) also postulated that the hemispheres shared an equipotentiality in functions starting at the organism's birth. However, Krashen (1973) moved the critical period forward to age

5 or 6 (instead of at puberty), based on his reanalysis of the clinical literature. Specifically, he found that if the right hemisphere was damaged before 5 years of age, aphasic symptoms resulted. But, if injury to that brain side occurred after that critical age, no (or very little) speech loss was evidenced. Thus, Krashen (1973) hypothesized that a much earlier period for brain lateralization was in order, although equipotentiality still remained a necessary prerequisite for this hemispheric specialization.

Lenneberg's (1967) doctrines of equipotentiality and progressive lateralization have not died out, but continue to shape the formulations of current researchers. For instance, Corballis and Morgan's (1978) gradient of brain lateralization is an extension of Lenneberg's (1967) basic principles. These authors have maintained that a maturational gradient favors the left hemispheric side as well as certain contralateral body functions such as right-handedness (see chapter 9 for more details). Although specialization of the left brain takes place relatively early on in development, the right side lags behind; because of this immaturity and lack of specialization in the right brain, it still is able to demonstrate a functional plasticity for language until it catches up developmentally with its cortical mate.

Corballis and Morgan's (1978) model is a remodification of the Lenneberg (1967) one in which equipotentiality now is equated with hemispheric immaturity. Other experimenters have transformed the original equipotential doctrine further to fit their own theories on developmental lateralization (Hiscock, 1988).

Clinical Studies with Children

Effects of Early Brain Damage. Perhaps the strongest evidence for the Lenneberg (1967) equipotentiality model comes from clinical studies investigating the effects of early unilateral lesions on subsequent speech development. Many reviews have indicated that the incidence of aphasia after damage to the right hemisphere in infancy is significantly higher than after similar damage to the same side in later years (Dennis & Whitaker, 1977; Woods, 1980a; Woods & Carey, 1979). In more specific studies, the same pattern of results generally has been obtained, although the critical time frame for equipotentiality seems to be of a much shorter duration than Lenneberg (1967) claimed. For instance, Woods (1980b) and Riva and Cazzaniga (1986) observed that if the lesion onset occurred before the first year, verbal deficits were present regardless of the side of damage. However, after age 1, only lesions restricted to the left hemisphere produced the aphasic symptoms. In addition, Krashen's (1973) earlier critical period of 5–6 years was confirmed recently by Vargha-Khadem, O'Gorman, and Watters (1985), who found that language impairments were most pronounced in left-lesioned groups when onset was after this particular age. Other studies (Kiessling, Denckla, & Carlton, 1983; Nass, Sadler, & Sidtis, 1984) showed that the right hemisphere is more capable of vocalization and discrimination of speech in early childhood than in adolescence and adulthood.

Before one accepts Lenneberg's (1967) position wholeheartedly, however, it is important to consider the number of shortcomings inherent in the clinical literature. First and foremost, many of the reports in which right-hemisphere damage in infancy resulted in aphasia actually involved injury to both hemispheres. As Witelson (1977c) and Kinsbourne (1975) argued, lesions are not localized as discretely within children as in older subjects, and they are more likely to include gross bilateral damage at younger ages. Furthermore, Woods and Teuber (1978) reexamined the incidence of childhood aphasias after the so-called lateralized lesions and discovered that the percentage of cases associated with right-brain injury was significantly higher before 1940 (i.e., approximately 33%), in comparison with periods after 1940, when the incidence dropped to under 10%. These authors attributed this changing pattern of aphasias to the use of antibiotics and mass immunizations that began in the 1940s. Apparently, the treatments more effectively controlled the number of infections that previously had led to bilateral hemispheric involvement. Thus, it was concluded that the hemispheres shared less of an equipotential nature than Lenneberg (1967) speculated.

Other criticisms raised with the clinical research have included the following: very little patient history on past and current types of seizure impairments (which may have introduced their own confounds); few specifics on the child's premorbid cognitive and linguistic status; a failure to compare the lesioned brain results to control populations; and, finally, the lack of uniformity in follow-up testing, making it difficult to distinguish between delayed development and permanent impairment. However, when such controls are instituted, two findings usually emerge: (a) recovery from early brain injury is rarely complete, and (b) functional asymmetries are present from the earliest measurable point in time, presumably at birth (Aram & Whitaker, 1988; Dennis, 1980b). I shall return to these more current research outcomes when evaluating the antiequipotentiality argument at a later point within the chapter.

Effects of Hemispherectomies.   Other clinical studies have focused on the effects obtained by more extensive types of brain damage. These operations, referred to as *hemispherectomies*, involve removal of the entire cortex of the brain. Although rarely performed with human subjects, the most likely reasons for their implementation are to remove fairly large and malignant tumors or to help reduce the crippling effects of epileptic seizures and/or other serious birth defects. Left hemispherectomies in adults generally have produced marked aphasias, with a significant return of certain cortical functions (Searleman, 1977; Smith, 1966; Smith & Burklund, 1966). Yet, some severe impairments have persisted, such as the inability to generate more complex syntactical sentences (Gott, 1973) and pronounced and lingering deficits in reading and writing skills (Zaidel, 1973).

In contrast, if left hemispherectomies are performed in infancy before language is acquired, recovery of almost all lost functions by the intact right hemisphere often is reported (Searleman, 1977). On first glance, the data suggest that the two hemispheres are equipotential at birth, and that, over time, progressive lateralization of the left hemisphere for language takes place. The Lenneberg (1967) view has been questioned of late, especially because subtle deficits have been seen in children as young as 5 months who experienced hemispherectomies involving the left brain.

Dennis (1980a, 1980b) found that syntactic competence was affected significantly in these subjects, along with the ability to employ rhyming cues for identification of common words. Although these results require further replication (Bishop, 1983), they indicate that there are identifiable limits to functional plasticity. Even if the young brain can reorganize itself to a greater degree than the adult version after experiencing fairly extensive damage, some lateralization of linguistic functions still can be evidenced early on in life, certainly much earlier than Lenneberg (1967) originally theorized.

Normal Studies with Children

Findings with Lateralized Tasks. The hypothesis that lateralization is established by a critical age, either at puberty or even earlier (e.g., by age 5), also has been strengthened by the behaviors manifested on basic laterality tasks. The most commonly used procedures involving normal children have included the dichotic, tachistoscopic, and related tactile/haptic assignments. These are examined in sufficient detail to make a partial case for the Lenneberg (1967) and Krashen (1973) positions, respectively.

Dichotic Effects. To answer the question of whether lateralization increases with age, as Lenneberg (1967) had stated, the dichotic listening procedure has been employed most extensively. A number of investigators (Bryden & Allard, 1978; Larsen, 1984; Lewandowski, 1982) found ear advantages to be more frequent or more pronounced with increasing subject maturity. The Satz, Bakker, Teunissen, Goebel, and Van der Vlugt (1975) study revealed that the magnitude of REAs for verbal materials increased substantially from ages 9 to 11, with nonsignificant advantages demonstrated prior to this developmental period. Based on their results, the authors concluded that "the ear asymmetry, regardless of its age of onset, does undergo [some] major changes after five years of age" (p. 184), with the most dramatic ones occurring near the time of puberty.

However, not all dichotic listening tasks have generated these age-related changes in REAs (Bissell & Clark, 1984; Bryden & Allard, 1981; Hynd & Obrzut, 1977; Mirabile, Porter, Hughes, & Berlin, 1978; Van Duyne, Gargiulo, & Gonter, 1984). For instance, Berlin, Hughes, Lowe-Bell, and Berlin (1973) identified consistent REAs for consonant–vowel syllables in children across ages 5–13 years (Fig. 10.1). Age-related increases in overall performance also were identified, but they did not affect the degree of the dichotic asymmetry. As opposed to some of the previous cross-sectional designs favoring the Lenneberg (1967) view, more recent longitudinal studies have shown that auditory lateralization does not increase in a simple linear fashion with the passage of time. One experiment (Bakker, Hoefkens, & Van der Vlugt, 1979) produced results directly opposite to those of Satz's, using the exact same stimulus materials. As Hiscock (1988) summarized, although not discounting the occasional reports of developmental change in REAs, the preponderance of current evidence seems to suggest that auditory laterality does not rise significantly prior to the adolescent years, as Lenneberg (1967) assumed.

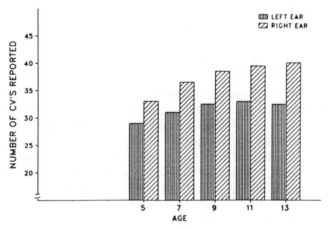

FIG. 10.1   Mean number of verbal stimuli reported from left and right ears as a function of age. Children consistently identified more CVs in the right ear across ages 5–13. Although performance generally improved as age increased, this effect did not interact with the ear advantage, questioning Lenneberg's (1967) progressive lateralization argument. From "Dichotic Right Ear Advantage in Children 5 to 13" by C. Berlin, L. Hughes, S. Lowe-Bell, and H. Berlin, 1973, *Cortex, 9*, p. 397. Copyright 1973 by Masson Italia Periodici. Reprinted by permission.

There is some evidence that these ear advantages begin close to Krashen's (1973) critical age of 5 years. Kimura's (1963) initial studies in dichotic listening identified a significant REA for digit names starting at approximately age 4. Other experimenters replicated these trends with CV stimuli (Geffner & Dorman, 1976; Studdert-Kennedy & Shankweiler, 1970) as well as actual word units and sentences (Saxby & Bryden, 1984; Tegano, 1982). Given the aforementioned observations, Porter and Berlin (1975) theorized that the ear asymmetry effect is established firmly by the fifth year, and that if any enhanced REAs are revealed in older children (Satz et al., 1975), they are probably due to more developed mnemonic processes to recall additional items from short-term memory.

Although Krashen's (1975) position can be confirmed more easily than Lenneberg's (1967), one must not discount the possibility that cerebral dominance might occur earlier, perhaps even shortly after birth (as is discussed later in this chapter). For now, one can conclude that the left hemisphere is more lateralized for verbal types of stimuli presented dichotically by age 5, if not sooner. Interestingly, the right hemisphere also shows signs of a similarly established preference (i.e., an LEA) for auditory emotional materials and sounds by approximately the same age (Saxby & Bryden, 1984).

Tachistoscopic Effects.   Many of the tachistoscopic studies with children have used facial stimuli to examine whether any visual field superiorities are present by a certain age. Some have produced the predicted LVF (right-hemispheric) advantage between ages 5 and 8 (Broman, 1978; Turkewitz & Ross-Kossak, 1984; Young & Bion, 1980), while others have not replicated this visual asymmetry (Carey, Diamond, & Woods, 1980; McQ. Reynolds & Jeeves, 1978b), even at later developmental periods (Saxby & Bryden, 1985). Nonverbal materials other than faces (i.e., dot detections, color identifications, and line orientations) also have resulted in the same general inconsistencies: namely, LVF superiorities sometimes were found as early as the fifth year (Witelson, 1977d; Young & Bion, 1979), others showed significant (and even curvilinear) age-related changes in laterality (Grant, 1980, 1981), and still others demonstrated the opposite asymmetrical pattern with these stimuli (Braine, 1968; Young & Bion, 1981).

In contrast, verbal inputs (e.g., letters, digits, and words) have produced the typical RVF (left-hemispheric) advantages, in keeping with the dichotic effects presented earlier. Forgays' (1953) classic experiment is a good starting point to begin a discussion with these types of materials. Specifically, he tested children at Grades 2–15 on a task that required them to recognize three- and four-letter words presented in either the left or right visual field. Forgays' (1953) results (Fig. 10.2) clearly illustrated that RVF

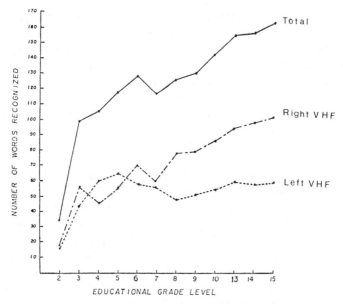

FIG. 10.2. Mean number of words recognized from left and right visual fields as a function of grade level. Forgays (1953) examined children's recognitions of three- and four-letter words presented unilaterally, with LVF and RVF trials mixed randomly. Findings indicated: (a) an increase in overall (total) performance with increasing educational level, (b) RVF advantages at all ages tested, and (c) an age x field interaction that reflected increasing right-field asymmetries with increasing age. "The Development of Differential Word Recognition" by D. G. Forgays, 1953, *Journal of Experimental Psychology*, *45*, p. 166. (In the public domain.)

recognitions exceeded LVF ones, with more pronounced asymmetries being displayed as the subjects matured. Subsequent studies have not confirmed this developmental trend, although they have shown the characteristic RVF superiorities to word stimuli, which Forgays (1953) originally reported (Ellis & Young, 1981; Garren, 1980; McKeever & Hurling, 1970). For instance, Olson (1973) replicated the former design and found a consistent RVF advantage across the age range of 7–11 years. Other investigators (Tomlinson-Keasey & Kelly, 1979; Tomlinson-Keasey, Kelly, & Burton, 1978) who have used related procedures have concluded that the tachistoscopic asymmetry is not evidenced until the onset of puberty, the critical period Lenneberg (1967) associated with the completed development of brain lateralization.

When multiple letters were the inputs to be processed (instead of words), significant as well as constant RVF superiorities were obtained again across all age levels of children, with the starting age approximately 5–8 years in most cases (Butler & Miller, 1979; Davidoff, Benton, Done,

& Booth, 1982; Davidoff & Done, 1984; Merola & Liederman, 1985). Although single letters have generated more variable outcomes, the trend in many of these studies was in the direction of a right-sided advantage (Corballis, Macadie, Crotty, & Beale, 1985; McQ. Reynolds & Jeeves, 1978a; Saxby & Bryden, 1985). Further, single digits presented unilaterally and bilaterally yielded the same right-field asymmetries at the same starting ages as for the letters (Kershner et al., 1977; Yeni-Komshian, Isenberg, & Goldberg, 1975).

The tachistoscopic results just cited tend to suggest that different categories of verbal stimuli produce the most consistent visual asymmetries. Language acquisition plays an instrumental role in the development of the RVF superiority, but it appears that the Krashen (1973) critical age of 5 years is the more compatible period for this asymmetry's establishment, rather than puberty. As some researchers (Beaumont, 1982; Young, 1982) stated, the contradictory findings involving nonverbal materials probably are based more on children's unfamiliarity with the stimulus items than their inability to express a lateralized function at an earlier age. Once more, there seems to be conclusive evidence to indicate that behavioral asymmetries shown in adulthood have their origins in early childhood, verifying the early lateralization hypothesis.

Haptic Effects. Because adults showed more sensitivity in their left hands as opposed to their right, Ghent (1961) wanted to know at what age children acquired this asymmetrical pattern. He discovered that these tactile asymmetries developed by age 6 in girls, but were delayed until approximately age 11 in boys. Since the time that Ghent's (1961) research was conducted, unilateralized stimulation tasks (Brizzolara, DeNobili, & Ferretti, 1982; Hatta, Yamamoto, Kawabata, & Tsutui, 1981; Yamamoto, 1980, 1984) have revealed that the left hand often is more adept than the right at making judgments involving spatial orientation, but the critical age when this asymmetry first appears has varied across studies (i.e., anywhere from age 5 to 12). In addition, gender differences have not been consistently expressed from one design to the next.

The most popular paradigm for examining the effects of bilateral stimulation on children's tactile performance has been the *dichaptic task*. Similar to the dichotic listening procedure, it relays different inputs to each body side simultaneously. In this case, the child palpates a different object in each hand and then has to choose from among a series of visual shapes the two that were just felt. When Witelson (1974) originally employed this dichaptic procedure, he obtained significant LHAs (i.e., left-hand advantages) in his 6- and 13-year-old male subjects. A replication of these findings with a larger group of children convinced Witelson (1976) that there was a later onset of asymmetric performance in females than males. Since the Witelson (1974, 1976) experiments, refinements have occurred in the dichaptic procedure, with the end result that the left-hand superiority has been evidenced in both genders (Klein & Rosenfield, 1980; Posluszny & Barton, 1981), sometimes at a much earlier age (i.e., 4 and 5 years) than supposed previously (Denes & Spinaci, 1981; Etaugh & Levy, 1981).

More recently, Rose (1984, 1985) modified Witelson's (1974) cross-modal task so that it could be used with very young children. Specifically, she placed an object in the child's hand for approximately 25 seconds and then presented each object along with a novel one for visual inspection. Fixation times generally were longer to the novel stimuli, with left-hand palpations enhancing the duration of fixation in older children between the ages of 2 and 5 years. Younger subjects did not show this LHA, however, signifying that there was a critical age for tactile lateralization close in time to the Krashen (1973) period.

With respect to interference produced by concurrent motor tasks, Kinsbourne and McMurray (1975) found that recitation of nursery rhymes and animal names slowed right-handed (left-hemispheric) tapping more than left-handed in kindergarten children. Duplications of this effect have abounded in the literature, with the start of the laterality typically being placed at age 3 and its continuance generally extending into the early adolescent years (Hiscock & Kinsbourne, 1980; Hiscock, Antonink, Prisciak, & van Hessert, 1985; Hiscock, Kinsbourne, Samuels, & Krause, 1987; Obrzut, Hynd, Obrzut, & Leitgeb, 1980; Willis & Hynd, 1987). For the most part, developmental increases have not been noted in these concurrent assignments, once again making a case for the early lateralization of the left hemisphere for linguistic functions.

Acquisition of Bilingual Skills.   In acquiring a second language, children usually appear to develop grammatical structures in the same order and at the same rate as their first language. Because of these observations, some theorists (Bailey, Madden, & Krashen, 1974; Dulay & Burt, 1974; Fatham, 1975) have speculated that there is some type of cortical processing mechanism that is universally operative in any type of language to be learned. Further claims have implicated the left hemisphere in the acquisition of these additional languages, so that the asymmetries exhibited by bilingual children should resemble those of monolingual controls for the most part. Although several experimental studies have supported this argument (Gordon, 1980; Ojemann & Whitaker, 1978), more current research has tended to emphasize the role that the right hemisphere plays in attaining bilingual proficiency.

In her critical review of second-language acquisition, Obler (1979) identified more behavioral asymmetries favoring the left body side (or right hemisphere) in children who initially were learning these new languages. As Obler (1979) mentioned, proficiency in the second language seems to be strongly dependent on pattern recognition cues that only the right hemisphere could provide to aspiring bilinguals (e.g., guessing the meaning of particular utterances within a particular environmental context or determining whether the new words rhymed with already acquired units).

Considering all the evidence in favor of this view (Gaziel, Obler, & Albert, 1978; Obler, Albert, & Gordon, 1975; Vaid & Genesee, 1980), including the most recent clinical reports on the elevated incidence of aphasias in bilinguals who experienced right-hemispheric lesions (Hakuta, 1986), I believe that brain lateralization is not as advanced in second-language learners as it is in monolinguals; and, additionally, that a Lennebergian type of equipotentiality might exist in this group of subjects up until the onset of puberty. I am not alone in these convictions either, because Genesee, Hamers, Lambert, Seitz, and Stark (1978) clearly stated that the right hemisphere can be involved in the later stages of bilingual acquisition (as well as the beginning ones), extending the time frame for cortical equivalency considerably.

Morphological Evidence for Progressive Lateralization. As already described in the introductory chapter to this text, the corpus callosum undergoes some rather dramatic changes in overall size as the organism matures from fetal to adult life. Based on a review of the available literature, Witelson and Kigar (1988) proposed a hypothetical model of callosal growth that includes three major developmental phases: a fetal stage, in which there is rapidly accelerating growth (Clarke, Kraftsik, Innocenti, & van der Loos, 1986; de Lacoste, Holloway, & Woodward, 1986); an infancy stage, extending from birth to approximately 2 years of age, where there is relatively constant callosal growth (Bell & Variend, 1985); and a childhood stage, in which the callosum either reaches its optimal size by age 4, or continues to grow at a very slow rate until it reaches its full adult size by approximately 10 years of age (Yakovlev & Lecours, 1967).

In the final stage of their model, Witelson and Kigar (1988) argued that the slow growth posited during early and middle childhood corresponds quite closely to other neuroanatomical changes that also take place at this time, such as callosal myelination and synaptic density of neurons (Huttenlocher, 1984). Moreover, when one considers the growth pattern of the entire brain, one can see that there is an initial growth spurt up until 3 years of age, followed by much slower increases in size at subsequent intervals (with interspersed smaller spurts) until age 18 (DeKaban, 1978; Grow & Johnson, 1983). Some educators (Epstein, 1978, 1980) assumed that left-hemisphere functions are stimulated more during these "spurt cycles," whereas right-hemisphere functions are maximized to a greater extent during the plateau periods between the spurts.

Callosal anatomy can be correlated strongly to overall brain size, with peak growth in both structures occurring somewhere in early childhood. According to Witelson and Kigar (1988), these consistently expressed morphological patterns appear to be quite compatible with the Lenneberg (1967) and Krashen (1973) theories of decreasing hemispheric plasticity with increasing chronological age, suggesting that a physiological base can be implicated with these views.

THE ANTI-EQUIPOTENTIALITY ARGUMENT: EVIDENCE FOR LATERALIZATION AT INFANCY

In recent years, several findings have questioned seriously the validity of Lenneberg's (1967) equipotentiality argument, especially its extension into the adolescent years. The reader might recall that many of the experimental studies presented, involving clinical as well as normal groups, were generally more supportive of the Krashen (1973) view that brain lateralization was established as early as age 5. Current thinking reflects that cerebral dominance could be established even closer to the time of birth, before language is acquired.

Some initial observations in favor of this *lateralization by age zero* approach, a label coined by Krashen (1975), have dealt with the behavioral measures of head turning and the onset of handedness in infancy. As already referenced in chapter 9, Turkewitz (1977, 1988) discovered that infants turned their heads more reliably to the right if that particular side was stimulated tactually. It was reasoned subsequently that the left hemisphere demonstrated an obvious (and fairly early) superiority in registering external stimuli, especially auditory inputs presented to the right ear. A further asymmetrical trend eventually was uncovered by Young (1977) and Witelson (1977c): namely, that young infants reached more often with the left hand, but were more likely to grasp objects with the right hand. Taking their cue from these pioneers, other researchers have traced the onset of this right-hand grasp to approximately 7 months of age (Ramsay, 1980), whereas still others have placed the origins even earlier, to 2 months of age (Caplan & Kinsbourne, 1976; Hawn & Harris, 1979).

Based on these preliminary data, one might see that body-side asymmetries can be expressed even earlier than Lenneberg (1967) or Krashen (1973) speculated. It seems that the most compelling findings for the lateralization of language at infancy have come from the dichotic and electrophysiological experiments; thus I direct attention mainly to these studies.

Studies with Infants

Dichotic Asymmetries. Experimenters have demonstrated effectively that REAs can be shown to verbal stimuli in children as young as 2½–3 years of age (Gilbert & Climan, 1974; Harper & Kraft, 1986; Kraft, 1984). Since then, work has proceeded at a vigorous pace to apply the dichotic listening procedure to even younger subjects to determine the earliest possible age for the expression of this lateralized ability. Entus (1977) was one of the first to examine ear differences in infants averaging 50 days of age. In her first phase of the experiment, the infants learned to suck on a nipple at a constant rate to hear the same dichotic pair of stimuli (whether musical notes or CVs) over and over again.

Eventually, a pattern of habituation was reached to each dichotic pair; then, a new element was introduced in either the infants' left or right ear while the other ear continued to register its habituated stimulus. Changes in the rate of sucking responses were monitored continuously to each new stimulus presented, with some interesting asymmetries being identified. Infants typically showed a greater increase in sucking when the syllable was altered in the right ear or when the musical note was varied in the left ear. These findings imply that brain differences can be evidenced in subjects soon after birth, lending some credence to the genetic approach of lateralization.

Although Entus's (1977) results have not always been replicated (Vargha-Khadem & Corballis, 1979), more times than not the same pattern of ear superiorities have been reported at approximately the same age levels (Best, Hoffman, & Glanville, 1982; Glanville, Best, & Levenson, 1977). Obviously, more behavioral studies need to be conducted at these earlier ages before any definite conclusion can be reached with respect to the duration of the critical period for brain lateralization. Further, most of the research has focused overwhelmingly on dichotic asymmetries, as opposed to other lateralized measures. This is due in part to the dichotic task being more compatible with infant skills and abilities (Best, 1988). However, other procedures (e.g., tachistoscopic and dichaptic) should continue to be refined to determine if there are any right-hemispheric advantages in the infants' holistic perception of faces as well as other nonverbal stimuli, as Levine (1985) suggested. In this way, the bias toward assessing only language-related functions can be avoided so that a more complete and accurate picture of the infants' capabilities across a wide range of activities can be obtained eventually.

Electrophysiological Asymmetries. Another area of research that strongly supports the lateralization of language by birth hypothesis involves taking direct, electrophysiological readings of hemispheric functioning to specific speech-related stimuli. Molfese (1972, 1973) strongly believed that if young infants could discriminate between speech sounds by 3 months of age, then the brain might be equipped with specialized left-language centers already, even before an understanding of those sounds is achieved fully. If this were the case, event-related potentials (ERPs) would show differential patterns between the two hemispheres, primarily to speech sounds, early on in development.

Molfese (1972, 1973) consistently found asymmetrical responses in this brain index whenever CVs (e.g., *ba* and *da*) and monosyllabic words were presented to infants. Specifically, the magnitude of the left hemisphere ERP was generally greater than that for the right hemisphere to these particular stimuli. Most importantly, Molfese (1972, 1973) noted that these differences were evidenced as early as 1 day of age, clearly indicating that language lateralization took place long before the periods predicted by Lenneberg (1967) and Krashen (1973). Other investigators (Davis & Wada, 1977a) obtained similar results, even when nonverbal sounds (e.g., auditory clicks) were introduced. As Wada and Davis (1977) remarked, a fundamental asymmetry of the brain neurocircuit presumably exists before the acquisition of language. This neurocircuit initially is more lateralized for any type of sound relayed to the left hemisphere, but, over time, it becomes more specialized for speech inputs.

Once it was determined that ERP asymmetries could be elicited in newborns, the next research phase basically consisted of identifying which stimulus characteristics actually evoked these lateralized responses. It appears that infants as young as 2 months can discriminate between speech sounds varying in *voice onset time* (VOT). VOT is the period it takes to voice particular stop consonants such as b and p. Analysis of infants' auditory ERPs revealed that the categorical discriminations included two major components: first, a relatively early onset bilateralized response (starting at approximately 100 milliseconds), followed by a more lateralized right-hemispheric response, which occurred at roughly 400 milliseconds (Molfese & Molfese, 1979b). These effects have been replicated with older preschoolers (Molfese & Hess, 1978; Molfese & Molfese, 1988), whereas in adults, only the right-hemisphere mechanism was found to be operative at times (Molfese, 1978). A developmental interval might be required to lateralize more fully the VOT cue to one brain side; curiously, this side just happens to be the right one, questioning previous notions that only the left hemisphere is implicated in language acquisition and its subsequent development.

Another important speech discrimination cue has to do with the phonetic expression of stop consonants combined with different vowel sounds, referred to as *place of articulation* (POA). Molfese and Molfese (1979a, 1980) also observed a similar two-phase pattern of bilateralized and lateralized activity in the auditory ERPs of newborns as well as pre-term infants, except that the left hemisphere was more functionally oper-ative than the right for the POA discriminations. Some studies showed a reverse trend, with the left-lateralized effect coming before the bilater-alized one (Molfese & Molfese 1985).

Based on these results, one might conclude that different regions of the auditory ERP are more lateralized than others, depending on the par-ticular speech characteristic. If the cue were more temporal (e.g., VOT), a right-hemispheric response was evoked more often; if the cue were more acoustic (e.g., POA), however, a left-hemispheric response typically was elicited. Again, it should be emphasized that these brain asymmetries were present in the youngest of subjects as well as older children and adults; thus it has been theorized subsequently that infant ERP lateralities are correlated directly with later language (and even cognitive) development (Molfese & Best, 1988).

Affective Asymmetries. Research with human infants also confirms the lateralization for the expression of emotion during the first year of life. Initially, Davidson and Fox (1982) examined 10-month-old infants' reactions to videotapes of an actress alternately laughing and crying via standard EEG measures. Although the parietal lobes did not discriminate between the happy and sad segments, frontal lobes displayed the adult asymmetrical pattern, with left-hemisphere activity more pronounced to the positive affective segments compared with the negative ones.

More natural emotion-producing conditions were then studied, such as infants' responses to maternal separation. Those who cried as a result of the separation exhibited an increase in right frontal lobe activation, whereas those who remained outwardly calm showed a corresponding inhibition of activity in that respective region (Fox & Davidson, 1987). Other designs have introduced a stranger to the infant, followed by the mother approaching her child before she left the room. Again, criers differed from noncriers in EEG lobe activity, with more right-sided fron-tal activation occurring in the distressed infants (Davidson & Fox, 1988b). Readings also taken at the time the mother approached the infant just before the separation episode induced an EEG reversal to greater left (as opposed to right) frontal activity (Fox & Davidson, 1987). In summariz-ing these major findings, it seems that the left hemisphere governs more positive affects (associated with mother presence), whereas its comple-ment controls more negative moods (associated with mother absence) even as early as 10 months of age.

Although the evidence presented here suggests that frontal lobe asym-metries are "hard-wired" in the human species, one cannot rule out the influence of environmental factors, especially learning, on the expression of various types of emotions (Davidson & Fox, 1988a). However, research is just beginning to show that these asymmetrical differences between positive and negative affects can be extended back even further, right to the start of the newborn period.

To elicit approach and withdrawal reactions in two day olds, Fox and Davidson (1986) exposed each newborn to different tastes presented via pipette on the tongue surface. The facial behavior of each child was recorded subsequently; EEG readings in the respective left and right frontal lobes were performed simultaneously as well. Sugar tastes produced the corresponding activity in the left frontal lobe, along with pleasurable facial expressions. The more unpleasant citric acid tastes, however, did not generate more right frontal activation, even when disgustful expressions were conveyed.

Although their experimental hypothesis was not verified completely, Fox and Davidson (1986) still concluded that there are hemispheric asymmetries to affective stimuli at birth (or shortly afterward). It may be that some developmental period (however short it may be) is necessary to establish right-hemispheric lateralization for more negative types of emotional states, in comparison with the positive types.

Several researchers (Tomarken & Davidson, 1988) posed a fascinating question: "Why is the right hemisphere associated with negative affect at all?" One of the more convincing explanations is that whereas subjects appraise situations in the same manner with either left or right frontal activation, the level of coping response might differ between brain sides. When the left hemisphere is activated, an extreme reaction might be terminated rather quickly; conversely, when the right hemisphere is activated, the strongly aversive reaction might not be coped with in the same efficient manner; hence negative feelings persist for some time. Perhaps subjects cannot help themselves from being carried away by these feelings whenever the right frontal lobes are stimulated.

In support of this argument, it should be recalled that the infant crying reactions to strangers involved more right-hemispheric activity, in comparison with the more copeworthy noncrying reactions in which this activity was inhibited. If one accepts these theoretical reflections, this might mean that: (a) certain coping responses (primarily in the left hemisphere) are present early on in life, and (b) infants experience a greater vulnerability to more negative affective states in their right hemisphere, which persists throughout the later stages of development.

Anatomical Asymmetries.   As already discussed in chapter 1, there are a number of morphological asymmetries in the human brain, some of which are present either at infancy or even before this period (i.e., in the fetus). The longer left temporal planum is found not only in the majority of adult brains (Witelson & Pallie, 1973), but also in fetal brains (Chi et al., 1977; Wada et al., 1975). By approximately the 16th week of fetal life, sylvian fissure asymmetries also can be detected, with left sides typically being more extended than right (LeMay & Culebras, 1972). Moreover, the smaller-sized Broca area of the adult left brain can be evidenced in the fetal one when the overall structure is measured (LeMay, 1977). However, if the buried cortex of Broca's area is examined, one immediately sees that this region is larger and more extensive on the left than the right side (Falzi, Perrone, & Vignolo, 1982). Based on these latter observations, scientists have speculated that the left hemisphere is fissured (i.e., folded) more deeply in comparison with its mate (Galaburda, 1984; Gur et al., 1980).

Although a preprogrammed bias might exist to show hemispheric asymmetries (especially within linguistic structures of the left brain) prior to birth, a maturational process still is required to develop the more intricate and highly detailed convolutions of each cerebrum. One hypothesized maturational gradient of lateralization is reviewed in more detail.

The Maturational Gradient Hypothesis for Lateralization

According to Best (1988), brain development normally proceeds in a general anterior-to-posterior direction. The effect of this growth vector is that frontal regions in the right hemisphere develop well before occipital ones located in the left hemisphere (Fig. 10.3). Best's (1988) proposed gradient has received some support from fetal brain observations. First, major fissures appear at least 2 weeks earlier on the right hemisphere, as opposed to the left. More importantly, the counterclockwise torque (with left hemisphere twisted back and right twisted forward) has been evidenced in fetal brains 34 weeks of age (Dooling, Chi, & Gilles, 1983). A more striking right frontopetalia is seen in fetuses and neonates (LeMay, 1977), whereas a more pronounced left occipitopetalia is displayed in adults (LeMay, 1976), possibly indicating that earlier emerging right frontal regions may become attenuated by later growth in the left posterior regions.

The morphological growth vector proposed by Best (1988) has obvious implications for functional asymmetries associated with the cerebral hemispheres. Specifically, right-hemisphere functions should be acquired much earlier than left hemisphere ones because of the faster maturational rate of the right frontal areas. This contention is supported mainly by the dichotic finding that LEAs for musical notes occur much sooner (i.e., at least 1 month earlier) than the complementary REAs for speech syllables (Best et al., 1982). Further, numerous reports have indicated that

PROPOSED GROWTH VECTOR

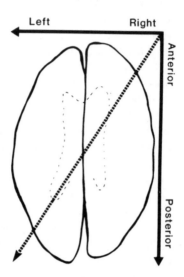

FIG. 10.3.   Schematic diagram of Best's (1988) morphological growth vector. The developmental gradient proceeds in an anterior-to-posterior direction, and from right-hemispheric frontal regions to left-hemispheric
posterior ones. Best's (1988) growth vector has obvious implications for
functional asymmetries, which also are hypothesized to follow the same
developmental pattern of earlier right-biases and later left-biases. From "The
Emergence of Cerebral Asymmetries in Early Human Development: A Literature Review and a Neuroembryological Model" by C. T. Best, D. L. Molfese, and S. J. Segalowitz in *Brain Lateralization in Children: Developmental Implications* by D. L. Molfese and S. J. Segalowitz (p. 23), New
York: Guilford. Copyright 1988 by Guilford Press. Reprinted by permission.

children can comprehend and produce the emotional, intonational
properties of language earlier than the actual word units (Best, 1988),
signifying once again the presence of right-hemispheric functions before
left.

Although Best's (1988) theory is an intriguing one, one must remember that morphological asymmetries are not necessarily reflective of functional differences between hemispheres (Springer & Deutsch, 1989), and
other researchers have argued respectably that the maturational gradient
favors left brain development over right (Corballis & Morgan, 1978), with
more recent ERP results tending to favor this approach. Until more empirical evidence is provided, it seems wise to dissociate behavioral outcomes from the more confirmable morphological differences identified
by Best (1988).

AN INTEGRATION OF THE EARLY
AND LATE LATERALIZATION VIEWS

In this author's opinion, it is probably best to combine the two models of developmental lateralization. There is a genetic base for brain differences that can be expressed relatively early on in development, especially for speech materials. However, this is not to say that the environment exerts no influence on the asymmetry's magnitude as the organism advances in years. Quite the contrary, changes can still occur in left- and right-brain processing from the earliest days up until approximately 5 years of age (the Krashen [1973] critical period), with some variations extending well into adolescence. These changes are brought about mainly by the presence (or absence) of experiential factors (e.g., learning one or more languages, imitating motor movements and other spatial skills). Hence the inborn components required for later lateralization can be modified as well as reshaped by exposure to particular stimulus conditions.

One such environmental condition has to do with whether children receive the necessary training to acquire a workable linguistic structure. The case study of Genie, an adolescent girl who spent most of her life in almost complete deprivation of social contacts, encountered some serious difficulties in acquiring a first language once she was removed from the aversive environment. This study (Fromkin, Krashen, Curtiss, Rigler, & Rigler, 1974) raised the question "Can children show language learning *after* the onset of puberty if they have been deprived of the basics early on in development?" Genie demonstrated some comprehension and production gains, although the former was almost always superior to the latter. Even with these advances, her articulation of sounds still remained impaired. In addition, she did not appear to use language for purely communicative purposes; given the opportunity, she would avoid speech altogether.

With respect to her hemispheric dominance, the same researchers (Curtiss, Fromkin, Rigler, Rigler, & Krashen, 1975) theorized that Genie represented linguistic elements in her right (not left) hemisphere. The dichotic listening tests that were administered to her reflected very strong LEAs for verbal inputs, far exceeding those of more normal subjects. The information to date suggests that Genie's right brain had acquired control of more linguistic functions once the left brain was deprived of the proper outside stimulation. In other words, a reversal in functional dominance occurred as a direct result of the environmental deprivation.

Other studies with deaf subjects have lent their support to the environmental influence argument for brain lateralization. Tachistoscopic findings have revealed that those born deaf generally displayed equivalent processing capabilities for words in both left and right visual fields, in comparison with normal hearing subjects who exhibited RVF advantages for these same stimuli (Manning, Goble, Markman, & LaBreche, 1977; Vargha-Khadem, 1983). Those who became deaf in early and middle childhood usually have responded in a manner similar to the congenitally deaf (Manning et al., 1977). It was concluded that auditory experience was (and is) a major determinant of cerebral lateralization for language within the left hemisphere.

Obviously, environmental factors interact with genetic components to produce the typical asymmetrical patterns of behavior. But if, for some reason, the given environment in which one is reared is altered, the expression of these lateralized responses is subsequently affected. Moreover, although a fairly early critical period can be established for brain lateralization, external factors still can exert an influence over subjects' performance for some extended length of time, as the clinical literature implies.

SUMMARY AND CONCLUSIONS

This chapter focused on the question "Are there developmental differences in brain lateralization?" Upon review of the literature, I identified a more serious inquiry that needed to be addressed, namely "When are these differences first shown?" Traditional views on the development of lateralization were critiqued, and new evidence was presented in favor of an early lateralization model for cerebral asymmetries. Similar to chapters 8 and 9, environmental factors were emphasized, along with genetic components, in the ultimate expression of these lateralized behaviors. One derived outcome of this developmental research was that terms such as *hemispheric equipotentiality* and *functional plasticity* were found to be extremely limited in their applications and did not convey adequately the true state of affairs when it came to analyzing infants' responses on lateralized tasks (as well as other related procedures).

To highlight the major themes of chapter 10:

1. Brain lesion and hemispherectomy studies have indicated that recovery from early brain damage rarely is complete. Dichotic, tachistoscopic, and haptic procedures with normal children have verified further that lateralization of functions is established firmly by age 5 (if not earlier), with little noticeable gains being evidenced at later periods. Morphological changes in callosal growth and overall brain size appear to be most pronounced at these earlier ages as well. In light of these findings, the Lennebergian view of decreasing equipotentiality with age would require some necessary modification.

2. The newer lateralization at birth argument suggests that if a critical period for equipotentiality exists, it is of an extremely short duration. Functional asymmetries, especially for language, have been noted as early as the first months of life (see the habituation sucking and heart-rate procedures). In addition, ERP changes in hemispheric activity for speech-related stimuli have been displayed in the 1- to 2-day-old neonate, along with frontal lobe EEG differences for positive affective stimuli. Finally, fetal brain asymmetries (e.g., longer left temporal planums, more extended left sylvian fissures) have been correlated closely with those of the adult human. Taken all together, these results imply that a preprogrammed bias exists for cerebral asymmetries, and that if any changes take place with age, they are due to the child's ever-growing cognitive and mnemonic skills, coupled with the gradual unfolding of particular maturational processes (e.g., more striking left occipitopetalia).

Now that I have considered brain differences in various normal subgroups classified by gender, handedness, or age, I am in a position to state some general conclusions about human cerebral asymmetries, based on data obtained in this part as well as earlier chapters. I also offer some guidelines as to the direction in which future research should proceed with respect to brain lateralization in Part IV.

PART FOUR

NEW APPROACHES TO AND CONCLUDING COMMENTS ON CEREBRAL ASYMMETRIES

This last part of the text is designed to provide the reader with the proper perspective as to where the research is currently in reference to brain differences, and also where it is going in future decades on this specialized topic. Specifically, chapter 11 attempts to clarify some of the asymmetry issues that still remain and offers several sound experimental methodologies that show the most promise in answering these issues. Although it is not intended to be the final statement on cerebral asymmetries, this final part should serve as a useful springboard to new avenues of study as well as associated theoretical formulations.

CHAPTER ELEVEN

What New Techniques Will
Be Used in Studying
Cerebral Asymmetries?

In this concluding chapter, the reader is given the opportunity to reflect on the future status of cerebral asymmetries within three major areas of interest: new theoretical formulations, refined experimental procedures, and potential educational applications. Similar to previous chapters, relevant inquiries are posed in each of these areas, along with interesting replies to stimulate further research and study. In addition, references are provided wherever possible so that an appropriate literature base can be obtained and subsequently consulted with respect to the research inquiries. I begin with a discussion of the more theoretical aspects associated with left brain–right brain differences.

NEW THEORETICAL FORMULATIONS

Are Cerebral Asymmetries Worthy
of Continued Study?

Several scientists have criticized the asymmetrical research, identifying a wide range of problems inherent in the discipline. Some, like Efron (1990), even have begun to doubt the validity of continued investigations with brain differences and have advocated that concepts such as *hemispheric specialization* be put to rest as quietly as possible. Efron's (1990) approach is critiqued to determine whether there is any merit to following his suggestions.

In his most recently published text, *The Decline and Fall of Hemispheric Specialization*, Efron (1990) firmly expressed his belief that cortical lateralization is simply one of many factors that can account for the performance asymmetries shown in dichotic and tachistoscopic tasks, and so it should not continue to maintain its highly exalted status. If anything, Efron (1990) stated that models that emphasize hemispheric lateralization should be abandoned entirely, because they are so confounded with other *modulating factors* (e.g., gender, age, handedness, task complexity, and information-processing strategy) that any explanation for the behavioral asymmetries is difficult to achieve in the foreseeable future.

Efron's (1990) interpretation was based largely on three points: (a) brain circuits in each hemisphere can support both verbal and spatial functions, (b) ear and field advantages do not always exhibit a consistent lateralized pattern, and (c) any performance asymmetries are not necessarily reflective of cerebral ones. In reviewing these points, I do not contest any of the claims that Efron (1990) mentioned. In fact, these are the very same themes that recur in this book (e.g., relative lateralization, within- and between-subject variability). Rather, I disagree with the jump in logic that Efron (1990) intentionally took from these ideas to the conclusion that it is not worthwhile to pursue the concept of cerebral dominance any further.

Returning to Efron's (1990) list of modulating factors, one should see immediately that I have discussed many of his variables while still retaining my lateralization model. Perhaps I even have made a case that these other factors are derived from inherent differences in the two brain hemispheres, implying that specialization still should be regarded as a necessary ingredient (perhaps even a prime mover) for the behavioral asymmetries.

The other, and perhaps more disconcerting, aspect to Efron's (1990) theory is that it basically ignored a massive body of literature pertaining to measures that more directly assess hemispheric functioning (i.e., electrophysiological measures, brain scans, and metabolic activity indices) and that have revealed some striking asymmetries. Instead, Efron (1990) consulted the more traditional findings and argued that the dichotic and tachistoscopic procedures are so physiologically imprecise that it is hard to arrive at any solid evidence supporting brain differences. In light of this narrow sightedness, it is not surprising that Efron (1990) arrived at his conclusion, given the outdated research base behind his arguments.

Therefore, continued work on cerebral lateralization is in order. The confounds notwithstanding, one should not exclude a number of conceptual variables merely to arrive at a "quick and easy" explanation for any task asymmetries. The more difficult strategy that lies before me and future theorists is whether we can more effectively integrate those factors already identified as significant into a framework (albeit complex) that truly captures the essence of subjects' processing capabilities. I feel that lateralization is one of those significant variables that cannot (nor should not) be eliminated in this model just because of a whim or personal bias.

Did Right Brain Functions Precede Left Ones?

Many theories on the origin of cerebral asymmetries have correlated language usage to the development of tools. Most have related that as our ancestors started to use tools, they uttered accompanying sounds (i.e., barks and babbles) that eventually evolved into the distinctively human spoken language (Hewes, 1973; Kimura, 1973a, 1973b). As Harris (1989) so eloquently described in his text, *Our Kind: Where We Are, Where We Came From, Where We Are Going,* when primitive humans relied

> more and more on tool-making and tool-usage [skills] . . . their genetically controlled repertory of grunts, grimaces, and tantrums no longer sufficed to convey the expanded range of requests that they needed to make. [Thus] culturally invented gestures and sounds . . . had to increase proportionately [to meet these new and ever-growing demands]. . . . This was not language as we know it, but it was certainly a *beginning* from which language as we know it could have evolved. (p. 79)

It then appears that the cerebral lateralization of language was, to a certain degree, dependent on the expression of tool-related behaviors and other manipulative skills that went along with them (Lieberman, 1984, 1985).

Instead of continuing to emphasize the dominant role of the left hemisphere, I propose that the evolution of cerebral lateralization really began with the specialization of the right hemisphere, not the left. Some researchers (Corballis & Beale, 1976, 1983; Webster, 1977) suggested that spatial representation needed to develop before linguistic representation so that primitive humans could make the appropriate left–right discriminations, ensuring successful navigation over familiar (and especially unfamiliar) territories.

Although counterarguments have emphasized the importance of language for acquiring the labels of *left* and *right*, I advance that there was a prelinguistic structure that strongly relied on spatial skills to move about the environment. (Labels at that point were unnecessary to effective locomotion.) This prelinguistic structure may have been lateralized in the right brain, which also controlled for the expression of signing behaviors and other gestures insofar as they related to the spatial. As humans evolved as a species, the left hemisphere eventually regulated those manipulative abilities that were connected intimately to more basic speech patterns.

This reversed specialization hypothesis for describing asymmetrical origins should in no way be threatening to proponents who adhere to a relative lateralization model. If components of language can be represented in both hemispheres, who is to say whether the right brain played as important a role in their eventual lateralization as the left did, maybe even more so if the right were able to mediate prelinguistic behaviors. In further reference to this prelinguistic system, anthropologists like Margaret Mead even suggested that "special supernatural powers" like extrasensory perception (ESP) could have existed in very primitive cultures. This implies that perhaps, at one point in the species' development, extrasensory abilities were the major means of communication between the members before language was acquired (Time-Life Books, 1987). Several investigators (e.g., Tart, 1976, 1990) reinterpreted these ideas in terms of cerebral dominance, explaining that such altered states of consciousness were (and continue to be) controlled primarily by the right hemisphere.

Although the conclusions presented here are highly speculative, they still are indicative of a need to describe our cortical origins according to a wide variety of perspectives. One of the advantages of highlighting right-brain lateralization before the traditionally accepted left is to provide a more realistic view of both hemispheres as major units to one's overall cognitive development. By deemphasizing the right's importance, even in theoretical formulations, one risks seeing him or herself as less than complete—fragmented in functions and separated in nature.

What Does Relative Lateralization Really Mean?

At this point, it probably is a good idea to redefine what we mean by *relative lateralization*. According to most experimental sources, interhemispheric differences are more a matter of degree than of kind (for a review, see Bradshaw & Nettleton, 1983). Although both hemispheres share most cortical functions, each brain side is more or less equipped to handle particular ones, with the left more specialized for linguistic and verbal elements and the right more spatial and nonverbal elements. In physiological terms, both hemispheres possess the same type of topographic arrangement, but the organization is different for each cortical side, with more space taken up for analytical processing on the left side and more area designated for holistic processing on the right side.

Given these inherent functional asymmetries, many of the posited left brain–right brain dichotomies soon fall apart when one considers real-world applications. Simply put, both hemispheres typically are involved in most (if not all) processing activities. As educators Caine and Caine (1991) summarized:

> The "left brain" processes are enriched and supported by "right brain" processes. [For example] great artists do not just set up an easel and paint; they may do a significant amount of preliminary design and analytical thinking. That is why we have so many sketches from, say, Picasso and da Vinci, before the final product was painted. The artistic process [would then] involve a substantial amount of analytical and segmented thinking. The "right side" relies on the left [for its] success. (p. 34)

This cross-hemispheric involvement makes it extremely difficult to distinguish exclusively left-brain from exclusively right-brain functions, especially because the corpus callosum merges the two hemispheric inputs together. Via the callosum (or other connecting commissure), patterns that are recognized by the right cortex are analyzed almost simultaneously and interpreted by the left cortex (Sagan, 1977). It would seem then that relative lateralization is a good concept to begin an understanding of cerebral asymmetries. But, at some later point, it needs to be treated much more relatively when one considers that most human functions require the activity of both hemispheres, not just one brain side.

Should one still adhere to the relative lateralization model (as I strongly encourage until a better one comes along), then obviously a certain amount of flexibility needs to be associated with the asymmetrical process. Cerebral differences are not so set or predetermined that they cannot be modified by environmental variables. As we have noticed in our research, LEAs even can occur for apparently incompatible verbal materials if enough time is provided to subjects to master the task of shadowing those inputs on that respective side. To give another example, exposing children to a series of languages by a certain critical period makes them more proficient and more bilateralized in those languages, compared with their monolingual controls.

Therefore, the asymmetrical blueprint can be changed, for the better or the worse, depending on the type of experiential agents administered to subjects. Because lateralization is never absolute, no single asymmetrical pattern ever will be found for a particular group of subjects. There will be as many blueprints as there are individual variations, and, sad but true, scientists may never be able to account for all of the patterns, even within a theoretical framework.

REFINED EXPERIMENTAL PROCEDURES

Some of the experimental techniques that will be employed in the study of cerebral asymmetries within the next decade and beyond are reviewed next.

What Will Be the Most Rigorous Methodologies to Studying Asymmetries in the 1990s?

PET Scans.   Springer and Deutsch (1989) recommended that

> studies with *PET* [scans] are only [just] starting to explore their potential
> in mapping brain activity during different behavioral states. . . . Experi-
> ments will have to be conducted with techniques such as *PET* to tease apart
> the many stages and confounding variables involved in studying basic brain
> activity–behavior relationships. . . . It is hopeful that these techniques will
> provide a great deal of new insight into the [various] functions of the
> hemispheres in the near future. (pp. 125–126)

I wholeheartedly agree with these sentiments, and so would like to spend
a few moments speculating on what the future holds in store for this precise brain index, the PET scan.

The recent methodologies executed by Petersen et al. (1988, 1989)
showed a most promising avenue for scientists to follow in the years to
come. To summarize their basic format, Petersen and his colleagues
presented single-word units either through a visual or auditory modality
across a series of tasks that increased in informational complexity. For
instance, in the series of visual conditions, subjects had to look first at
the printed words, then repeat aloud the nouns that they had just viewed,
and, finally, select an appropriate verb to go along with each printed
noun. The auditory conditions resembled the visual, except that here the
nouns were heard instead of seen.

Petersen and his research team (1988, 1989) assessed subjects' brain
activity throughout these conditions via a number of PET scan readings.
Specifically, they developed a computer program that effectively screened
out changes in cortical activity from one task to the next, thus allowing
for an easier determination as to which brain areas were involved for
particular functions.

The results of these PET scan subtraction tests revealed that seeing
printed words generated cortical activity in the subjects' left and right
visual corti, whereas hearing those same nouns activated auditory corti
centers in both brains. When the task was changed to having subjects
repeat the words aloud, the same general brain areas were activated,
regardless of modality. In this case, activation occurred along the central fissures of both left and right hemispheres. Finally, when the verb-
association conditions were introduced, the prefrontal cortex of the left
hemisphere immediately ventral to Broca's area generated the most activity. In addition, a region in the medial cortex directly superior to the
corpus callosum was implicated for both left and right brain sides.

Such impressive findings like these should cue the reader that no language test is exclusively left-brain oriented. Rather, bilateral involvement appears to be the norm (rather than the exception) for many different types of verbal assignments presented across a variety of stimulus modalities. Research like that of Petersen et al. (1988, 1989) should be viewed as paving the way for scientists to map the "biological topography underlying language use" (Montgomery, 1989) as well as helping them develop cortical maps for myriad other functions.

By utilizing PET scans with accompanying computer-generated subtraction procedures, further investigators will be able to determine more clearly how many regions bilaterally interact with one another in the control and expression of specific behaviors. Perhaps other modalities (e.g., the haptic) also will be examined in the hopes of uncovering similar cortical patterns of activity across an even wider range of sensory channels. Only time and continued work with PET scans will give a more definite idea as to how the brain truly works.

Attentional Measures: Instructional Manipulations. Following in Bryden's footsteps, I have discovered that a number of behavioral asymmetries can be enhanced when experimental instructions are provided to attend to a certain body side. In those studies where the focus of attention alternated between the left and right body sides across a series of counterbalanced blocks of trials, the following effects were obtained: REAs in right-handed males for CV inputs (Iaccino & Sowa, 1989), RVF advantages in dextral males for single consonant units, and complementary LVF advantages in dextral subjects for position identifications of those consonants (Iaccino, 1990). Curiously, and quite unexpectedly, when a greater number of focused trials was administered on each body side, these asymmetrical patterns tended to change rather dramatically. LEAs as well as REAs were observed in both right-handed men and women with the CV stimuli (Iaccino & Houran, 1989, 1991). More recently, although no field superiorities were evidenced, dextral females were more likely to recall consonant positions shown tachistoscopically even better than their male counterparts (Iaccino & Houran, in press).

Making sense of these rather complex findings, it appears that, depending on the instructional manipulation, ear and field advantages could be either present or absent. A more consistent outcome was that only dextral subjects were affected by the attentional variations, perhaps indicating that this group's cortical organization could be modified, at least to a certain degree, by experiential factors such as task demands. Sometimes comparisons could not be made with sinistral subjects, because it proved particularly hard to identify these hand-dominant individuals within the population. In light of this information, any conclusions reached tend to show a strong bias toward the dextral group.

Obviously, more work should be undertaken with the attentional set variable, if for no other reason than to see that particular subject groups might not deploy the same type of information-processing strategy from one lateralized task to the next. Possibly with additional focus time and trial practice, subject groups (e.g., men and women) might even reach comparable levels of performance.

As stated in an earlier chapter, one needs to be reminded that a tremendous amount of variability exists in the way each individual member interprets the task requirements and subsequently processes the respective information (refer to my attentional variability model in chapter 7). Only by bringing some of these individual differences under more strict experimental control can one hope to understand more fully how flexible cerebral organizations can be and to what extent hemispheric asymmetries are hard wired into the human species. One way to achieve this is to give subjects more directed, precuing instructions before the start of each experimental trial to determine more effectively which attentional sets are the best (or worst) for processing the information at hand.

Attentional Measures: Electrophysiological Indices.   A related brain measure to the instructional manipulations is the contingent negative variation (CNV). As described in chapter 7, the CNV is a negatively charged, event-related potential that occurs immediately prior to the expectancy of a particular stimulus. Some investigators have identified CNVs as reflective of the subjects' attentional set, because larger potentials have been observed in the left hemisphere when verbal material was anticipated, and, conversely, greater magnitude waves in the right hemisphere when nonverbal input was expected (Butler & Glass, 1974, 1976; Donchin et al., 1977). Recent research undertaken by Kesner (1990) and Woods (1990) has tended to confirm these earlier results that a physiological index for selective attention could be obtained directly, which accurately represented the degree of cognitive processing executed by a single hemisphere in anticipation of a highly specialized input.

Although the CNV effects are not always replicable (see Bradshaw & Nettleton, 1983, for a more detailed critique), this should not discourage experimenters from continuing their studies with this measure. As already mentioned, subjects vary in their attentional and cognitive capabilities, and so one cannot (and should not) expect consistent results from one design to the next. Despite its limitations, the CNV still appears to be an effective way of tapping into the internal processing mechanisms of the human species, and hopefully, if combined with more externally focused instructions, can provide the researcher with the missing link between behavioral asymmetries and physiological ones. (It would be interesting to see whether the CNV asymmetry would change from one hemisphere to the other as subjects' attentional processes switched from the left to the right body side.) Similar to the PET scan, this specific type of ERP can help us interpret more easily what the brain is really doing, especially when it expects certain stimuli within its environment. One derived outcome is that as the cortical measurement techniques become more refined, the amount of guesswork attributed to brain differences is significantly reduced, thus allowing for the study of cerebral asymmetries to become a more precise science in decades to come.

Perceptual Scanning Mechanisms.　　Although Efron (1990) did not see the benefits of continuing research along the lines of hemispheric specialization, he made some important contributions to the way subjects perceptually scan bilateralized stimuli. These effects should be noted here, because they bear some relationship to the attentional manipulations already discussed. In one experimental paradigm employed by Efron, Yund, and Nichols (1987), subjects were tachistoscopically exposed to six different visuospatial patterns that were enclosed in boxes, three of which were located at various positions in the LVF and the remaining three at locations in the RVF. After each bilateralized exposure, subjects were required to report the box number in which the target stimulus was presented.

Target and nontarget patterns were counterbalanced across each of the six possible locations to reduce any interactive effects attributed to distance between the stimuli. Results clearly showed a gender effect, with females demonstrating an RVF superiority in the detection of the targets and males exhibiting a nonsignificant trend in the same direction. Target errors increased linearly from central to more peripheral locations in the RVF, followed by sequential locations in the LVF.

The relevance of these observations to cerebral laterality is interpreted next. The Efron (1990) study seems to indicate that the left, not the right, hemisphere was more specialized to process the spatial inputs, and that, even more surprisingly, women were more lateralized in this tachistoscopic task. Of course, my attentional variation model accounts for this supposedly discrepant gender difference. The sequential increase in errors per position further suggest that subjects, especially women, intentionally were scanning the stimuli and making progressively more mistakes at each step of the serial scan. In this case, there was a greater tendency to examine the contents of the RVF much earlier than the LVF, thereby reducing the number of errors from the former body side.

As Efron (1990) concluded, operation of such a scanning mechanism "would result in a right/left performance asymmetry *without* [necessarily] involving [or invoking] any hemispheric differences in processing capacity" (pp. 63–64). Although I tend to disagree with this rather extreme position, because it does not really explain why this scan favored the right field in the first place, I present some additional investigations by the Efron team for further analysis and scrutiny.

In a follow-up set of experiments (Yund, Efron, & Nichols, 1990), it soon was discovered that the RVF detection superiority also existed for the same stimulus patterns arranged in different configurations (e.g., circular), with six of the patterns presented in a half circle within the RVF and the remaining number organized similarly in the LVF. Like the preceding study, target detections were best in both fields for certain locations, namely the topmost parts of the circles, and worst in the bottommost areas. Moreover, as the number of nontarget patterns decreased in progressive stages from 11 to 0 stimuli, detectability of the target subsequently improved in a linear fashion.

As summarized by Efron, Yund, and Nichols (1990a), there remained little doubt that a serial processing mechanism was being deployed by subjects that: (a) favored the right body side, (b) permitted a scanning of that visual information in memory before it neuronally decayed, and (c) allowed for a more effective recall of that information when fewer nontarget locations had to be perceived. Curiously, the RVF advantage eventually disappeared as the number of nontargets decreased to essentially zero stimuli, but, as the authors speculated, with fewer stimuli to be scanned, LVF detection should not be impaired as greatly because the information would have had less time to decay in that particular field.

Efron's (1990) visual scanning mechanism appropriately explained the effects obtained with multiple lateralized stimuli, and perhaps it can be modified for other experimental procedures in time (e.g., auditory scans for dichotic information). However, as imparted by Efron (1990), this perceptual mechanism really reveals

> nothing about how the scanning order is determined [i.e., from right to left], except that it is *not* completely random and that it is influenced by previous visual experience. . . . Needless to say, *no* dichotomous theory on hemispheric differences is a particularly promising candidate for a general explanation [of these results]. (p. 102)

At this point, I advance a model of my own, based on cerebral asymmetries, that could resolve satisfactorily some of these lingering (and quite disturbing) questions posed by Efron (1990).

As highlighted in chapter 3, the left hemisphere employs an analytic style of processing that breaks down stimulus configurations into their respective components. These parts then are analyzed, one at a time, in a very orderly and sequential fashion. Efron's (1990) configurations of spatial patterns were arranged in a number of sequential locations, either extending from left to right or top to bottom. Because of the recall demands on particular position locations, patterns lent themselves more amenably to an analytic style of processing than a spatially holistic one, thus accounting for the consistently strong RVF (or left-hemispheric) superiority.

As the number of patterns decreased, this modal strategy did not prove to be as effective (or efficient) as the more holistic one, which could grasp more easily the overall configuration(s) due to relatively fewer separate components to integrate together. In fact, Efron et al. (1990a) identified a statistically insignificant trend toward an LVF superiority in the one-target pattern condition, implying that a shift might have occurred from a left- to a right-hemispheric style of processing.

Although Efron (1990) did not adhere to my lateralized version of the results, I feel that he should (at the very least) reevaluate his data in light of the rather unique stimulus patterns he tachistoscopically presented to his subjects. Because of their expanding complexity as the number of locations increased, the stimuli presumably could not be correctly identified other than by a left-hemispheric cognitive style.

One final word should be mentioned about the Efron et al. (1990a) procedures. Quite recently it was found that the perceptual scan improved with repeated exposures to the same circular configurations (Efron, Yund, & Nichols, 1990b). Error analyses revealed that by the third block of trials, the subjects' search became much more efficient—not "jumping around" so much and moving systematically downward in the semicircular path portrayed in each visual field. This general improvement with practice should come as no surprise, because subjects probably had mastered the task requirements by this point and now were able to develop more effective and consistent attentional sets. In other words, attentional variability within, as well as between, subjects was reduced significantly as the number of trials increased. Although Efron (1990) emphasized the perceptual processes of the visual scanning mechanism, attentional ones should not be ruled out by any means. Maybe attentional and perceptual processes impact on each other in such lateralized procedures. This should be kept in mind when future studies are conducted around the scanning of multiple stimuli relayed through different sensory modalities.

POTENTIAL EDUCATIONAL APPLICATIONS

This chapter concludes with an examination of the possible ways in which the study of cerebral asymmetries can be integrated effectively within the educational environment. The discussion begins with a critical analysis of right-brain learning.

How Effective Is Continued Emphasis
on Right-Brain Learning?

In the late 1970s to mid-1980s, a prevailing educational view was that the school curriculum overdeveloped the left hemisphere, but did not pay too much attention to right-brain training. Regelski (1977) best summarized this thinking by stating that conventional education has more than adequately developed the left hemisphere to the detriment of the whole person. A number of books and articles published during this period focused on attempts to remedy this sorry state of educational affairs, specifically by promoting a greater range of mental exercises that deliberately stimulated right-brain learning to balance out the educational curriculum more effectively.

As referenced in chapter 3, some authors advocated highly detailed right-brain programs that involved listening to music during the presentation of lectures (Prince, 1978), looking at a variety of visuospatial mediums ranging from pictorial materials to televised programs and videos (Grady & Luecke, 1978), and drawing and creating more individually tailored projects that related the analytic information already learned (Edwards, 1979; Stanish, 1989). Still other educators noted more general techniques, such as coming up with a series of insight problems that would "unleash the right side of the brain" (Williams & Stockmyer, 1987) or forming "mind maps" in which an entire thought sequence could be represented holistically in the right brain by a complex linking of ideas together via an illustrated format (Buzan, 1983). The common denominator to all of these proposed procedures was that if the right hemisphere were stimulated properly, it would offset the traditional emphasis on the left-hemispheric 3R curriculum (Bogen, 1977).

Lately, the right-brain learning approach has been under attack by scientists and anatomists who feel that gross mistakes have been made about the nature of cerebral asymmetries. Harris (1988), among others, remarked that one of the more pervasive errors has been the tendency on the part of educators to consider highly complex, cognitive processes as if they were quite simple and under the direction of a single hemisphere. Harris (1988) went on to say that artistic and musical abilities should not be restricted to just the right brain side any more than language and related reading and writing functions should be contained solely within the complementary left brain. As repeatedly emphasized in our text, both hemispheres are involved intimately in all functions to various degrees. Therefore, it appears to be a misnomer to talk about right-brain training per se, because this side probably gets as much mental exercise as the left in the classroom environment. A movement already is underway among the scientific professions to present more accurate information about cerebral asymmetries so as not to mislead the general public, but, rather, to educate it correctly about the functions of the integrated brain, not the artificially constructed split brain of some educators' dream world.

What Are the Components
of a Holistic Brain-Based Learning Approach?

If the right-brain learning approach is abandoned, what should be substituted in its place? Caine and Caine (1989, 1990) urged that a more holistic two-brain doctrine be instituted, in which both left-analytic and right-spatial features are integrated together. Only by seeing the interactive relationship between the two hemispheres can more flexible and innovative teaching methods be developed that will be of ultimate benefit to students in the long run.

According to Caine and Caine (1991), this holistic (not lateralized) style of learning should contain the following three elements: orchestrated immersion, relaxed alertness, and active processing. The thrust of orchestrated immersion is to "take information off the page and blackboard and bring it to life in the minds of students" (p. 107). The best way to accomplish this is to integrate the curriculum by combining the content of several subject areas together. At the same time, students should be relating their own personally relevant and meaningful experiences to this expanded educational curriculum, teaching one another in the process of learning.

The second element, relaxed alertness, typifies a state of mind conducive to optimal learning that is generated in an environment of low threat, yet significant challenge. Students need to feel comfortable with themselves and confident in their own abilities if information is to be extracted successfully and internalized effectively. Finally, active processing requires students to reflect on important issues, allowing ideas to incubate and gestate until, hopefully, more critical thinking skills begin to emerge.

If holistic brain-based learning truly is taking place, then the 15 questions presented in Fig. 11.1 should be answered easily. Each inquiry is an indicator of the extent to which students: (a) are sufficiently immersed in the learning experiences (e.g., "Are life themes and metaphors being engaged?"), (b) have achieved a level of relaxed alertness (e.g., "Are there any signs of positive collaboration?"), and (c) are actively processing those experiences ("Are there opportunities to reflect in an open-ended way?"). As Caine and Caine (1991) related, "regardless of what particular model educators use, the key [to effective learning] is the adequate engagement of the *entire* brain" (p. 156). I hope that the future educational focus is

• Are students involved and challenged?
• Is there clear evidence of student creativity and enjoyment? Are students dealing appropriately with dissonance?
• Are students being exposed to content in many ways that link content to life?
• Are students' life themes and metaphors being engaged?
• Are there "hooks" that tie the content together in a big picture that itself can make sense to students?
• Is there some sort of continuity, such as through projects and ongoing stories, so that content is tied together and retains interest over time?
• Is there any sign of continuing motivation or student interest that expresses itself above and beyond the dictates of the class?
• Is the physical context being used optimally?
• What do the setting, decorations, architecture, layout, music, and other features of the context actually "say" to students?
• What sort of group atmosphere is emerging?
• Are there any signs of positive collaboration, and do they continue after the lesson and after school?
• Do students have opportunities to reorganize content in creative and personally relevant ways?
• Are there opportunities to reflect in an open-ended way on what does and does not make sense?
• Are students given the opportunity to apply the material in different contexts?
• Do students consciously and deliberately examine their performances in those different contexts and begin to appreciate their own strengths and weaknesses?

FIG. 11.1.   Checklist of useful questions to assess extent of holistic brain-based learning. If the brain is engaged fully in the learning process, then these questions should guide the evaluator in determining the degree of orchestrated immersion, relaxed alertness, and active processing on the part of students participating in such holistic programs. From *Making Connections: Teaching and the Human Brain* (p. 157) by R. Caine and G. Caine, 1991, Alexandria, VA: Association for Supervision and Curriculum Development. Copyright 1991 by R. Caine and G. Caine. Reprinted by permission.

on these integrated brain models, because they truly capture the essence of what cortical processing entails.

FUTURE OUTLOOK ON CEREBRAL ASYMMETRIES

The purpose of this chapter has been to show the reader that the future looks quite promising for cerebral asymmetries. Theoretical frameworks and models continue to be formulated to explain why lateralization of abilities evolved the way it did in the human species. Experimental techniques involving attentional manipulations and electrophysiological measures continue to be refined to determine how flexible (or hard wired) these asymmetries are. One factor that will guide the direction and focus of the asymmetrical research into the next century and beyond will be its continued application to educational settings and other learning environments.

The terminology and language pertaining to cerebral asymmetries will change with the cultural emphasis. For now, the distinction between left- and right-brain processing is an important one to make in Western society. But this may not always be the case. In time, scientists and other professional groups will consider the practicality of discussing more integrated (as opposed to lateralized) brain approaches. The public tide already is slowly turning in this direction.

However, one constant remains, regardless of the conceptualization that is adopted: namely, that the brain hemispheres are not mirror images of each other, structurally or functionally speaking. This point should be kept in mind when reaching any conclusion concerning cerebral asymmetries, both now and in future decades.

References

Aaron, P. G. (1978). Dyslexia, an imbalance in cerebral information-processing strategies. *Perceptual and Motor Skills, 47,* 699–706.

Adelson, J. (1985). What we don't know about sex differences. *New Perspectives, 17,* 9–14.

af Klinteberg, B., Levander, S., & Schalling, D. (1987). Cognitive sex differences: Speed and problem-solving strategies in computerized neuropsychological tasks. *Perceptual and Motor Skills, 65,* 683–697.

Ahern, G. L., & Schwartz, G. E. (1979). Differential lateralization for positive versus negative emotions. *Neuropsychologia, 17,* 693–697.

Alajouanine, T. (1948). Aphasia and artistic realization. *Brain, 71,* 229–241.

Albert, M. L., & Friedman, R. B. (1985). Alexia. In K. M. Heilman & E. Valenstein (Eds.), *Clinical neuropsychology* (pp. 49–73). New York: Oxford Press.

Albert, M. L., Sparks, R. W., & Helm, N. A. (1973). Melodic intonation therapy for aphasia. *Archives of Neurology, 29,* 130–131.

Allen, L. S., & Gorski, R. A. (1992, August). Anatomical differences in homosexual brains. *Proceedings of the National Academy of Sciences.*

Allen, L. S., Hines, M., Shryne, J. E., & Gorski, R. A. (1989). Two sexually dimorphic cell groups in the human brain. *Journal of Neuroscience, 9,* 497–506.

Anand, B., Chhina, G., & Singh, B. (1972). Some aspects of electroencephalographic studies in Yogis. In C. T. Tart (Ed.), *Altered states of consciousness* (pp. 515–518). New York: Doubleday.

Anderson, R. H., Fleming, D. E., Rhees, R. W., & Kinghorn, E. (1986). Relationships between sexual activity, plasma testosterone, and the volume of the sexually dimorphic nucleus of the preoptic area in prenatally stressed and nonstressed rats. *Brain Research, 370,* 1–10.

Andrews, G., Quinn, P. T., & Sorby, W. A. (1972). Stuttering: An investigation into cerebral dominance for speech. *Journal of Neurology, Neurosurgery, and Psychiatry, 35,* 414–418.

Annett, M. (1964). A model of the inheritance of handedness and cerebral dominance. *Nature, 204,* 59–60.

Annett, M. (1967). The binomial distribution of right-, mixed-, and left-handedness. *Quarterly Journal of Experimental Psychology, 29,* 327–333.

Annett, M. (1972). The distribution of manual asymmetry. *British Journal of Psychology, 63,* 343–358.

Annett, M. (1973). Handedness in families. *Annals of Human Genetics, 37,* 93–105.

Annett, M. (1978). Throwing loaded and unloaded dice. *Behavioral and Brain Sciences, 2,* 278–279.

Annett, M. (1983). Hand preference and skill in 115 children of two left-handed parents. *British Journal of Psychology, 74,* 17–32.

Annett, M., Hudson, P. T. W., & Turner, A. (1974). Effects of right and left unilateral ECT on naming and visual discrimination analyzed in relation to handedness. *British Journal of Psychiatry, 124,* 260–264.

Aram, D. M., & Whitaker, H. A. (1988). Cognitive sequelae of unilateral lesions acquired in early childhood. In D. L. Molfese & S. J. Segalowitz (Eds.), *Brain lateralization in children: Developmental implications* (pp. 417–436). New York: Guilford.

Arndt, S., & Berger, D. F. (1978). Cognitive mode and asymmetry in cerebral functioning. *Cortex, 14,* 78–86.

Ashbrook, J. B. (1988). *The brain and belief.* Bristol, IN: Wyndham Hall.

Ashton, G. S. (1982). Handedness: An alternative hypothesis. *Behavior Genetics, 12,* 125–148.

Asperger, H. (1979). Problems of infantile autism. *Communication, 13,* 45–52.

Ausburn, L. J., & Ausburn, F. (1978). Cognitive styles: Some information and implications for instructional design. *Educational Communication and Technology, 26,* 337–354.

Badian, N. A. (1983a). Birth order, maternal age, season of birth, and handedness. *Cortex, 19,* 451–463.

Badian, N. A. (1983b). Dyscalculia and nonverbal disorders of learning. In H. R. Mykelbust (Ed.), *Progress in learning disabilities* (Vol. 3, pp. 235–264). New York: Grune & Stratton.

Bailey, N., Madden, C., & Krashen, S. (1974). Is there a "natural sequence" in adult second language learning? *Language Learning, 24,* 235–243.

Bakan, P. (1969). Hypnotizability, laterality of eye movement, and functional brain asymmetry. *Perceptual and Motor Skills, 28,* 927–932.

Bakan, P. (1973). Left-handedness and alcoholism. *Perceptual and Motor Skills, 36,* 514.

Bakan, P. (1975). Are left-handers brain damaged? *New Scientist, 67,* 200–202.

Bakan, P. (1987). Effect of maternal cigarette smoking on offspring handedness. *Canadian Psychology, 28,* 2A. (Abstract No. 18)

Bakan, P., Dibb, G., & Reed, P. (1973). Handedness and birth stress. *Neuropsychologia, 11,* 363–366.

Bakker, D. J. (1973). Hemispheric specialization and stages in the learning-to-read process. *Bulletin of the Orton Society, 23,* 15–27.

Bakker, D. J., Hoefkens, M., & Van der Vlugt, H. (1979). Hemispheric specialization in children as reflected in the longitudinal development of ear asymmetry. *Cortex, 15,* 619–625.

Bakker, D. J., Smink, T., & Reitsma, P. (1973). Ear dominance and reading ability. *Cortex, 9,* 301–312.

Bakwin, H. (1973). Reading disability in twins. *Developmental Medicine and Child Neurology, 15,* 184–187.

Baron, I. S. (1987, February). *The childhood presentation of social-emotional learning disabilities on the continuum of Asperger's syndrome.* Paper presented at the 15th annual International Neuropsychological Society meeting, Washington, DC.

Barsley, M. (1979). *Left-handed people.* North Hollywood, CA: Wilshire.

Barton, M. I., Goodglass, H., & Shai, A. (1965). Differential recognition of tachistoscopically presented English and Hebrew words in right and left visual fields. *Perceptual and Motor Skills, 21*, 431–437.

Basser, L. S. (1962). Hemiplegia of early onset and the faculty of speech with special reference to the effects of hemispherectomy. *Brain, 85*, 427–460.

Bean, N. J., & Conner, R. (1978). Central hormonal replacement and home-cage dominance in castrated rats. *Hormones and Behavior, 11*, 100–109.

Bear, D. M., & Fedio, P. (1977). Quantitative analysis of intertictal behavior in temporal lobe epilepsy. *Archives of Neurology, 34*, 451–467.

Beaumont, J. G. (1982). Developmental aspects. In J. G. Beaumont (Ed.), *Divided visual field studies of cerebral organisation* (pp. 113–128). London: Academic Press.

Beaumont, J. G., & Dimond, S. (1972). Brain disconnection and schizophrenia. *British Journal of Psychiatry, 123*, 661–662.

Beck, C. H. M., & Barton, R. L. (1972). Deviation and laterality of hand preference in monkeys. *Cortex, 8*, 339–363.

Bell, A. D., & Variend, S. (1985). Failure to demonstrate sexual dimorphism of the corpus callosum in childhood. *Journal of Anatomy, 143*, 143–147.

Bell, A. D., Weinberg, M. S., & Hammersmith, S. K. (1981). *Sexual preferences: Its development in men and women.* Bloomington: Indiana University Press.

Benbow, C. P. (1988). Sex differences in mathematical reasoning ability in intellectually talented preadolescents: Their nature, effects and possible causes. *Behavioral and Brain Sciences, 11*, 169–232.

Benbow, C. P., & Stanley, J. C. (1980). Sex differences in mathematical ability: Fact or artifact? *Science, 210*, 1262–1264.

Benbow, C. P., & Stanley, J. C. (1983). Sex differences in mathematical reasoning ability: More facts. *Science, 222*, 1029–1031.

Benderly, B. L. (1987). *The myth of two minds: What gender means and doesn't mean.* New York: Doubleday.

Benton, A. L. (1975). Developmental dyslexia: Neurological aspects. In W. J. Friedlander (Ed.), *Advances in neurology: Vol. 7. Current reviews of higher nervous system dysfunction.* New York: Raven Press.

Benton, A. L. (1977). The amusias. In M. Critchley & R. A. Henson (Eds.), *Music and the brain.* London: Heinemann.

Benton, A. L. (1980). The neuropsychology of facial recognition. *American Psychologist, 35*, 176–186.

Benton, A. L. (1985). Visuoperceptive, visuospatial and visuoconstructive disorders. In K. M. Heilman & E. Valenstein (Eds.), *Clinical neuropsychology* (pp. 151–185). Oxford: Oxford University Press.

Benton, A. L., & Hecaen, H. (1970). Stereoscopic vision in patients with unilateral cerebral disease. *Neurology, 20*, 1084–1088.

Benton, A. L., & Joynt, R. J. (1960). Early descriptions of aphasia. *Archives of Neurology, 3*, 205–222.

Bergson, H. (1965). *Duration and simultaneity.* New York: Bobbs-Merrill.

Berlin, C. I. (1977). Hemispheric asymmetry in auditory tasks. In S. Harnad, R. W. Doty, L. Goldstein, J. Jaynes, & G. Krauthamer (Eds.), *Lateralization in the nervous system* (pp. 303–323). New York: Academic.

Berlin, C. I., Hughes, L. F., Lowe-Bell, S. S., & Berlin, H. L. (1973). Dichotic right ear advantage in children 5 to 13. *Cortex, 9*, 394–402.

Berlucchi, G., Brizzolara, D., Marzi, C. A., Rizzolatti, G., & Umilta, C. (1974). Can lateral asymmetries in attention explain interfield differences in visual perception? *Cortex, 10*, 177–185.

Berlucchi, G., Marzi, C. A., Rizzolatti, G., & Umilta, C. (1976). *Functional hemispheric asymmetries in normals: Influence of sex and practice.* Paper presented at the 21st annual meeting of the International Congress of Psychology, Paris.

Bermant, G., & Davidson, J. M. (1974). *Biological bases of sexual behavior.* New York: Harper & Row.

Best, C. T. (1988). The emergence of cerebral asymmetries in early human development: A literature review and a neuroembryological model. In D. L. Molfese & S. J. Segalowitz (Eds.), *Brain lateralization in children: Developmental implications* (pp. 5–34). New York: Guilford.

Best, C. T., Hoffman, H., & Glanville, B. B. (1982). Development of infant ear asymmetries for speech and music. *Perception and Psychophysics, 31,* 75–85.

Bever, T. G. (1980). Broca and Lashley were right: Cerebral dominance is an accident of growth. In D. Caplan (Ed.), *Biological studies of mental processes.* Cambridge, MA: MIT Press.

Bever, T. G., & Chiarello, R. J. (1974). Cerebral dominance in musicians and nonmusicians. *Science, 185,* 137–139.

Bever, T. G., Hurtig, R. R., & Handel, A. B. (1976). Analytic processing elicits right ear superiority in monaurally presented speech. *Neuropsychologia, 14,* 175–181.

Bishop, D. V. M. (1983). Linguistic impairment after left hemidecortication for infantile hemiplegia? A reappraisal. *Quarterly Journal of Experimental Psychology, 35,* 199–207.

Bishop, D. V. M. (1987). How sinister is sinistrality? In N. Geschwind & A. M. Galaburda (Eds.), *Cerebral lateralization: Biological mechanisms, associations and pathology* (pp. 85–86). Cambridge, MA: MIT Press.

Bissell, J. C., & Clark, F. (1984). Dichotic listening performance in normal children and adults. *American Journal of Occupational Therapy, 38,* 176–183.

Blau, T. H. (1977). Torque and schizophrenic vulnerability. As the world turns. *American Psychologist, 32,* 997–1005.

Blaustein, J. D., & Olster, D. H. (1989). Gonadal steroid hormone receptors and social behaviors. In J. Balthazart (Ed.), *Advances in comparative and environmental physiology* (Vol. 3). Berlin: Springer-Verlag.

Bloch, G. J., & Gorski, R. A. (1988). Cytoarchitectonic analysis of the SDN-POA of the intact and gonadectomized rat. *Journal of Comparative Neurology, 275,* 604–612.

Blumstein, S., & Cooper, W. E. (1974). Hemispheric processing of intonation contours. *Cortex, 10,* 146–158.

Bock, R., & Kolakowski, D. (1973). Further evidence of sex-linked major gene influence on human spatial visualizing ability. *American Journal of Human Genetics, 25,* 1–14.

Bogen, J. E. (1969). The other side of the brain, I, II, III. *Bulletin of the Los Angeles Neurological Societies, 34,* No. 3.

Bogen, J. E. (1975). Some educational aspects of hemispheric specialization. *UCLA Educator, 17,* 24–32.

Bogen, J. E. (1977). Some educational implications of hemispheric specialization. In M. C. Wittrock (Ed.), *The human brain.* Englewood Cliffs, NJ: Prentice-Hall.

Bogen, J. E. (1985). The callosal syndrome. In K. M. Heilman & E. Valenstein (Eds.), *Clinical neuropsychology* (pp. 295–338). Oxford: Oxford University Press.

Bogen, J. E., DeZare, R., TenHouten, W. D., & Marsh, J. F. (1972). The other side of the brain. IV: The A/P ratio. *Bulletin of the Los Angeles Neurological Societies, 37,* 49–61.

Bogen, J. E., & Gordon, H. W. (1971). Musical tests of functional lateralization with intracarotid amobarbital. *Nature, 230,* 524–525.

Bolter, J. F., & Hannon, R. (1986). Lateralized cerebral dysfunction in early- and late-stage alcoholics. *Journal of Studies on Alcohol, 47,* 213–218.

Borod, J. C., & Caron, H. S. (1980). Facedness and emotion related to lateral dominance, sex and expression type. *Neuropsychologia, 18,* 237–241.

Borod, J. C., Koff, E., & White, B. (1983). Facial asymmetry in posed and spontaneous expressions of emotion. *Brain and Cognition, 2,* 165–175.

Boucher, J. (1977). Hand preference in autistic children and their parents. *Journal of Autism and Childhood Schizophrenia, 7,* 177–187.

Bowers, D., Heilman, K. M., Satz, P., & Altman, A. (1978). Simultaneous performance on verbal, nonverbal and motor tasks by right-handed adults. *Cortex, 14,* 540–556.

Bracha, H. S., Seitz, D. J., Otemaa, J., & Glick, S. D. (1987). Rotational movement (circling) in normal humans: Sex difference and relationship to hand, foot and eye preference. *Brain Research, 411,* 231–235.

Bradshaw, J. L., Bradley, D., & Patterson, K. (1976). The perception and identification of mirror-reversed patterns. *Quarterly Journal of Experimental Psychology, 28,* 667–681.

Bradshaw, J. L., & Bradshaw, J. A. (1988). Reading mirror-reversed text: Sinistrals really are inferior. *Brain and Language, 33,* 189–192.

Bradshaw, J. L., Farrelly, J., & Taylor, M. J. (1981). Synonym and antonym pairs in the detection of dichotically and monaurally presented targets: Competing monaural stimulation can generate a REA. *Acta Psychologica, 47,* 189–205.

Bradshaw, J. L., & Gates, E. A. (1978). Visual field differences in verbal tasks: Effects of task familiarity and sex of subject. *Brain and Language, 5,* 166–187.

Bradshaw, J. L., & Nettleton, N. C. (1983). *Human cerebral asymmetry.* Englewood Cliffs, NJ: Prentice-Hall.

Bradshaw, J. L., Nettleton, N. C., & Taylor, M. J. (1981). The use of laterally presented words in research into cerebral asymmetry: Is directional scanning likely to be a source of artifact? *Brain and Language, 14,* 1–14.

Bradshaw, J. L., & Sherlock, D. (1982). Bugs and faces in the two visual fields: Task order, difficulty, practice, and the analytic/holistic dichotomy. *Cortex, 18,* 211–225.

Bradshaw, J. L., & Taylor, M. (1979). A word naming deficit in nonfamilial sinistrals? Laterality effects of vocal responses to tachistoscopically presented letter strings. *Neuropsychologia, 17,* 21–32.

Bradshaw, J. L., Taylor, M. J., Patterson, K., & Nettleton, N. C. (1980). Upright and inverted faces, and housefronts, in the two visual fields: A right and left hemisphere contribution. *Journal of Clinical Neuropsychology, 2,* 245–257.

Brady, J. P., & Berson, J. (1975). Stuttering, dichotic listening and cerebral dominance. *Archives of General Psychiatry, 32,* 1449–1452.

Braine, L. G. (1968). Asymmetries of pattern perception observed in Israelis. *Neuropsychologia, 6,* 73–88.

Briggs, G. G., & Nebes, R. D. (1976). The effects of handedness, family history and sex on the performance of a dichotic listening task. *Neuropsychologia, 14,* 129–134.

Brizzolara, D., DeNobili, G. L., & Ferretti, G. (1982). Tactile discrimination of direction of lines in relation to hemispheric specialization. *Perceptual and Motor Skills, 54,* 655–660.

Broman, M. (1978). Reaction-time differences between the left and right hemispheres for face and letter discrimination in children and adults. *Cortex, 14,* 578–591.

Brooks, L. R. (1973). *Treating verbal stimuli in a novel manner.* Paper presented at the Eastern Psychological Association meeting, Washington, DC.

Brust, J. C. M. (1980). Music and language: Musical alexia and agraphia. *Brain, 103,* 367–392.

Bryden, M. P. (1963). Ear preference in auditory perception. *Journal of Experimental Psychology, 65,* 103–105.

Bryden, M. P. (1965). Tachistoscopic recognition, handedness and cerebral dominance. *Neuropsychologia, 3,* 1–8.

Bryden, M. P. (1966). Accuracy and order of report in tachistoscopic recognition. *Canadian Journal of Psychology, 20,* 262–272.

Bryden, M. P. (1970). Laterality effects in dichotic listening: Relations with handedness and reading ability in children. *Neuropsychologia, 8,* 443–450.

Bryden, M. P. (1973). Perceptual asymmetry in vision: Relation to handedness, eyedness and speech lateralization. *Cortex, 9,* 419–435.

Bryden, M. P. (1976). Response bias and hemispheric differences in dot localization. *Perception and Psychophysics, 19,* 23–28.

Bryden, M. P. (1978). Strategy effects in the assessment of hemispheric asymmetry. In G. Underwood (Ed.), *Strategies of information processing* (pp. 117–149). London: Academic Press.

Bryden, M. P. (1979). Evidence for sex-related differences in cerebral organization. In M. A. Whittig & A. Peterson (Eds.), *Sex-related differences in cognitive functioning* (pp. 121–143). New York: Academic Press.

Bryden, M. P. (1980). Sex differences in brain organization: Different brains or different strategies? *Behavioral and Brain Sciences, 3,* 230–231.

Bryden, M. P. (1982). *Laterality: Functional asymmetry in the intact brain.* New York: Academic Press.

Bryden, M. P. (1986). Dichotic listening performance, cognitive ability and cerebral organization. *Canadian Journal of Psychology, 40,* 445–456.

Bryden, M. P., & Allard, F. A. (1978). Dichotic listening and the development of linguistic processes. In M. Kinsbourne (Ed.), *Asymmetrical function of the brain* (pp. 392–404). New York: Cambridge University Press.

Bryden, M. P., & Allard, F. A. (1981). Do auditory perceptual asymmetries develop? *Cortex, 17,* 313–318.

Bryden, M. P., Munhall, K., & Allard, F. A. (1983). Attentional biases and the right-ear effect in dichotic listening. *Brain and Language, 18,* 236–248.

Buffery, A. W., & Gray, J. A. (1972). Sex differences in the development of spatial and linguistic skills. In C. Ounsted & D. C. Taylor (Eds.), *Gender differences: Their ontogeny and significance* (pp. 123–157). Edinburgh: Churchill Livingstone.

Burnett, S. A., Lane, D. M., & Dratt, L. M. (1982). Spatial ability and handedness. *Intelligence, 6,* 57–58.

Burstein, B., Bank, L., & Jarvik, L. F. (1980). Sex differences in cognitive functioning: Evidence, determinants, implications. *Human Development, 23,* 289–313.

Burt, C. (1937). *The backward child.* London: London University Press.

Buschbaum, M., & Fedio, P. (1970). Hemispheric differences in evoked potentials to verbal and nonverbal stimuli on the left and right visual fields. *Physiology and Behavior, 5,* 207–210.

Butler, D. K., & Miller, L. K. (1979). Role of approximation to English and letter array length in the development of visual laterality. *Developmental Psychology, 15,* 522–529.

Butler, S. (1984). Sex differences in human cerebral function. In G. J. De Vries, J. De Bruin, H. Uylings, & M. Cormer (Eds.), *Progress in brain research* (Vol. 61). Amsterdam: Elsevier.

Butler, S., & Glass, A. (1974). Asymmetries in the CNV over left and right hemispheres while subjects await numeric information. *Biological Psychology, 2,* 1–16.

Butler, S., & Glass, A. (1976). EEG correlates of cerebral dominance. In A. H. Riesen & R. F. Thompson (Eds.), *Advances in psychobiology* (Vol. 3). New York: Wiley.

Buzan, T. (1983). *Use both sides of your brain.* New York: E. P. Dutton.

Cain, D. P., & Wada, J. A. (1979). An anatomical asymmetry in the baboon brain. *Brain, Behavior and Evolution, 16,* 222–226.

Caine, G., & Caine, R. N. (1989). Learning about accelerated learning. *Training and Development Journal, 43,* 65–73.

Caine, R. N., & Caine, G. (1990). Understanding a brain-based approach to learning and teaching. *Educational Leadership, 48,* 66–70.

Caine, R. N., & Caine, G. (1991). *Making connections: Teaching and the human brain.* Alexandria, VA: Association for Supervision and Curriculum Development.

Campbell, R. (1978). Asymmetries in interpreting and expressing a posed facial expression. *Cortex, 14,* 327–342.

Caplan, P., & Kinsbourne, M. (1976). Baby drops the rattle: Asymmetry of duration of grasp by infants. *Child Development, 47,* 532–534.

Carey, S., & Diamond, R. (1980). Maturational determination of the developmental course of face encoding. In D. Caplan (Ed.), *Biological studies of mental processes.* Cambridge, MA: MIT Press.

Carey, S., Diamond, R., & Woods, B. (1980). Development of face recognition—a maturational component? *Developmental Psychology, 16,* 257–269.

Carlson, N. R. (1991). *Physiology of behavior.* Boston: Allyn & Bacon.

Carmon, A. (1978). Spatial and temporal factors in visual perception of patients with unilateral cerebral lesions. In M. Kinsbourne (Ed.), *Asymmetrical function of the brain* (pp. 86–98). Cambridge, England: Cambridge University Press.

Carmon, A., & Gombos, G. M. (1970). A physiological vascular correlate of hand preference: Possible implications with respect to hemispheric cerebral dominance. *Neuropsychologia, 8,* 119–128.

Carmon, A., Gordon, H. W., Bental, E., & Harnes, B. Z. (1977). Retraining in literal alexia: Substitution of a right hemisphere perceptual strategy for impaired left hemisphere processing. *Bulletin of the Los Angeles Neurological Societies, 42,* 41–50.

Carmon, A., Harishanu, Y., Lowinger, E., & Lavy, S. (1972). Asymmetries in hemispheric blood volume and cerebral dominance. *Behavioral Biology, 7,* 853–859.

Carmon, A., & Nachshon, I. (1971). Effect of unilateral brain damage on the perception of temporal order. *Cortex, 7,* 410–418.

Carmon, A., & Nachshon, I. (1973). Ear asymmetry in perception of emotional nonverbal stimuli. *Acta Psychologica, 37,* 351–357.

Carmon, A., Nachshon, I., & Starinsky, R. (1976). Developmental aspects of visual hemifield differences in perception of verbal materials. *Brain and Language, 3,* 463–469.

Carr, B. M. (1969). Ear effect variables and order of report in dichotic listening. *Cortex, 5,* 63–68.

Carter-Saltzman, L. (1979). Patterns of cognitive functioning in relation to handedness and sex-related differences. In M. A. Whittig & A. C. Petersen (Eds.), *Sex-related differences in cognitive functioning.* New York: Academic Press.

Chi, J. G., Dooling, E. C., & Gilles, F. H. (1977). Left–right asymmetries of the temporal speech areas of the human fetus. *Archives of Neurology, 34,* 346–348.

Chiarello, C. (1980). A house divided? Cognitive functioning with callosal agenesis. *Brain and Language, 11,* 128–158.

Chui, H. C., & Damasio, A. R. (1980). Human cerebral asymmetries evaluated by computed tomography. *Journal of Neurology, Neurosurgery, and Psychiatry, 43,* 873–878.

Claridge, G. S. (1985). *Origins of mental illness: Temperament, deviance, and disorder.* New York: Basil Blackwell.

Clarke, S., Kraftsik, R., Innocenti, G. M., & van der Loos, H. (1986). Sexual dimorphism and development of the human corpus callosum. *Neuroscience Letters, 26,* S299. (Abstract)

Clementz, B. A., & Sweeney, J. A. (1990). Is eye movement dysfunction a biological marker for schizophrenia? A methodological review. *Psychological Bulletin, 108,* 77–92.

Cohen, G. (1972). Hemispheric differences in a letter classification task. *Perception and Psychophysics, 11,* 139–142.

Cohen, G. (1973). Hemispheric differences in serial versus parallel processing. *Journal of Experimental Psychology, 97,* 349–356.

Cohen, G. (1975). Hemispheric differences in the utilization of advance information. In P. M. A. Rabbitt & S. Dornic (Eds.), *Attention and performance* (Vol. 5). New York: Academic Press.

Collins, R. L. (1968). On the inheritance of handedness. I: Laterality in inbred mice. *Journal of Heredity*, *59*, 9–12.

Collins, R. L. (1969). On the inheritance of handedness. II: Selection for sinistrality in mice. *Journal of Heredity*, *60*, 117–119.

Collins, R. L. (1970). The sound of one paw clapping: An inquiry into the origins of left-handedness. In G. Lindzey & D. D. Thiessen (Eds.), *Contributions to behavior–genetic analysis—The mouse as a prototype*. New York: Meredith Corporation.

Collins, R. L. (1977). Toward an admissable genetic model for the inheritance of the degree and direction of asymmetry. In S. Harnard, R. W. Doty, L. Goldstein, J. Jaynes, & G. Krauthamer (Eds.), *Lateralization in the nervous system* (pp. 137–150). New York: Academic Press.

Coltheart, M. (1979). Mysteries of reading in brain defects. *New Scientist*, *8*, 368–370.

Coltheart, M. (1980a). Deep dyslexia: A right-hemisphere hypothesis. In M. Coltheart, K. Patterson, & J. C. Marshall (Eds.), *Deep dyslexia*. London: Routledge & Kegan Paul.

Coltheart, M. (1980b). Reading, phonological recoding and deep dyslexia. In M. Coltheart, K. Patterson, & J. C. Marshall (Eds.), *Deep dyslexia*. London: Routledge & Kegan Paul.

Conner, R. L., & Levine, S. (1969). Hormonal influences on aggressive behavior. In S. Garattini & E. B. Sigg (Eds.), *Aggressive behavior*. New York: Wiley.

Cook, N. D. (1984a). Callosal inhibition: The key to the brain code. *Behavioral Science*, *29*, 98–110.

Cook, N. D. (1984b). The transmission of information in natural systems. *Journal of Theoretical Biology*, *108*, 349–367.

Corballis, M. (1980). Is left-handedness genetically determined? In J. Herron (Ed.), *Neuropsychology of left-handedness* (pp. 159–176). New York: Academic Press.

Corballis, M. (1983). *Human laterality*. New York: Academic Press.

Corballis, M. (1989). Laterality and human evolution. *Psychological Review*, *96*, 492–505.

Corballis, M., & Beale, I. L. (1976). *The psychology of left and right*. Hillsdale, NJ: Lawrence Erlbaum Associates.

Corballis, M., & Beale, I. L. (1983). *The ambivalent mind: The neuropsychology of left and right*. Chicago: Nelson-Hall.

Corballis, M., Macadie, L., Crotty, A., & Beale, I. L. (1985). The naming of disoriented letters by normal and reading-disabled children. *Journal of Child Psychology and Psychiatry*, *26*, 929–938.

Corballis, M., & Morgan, M. J. (1978). On the biological basis of human laterality. I: Evidence for a maturational left-right gradient. *Behavioral and Brain Sciences*, *2*, 261–336.

Corballis, M., & Sergent, J. (1988). Imagery in a commissurotomized patient. *Neuropsychologia*, *26*, 13–26.

Coren, S. (1989a). Left-handedness and accident-related injury risk. *American Journal of Public Health*, *79*, 1–2.

Coren, S. (1989b). Southpaws—somewhat scrawnier. *Journal of the American Medical Association*, *262*, 2682–2683.

Coren, S., & Halpern, D. F. (1991). Left-handedness: A marker for decreased survival fitness. *Psychological Bulletin*, *109*, 90–106.

Coren, S., & Porac, C. (1977). Fifty centuries of right handedness: The historical record. *Science*, *198*, 631–632.

Coren, S., & Porac, C. (1980). Family patterns in four dimensions of lateral preference. *Behavior Genetics*, *10*, 333–348.

Coren, S., & Porac, C. (1981). *Lateral preferences and human behavior*. New York: Springer-Verlag.

Coren, S., & Searleman, A. (1985). Birth stress and self-reported sleep difficulty. *Sleep, 8,* 222–226.

Coren, S., & Searleman, A. (1987). Left-sidedness and sleep difficulty: The alinormal syndrome. *Brain and Cognition, 6,* 184–192.

Coren, S., Searleman, A., & Porac, C. (1982). The effects of specific birth stressors on four indices of lateral preference. *Canadian Journal of Psychology, 36,* 478–487.

Coren, S., Searleman, A., & Porac, C. (1986). Rate of physical maturation and handedness. *Developmental Neuropsychology, 2,* 17–23.

Critchley, M. (1970). *Aphasiology and other aspects of language.* London: Edward Arnold.

Cummings, J. L., Benson, D. F., Walsh, M. J., & Levine, H. L. (1979). Left-to-right transfer of language dominance: A case study. *Neurology, 29,* 1547–1550.

Curry, F. K. W. (1967). A comparison of left-handed and right-handed subjects on verbal and nonverbal dichotic listening tasks. *Cortex, 3,* 343–352.

Curtiss, S., Fromkin, V., Rigler, D., Rigler, M., & Krashen, S. (1975). An update on the linguistic development of Genie. In D. P. Dato (Ed.), *Developmental psycholinguistics: Theory and applications.* Washington, DC: Georgetown University Press.

Cutting, J. E. (1974). Two left-hemisphere mechanisms in speech perception. *Perception and Psychophysics, 16,* 601–612.

Dabbs, J. (1980). Left–right differences in cerebral blood flow and cognition. *Psychophysiology, 17,* 548–551.

Damasio, A. (1983). Language and the basal ganglia. *Trends in Neurosciences, 6,* 442–444.

Dart, R. A. (1949). The predatory implementary techniques of Australopithecus. *American Journal of Physical Anthropology, 7,* 1–38.

Davidoff, J. B. (1977). Hemispheric differences in dot detection. *Cortex, 13,* 434–444.

Davidoff, J. B., Benton, A. A., Done, D. J., & Booth, H. (1982). Information extraction from brief visual displays: Half-field and serial position effects for children, normal and illiterate adults. *British Journal of Psychology, 73,* 29–39.

Davidoff, J. B., & Done, D. J. (1984). A longitudinal study of the development of visual field advantage for letter matching. *Neuropsychologia, 22,* 311–318.

Davidson, R. J., Chapman, J. P., & Chapman, L. J. (1987). Task-dependent EEG asymmetry discriminates between depressed and nondepressed subjects. *Psychophysiology, 24,* 585.

Davidson, R. J., & Fox, N. A. (1982). Asymmetrical brain activity discriminates between positive versus negative affective stimuli in human infants. *Science, 218,* 1235–1237.

Davidson, R. J., & Fox, N. A. (1988a). Cerebral asymmetry and emotion: Developmental and individual differences. In D. L. Molfese & S. L. Segalowitz (Eds.), *Brain lateralization in children: Developmental implications* (pp. 191–206). New York: Guilford Press.

Davidson, R. J., & Fox, N. A. (1988b). *Frontal brain asymmetry predicts infants' response to maternal separation.* Paper submitted for publication.

Davidson, R. J., & Schwartz, G. E. (1976). Patterns of cerebral lateralization during cardiac feedback versus the self-regulation of emotion: Sex differences. *Psychophysiology, 13,* 62–68.

Davidson, R. J., Schwartz, G. E., Saron, C., Bennett, J., & Galeman, D. J. (1979). Frontal versus parietal EEG asymmetry during positive and negative affect. *Psychophysiology, 16,* 202–203.

Davidson, R. J., Shaffer, C. E., & Saron, C. (1985). Effects of lateralized presentations of faces on self-reports of emotion and EEG asymmetry in depressed and nondepressed subjects. *Psychophysiology, 22,* 353–364.

Davis, A. E., & Wada, J. A. (1977a). Hemispheric asymmetries in human infants: Spectral analysis of flash- and click-evoked potentials. *Brain and Language, 4,* 23–31.

Davis, A. E., & Wada, J. A. (1977b). Hemispheric asymmetries of visual and auditory information processing. *Neuropsychologia, 15,* 799–806.

Dawson, G., Warrenburg, S., & Fuller, P. (1982). Cerebral lateralization in individuals diagnosed as autistic in early childhood. *Brain and Language, 15,* 353–368.

Day, M. E. (1964). An eye movement phenomenon relating to attention, thought, and anxiety. *Perceptual and Motor Skills, 19,* 443–446.

Dee, H. L. (1971). Auditory asymmetry and strength of manual preference. *Cortex, 7,* 236–245.

Deikman, A. (1972). Deautomatization and the mystical experience. In C. T. Tart (Ed.), *Altered states of consciousness* (pp. 25–46). New York: Doubleday.

DeKaban, A. S. (1978). Changes in brain weights during the span of human life: Relation of brain weights to body heights and body weights. *Annals of Neurology, 4,* 345–356.

de Lacoste, M. C., Holloway, R. L., & Woodward, D. J. (1986). Sex differences in the fetal human corpus callosum. *Human Neurobiology, 5,* 93–96.

Delis, D. C., Robertson, L. C., & Efron, R. (1986). Hemispheric specialization of memory for visual hierarchical stimuli. *Neuropsychologia, 24,* 205–214.

Demarest, J., & Demarest, L. (1980). Auditory asymmetry and strength of manual preference reexamined. *International Journal of Neuroscience, 11,* 121–124.

Denckla, M. B. (1978). Minimal brain dysfunction. In J. S. Chall & A. F. Mirsky (Eds.), *Education and the brain* (pp. 223–268). Chicago: University of Chicago Press.

Denckla, M. B., Rudel, R. G., & Broman, M. (1980). The development of a spatial orientation skill in normal, learning-disabled, and neurologically impaired children. In D. Caplan (Ed.), *Biological studies of mental processes.* Cambridge, MA: MIT Press.

Denenberg, V. H. (1981). Hemispheric laterality in animals and the effects of early experience. *Behavioral and Brain Sciences, 4,* 1–49.

Denenberg, V. H., Garbanati, J., Sherman, G., Yutzey, D. A., & Kaplan, G. (1978). Infantile stimulation induces brain lateralization in rats. *Science, 201,* 1150–1152.

Denes, G., & Spinaci, M. P. (1981). Influence of association value in recognition of random shapes under dichaptic presentation. *Cortex, 17,* 597–602.

Dennis, M. (1980a). Capacity and strategy for syntactic comprehension after left or right hemidecortication. *Brain and Language, 10,* 287–317.

Dennis, M. (1980b). Language acquisition in a single hemisphere: Semantic organization. In D. Caplan (Ed.), *Biological studies of mental processes.* Cambridge, MA: MIT Press.

Dennis, M., & Whitaker, H. A. (1977). Hemispheric equipotentiality and language acquisition. In S. J. Segalowitz & F. A. Gruber (Eds.), *Language development and neurological theory* (pp. 93–106). New York: Academic Press.

Deutsch, G., Bourbon, W. T., Papanicolaou, A. C., & Eisenberg, H. M. (1988). Visuospatial tasks compared via activation of regional cerebral blood flow. *Neuropsychologia, 26,* 445–452.

Deutsch, G., Papanicolaou, A. C., Bourbon, W. T., & Eisenberg, H. M. (1987). Cerebral blood flow evidence of right frontal activation in attention-demanding tasks. *International Journal of Neuroscience, 36,* 23–28.

Deutsch, G., Tweedy, J., & Lorinstein, B. (1980). *Some temporal and spatial factors affecting visual neglect.* Paper presented at the 8th Annual Meeting of the International Neurological Society, San Francisco, CA.

Dewson, J. H. (1977). Preliminary evidence of hemispheric asymmetry of auditory function in monkeys. In S. Harnad, R. W. Doty, L. Goldstein, J. Jaynes, & G. Krauthamer (Eds.), *Lateralization in the nervous system* (pp. 63–71). New York: Academic Press.

Dewson, J. H., Cowey, A., & Weiskrantz, L. (1970). Disruptions of auditory sequence discrimination by unilateral and bilateral cortical ablations of superior temporal gyrus in the monkey. *Experimental Neurology, 28,* 529–548.

Diamond, M. C. (1984). Age, sex, and environmental influences on anatomical asymmetry in rat forebrain. In N. Geschwind & A. M. Galaburda (Eds.), *Cerebral dominance: The biological foundations.* Cambridge, MA: Harvard University Press.

Diamond, M. C., Dowling, G. A., & Johnson, R. E. (1981). Morphological cerebral cortical asymmetry in male and female rats. *Experimental Neurology, 71*, 261–268.

Dimond, S. J. (1980). *Neuropsychology: A textbook of systems and psychological functions of the human brain*. London: Butterworths.

Dimond, S. J., & Farrington, J. (1977). Emotional response to films shown to the right or left hemisphere of the brain measured by heart rate. *Acta Psychologica, 41*, 255–260.

Dirks, D. (1964). Perception of dichotic and monaural verbal material and cerebral dominance for speech. *Acta Oto-Laryngologica, 58*, 73–80.

Donchin, E., Kutas, M., & McCarthy, G. (1977). Electrocortical indices of hemispheric utilization. In S. Harnad, R. W. Doty, L. Goldstein, J. Jaynes, & G. Krauthamer (Eds.), *Lateralization in the nervous system* (pp. 339–384). New York: Academic Press.

Donchin, E., McCarthy, G., & Kutas, M. (1977). Electroencephalographic investigations of hemispheric specialization. In J. E. Desmedt (Ed.), *Language and hemispheric specialization in man: Cerebral event-related potentials*. Basel: Karger.

Dooling, E. C., Chi, J. G., & Gilles, F. H. (1983). Telencephalic development: Changing gyral patterns. In F. H. Gilles, A. Leviton, & E. C. Dooling (Eds.), *The developing human brain: Growth and epidemiologic neuropathy* (pp. 94–104). Boston: John Wright.

Dorman, M., & Porter, R. (1975). Hemispheric lateralization for speech perception in stutterers. *Cortex, 11*, 181–185.

Duda, P. D., & Kirby, H. W. (1980). Effects of eye-movement controls and frequency levels on accuracy of word recognition. *Perceptual and Motor Skills, 50*, 979–985.

Dulay, H., & Burt, M. (1974). A new perspective on the creative construction processes in child second language acquisition. *Language Learning, 24*, 253–278.

Dunlop, D. B., Dunlop, P., & Fenelon, B. (1973). Vision-laterality analysis in children with reading disability: The results of new techniques of examination. *Cortex, 9*, 227–236.

Eberle, B. (1982). *Visual thinking: A SCAMPER tool for useful imaging*. Buffalo, NY: D. O. K.

Eberle, B. (1987). *Scamper on: Games for imagination development*. Buffalo, NY: D. O. K.

Eccles, J. C. (1973). Brain, speech, and consciousness. *Naturwissenschaften, 60*, 167–176.

Edwards, B. (1979). *Drawing on the right side of the brain*. Los Angeles: J. P. Tarcher.

Edwards, D. A. (1968). Mice: Fighting by neonatally androgenized females. *Science, 161*, 1027–1028.

Edwards, D. A. (1969). Early androgen stimulation and aggressive behavior in male and female mice. *Physiology and Behavior, 4*, 333–338.

Efron, R. (1990). *The decline and fall of hemispheric specialization*. Hillsdale, NJ: Lawrence Erlbaum Associates.

Efron, R., Yund, E. W., & Nichols, D. R. (1987). Scanning the visual field without eye movements—a sex difference. *Neuropsychologia, 25*, 637–644.

Efron, R., Yund, E. W., & Nichols, D. R. (1990a). Serial processing of visual spatial patterns in a search paradigm. *Brain and Cognition, 12*, 17–41.

Efron, R., Yund, E. W., & Nichols, D. R. (1990b). Detectability as a function of target location: Effects of spatial configuration. *Brain and Cognition, 12*, 102–116.

Ehrhardt, A. A., & Meyer-Balburg, H. F. L. (1981). Effects of prenatal sex hormones on gender-related behavior. *Science, 211*, 1312–1318.

Ehrlichman, H., & Weinberger, A. (1978). Lateral eye movements and hemispheric asymmetry: A critical review. *Psychological Bulletin, 85*, 1080–1081.

Ellenberg, L., & Sperry, R. W. (1980). Lateralized division of attention in the commissurotomized and intact brain. *Neuropsychologia, 18*, 411–418.

Ellis, A. W., & Young, A. W. (1981). Visual hemifield asymmetry for naming concrete nouns and verbs in children between seven and eleven years of age. *Cortex, 17*, 617–624.

Ellis, R. J., & Oscar-Berman, M. (1989). Alcoholism, aging, and functional cerebral asymmetries. *Psychological Bulletin, 106*, 128–147.

Entus, A. K. (1977). Hemispheric asymmetry in the processing of dichotically presented speech and nonspeech sounds by infants. In S. J. Segalowitz & F. A. Gruber (Eds.), *Language development and neurological theory* (pp. 63–73). New York: Academic Press.

Epstein, H. (1978). Growth spurts during brain development: Implications for educational policy and practice. In *Education and the brain*. Chicago: National Society for the Study of Education.

Epstein, H. (1980, June). *Cognitive growth and development*. Paper presented at Institute on the Middlescent Learner, Kent, OH.

Erickson, T. C. (1940). Spread of epileptic discharge. *Archives of Neurology and Psychiatry*, *43*, 429–452.

Erlenmeyer, D. (1883). Quoted by *British Medical Journal*, *1*, 1161.

Erlichman, H., & Barret, J. (1983). Right hemisphere specialization for mental imagery: A review of the evidence. *Brain and Cognition*, *2*, 55–76.

Erman, A. (1894). *Life in ancient Egypt* (H. M. Tirard, Trans.). London: MacMillan.

Etaugh, C., & Levy, R. B. (1981). Hemispheric specialization for tactile-spatial processing in preschool children. *Perceptual and Motor Skills*, *53*, 621–622.

Ettlinger, G., & Gautrin, D. (1971). Verbal discrimination performance in the monkey: The effect of unilateral removal of temporal cortex. *Cortex*, *7*, 315–331.

Fagot, J., & Vauclair, J. (1991). Manual laterality in nonhuman primates: A distinction between handedness and manual specialization. *Psychological Bulletin*, *109*, 76–89.

Fairweather, H. (1982). Sex differences: Little reason to play midfield. In J. Beaumont (Ed.), *Divided visual field studies of cerebral organization* (pp. 147–190). New York: Academic Press.

Falzi, G., Perrone, P., & Vignolo, L. A. (1982). Right–left asymmetry in anterior speech region. *Archives of Neurology*, *39*, 239–240.

Fancher, R. E. (1990). *Pioneers of psychology*. New York: W. W. Norton.

Farah, M. J. (1990). *Visual agnosia: Disorders of object recognition and what they tell us about normal vision*. Cambridge, MA: MIT Press.

Farah, M., Gazzaniga, M. S., Holtzman, J. D., & Kosslyn, S. M. (1985). A left-hemisphere basis for visual imagery? *Neuropsychologia*, *23*, 115–118.

Fatham, A. (1975). *Language, background, age, and the order of acquisition of English structures*. Paper presented at the annual TESOL convention, Los Angeles, CA.

Feder, H. H. (1981). Estrous cyclicity in mammals. In N. T. Adler (Ed.), *Neuroendocrinology of reproduction*. New York: Plenum Press.

Feder, H. H. (1984). Hormones and sexual behavior. *Annual Review of Psychology*, *35*, 165–200.

Fein, D., Humes, M., Kaplan, E., Lucci, D., & Waterhouse, L. (1984). The question of left-hemisphere dysfunction in infantile autism. *Psychological Bulletin*, *95*, 258–281.

Ferguson, S. M., Rayport, M., & Corrie, W. S. (1985). Neuropsychiatric observations on the behavioral consequences of corpus callosum section for seizure control. In A. G. Reeves (Ed.), *Epilepsy and the corpus callosum*. New York: Plenum Press.

Field, M., Ashton, R., & White, K. (1978). Agenesis of the corpus callosum: A report of two preschool children and review of the literature. *Developmental Medicine and Child Neurology*, *20*, 47–61.

Fisher, F. W., Liberman, I. Y., & Shankweiler, D. (1978). Reading reversals and developmental dyslexia: A further study. *Cortex*, *14*, 496–510.

Fleminger, J. J., Dalton, R., & Standage, K. F. (1977). Age as a factor in the handedness of adults. *Neuropsychologia*, *15*, 471–473.

Flor-Henry, P. (1969a). Psychosis and temporal lobe epilepsy: A controlled investigation. *Epilepsia*, *10*, 363–395.

Flor-Henry, P. (1969b). Schizophrenic-like reactions and affective psychoses associated with temporal lobe epilepsy: Etiological factors. *American Journal of Psychiatry*, *26*, 400–403.

Flor-Henry, P. (1976). Lateralized temporal-limbic dysfunction and psychopathology. In S. Harnad, H. Steklis, & J. Lancaster (Eds.), *Origins and evolution of language and speech.* New York: New York Academy of Sciences.

Foldi, N. S., Cicone, M., & Gardner, H. (1983). Pragmatic aspects of communication in brain damaged patients. In S. J. Segalowitz (Ed.), *Language functions and brain organization.* New York: Academic Press.

Fontenot, D. J., & Benton, A. L. (1971). Tactile perception of direction in relation to hemispheric locus of lesion. *Neuropsychologia, 9,* 83–88.

Forgays, D. G. (1953). The development of differential word recognition. *Journal of Experimental Psychology, 45,* 165–168.

Fox, N. A., & Davidson, R. J. (1986). Taste-elicited changes in facial signs of emotion and the asymmetry of brain electrical activity in newborns. *Neuropsychologia, 24,* 417–422.

Fox, N. A., & Davidson, R. J. (1987). Electroencephalogram asymmetry in response to the approach of a stranger and maternal separation in 10-month-old infants. *Developmental Psychology, 23,* 233–240.

Fox, N. A., Petersen, S. E., Posner, M. I., & Raichle, M. E. (1987). Language-related brain activation measured with PET: Comparison of auditory and visual word presentations. *Journal of Cerebral Blood Flow and Metabolism,* 7(Suppl. 1), S294.

Franco, L., & Sperry, R. W. (1977). Hemispheric lateralization for cognitive processing of geometry. *Neuropsychologia, 15,* 107–114.

Friedlander, W. J. (1971). Some aspects of eyedness. *Cortex, 7,* 357–371.

Fromkin, V. A., Krashen, S., Curtiss, S., Rigler, D., & Rigler, M. (1974). The development of language in Genie: A case of language acquisition beyond the critical period. *Brain and Language, 1,* 81–107.

Fry, D. B. (1974). Right-ear advantage for speech presented monaurally. *Language and Speech, 17,* 142–151.

Gaddes, W. H. (1985). *Learning disabilities and brain function: A neuropsychological approach.* New York: Springer-Verlag.

Gaede, S. E., Parsons, O. A., & Bertera, J. H. (1978). Hemispheric differences in musical perception: Aptitude vs. experience. *Neuropsychologia, 16,* 369–373.

Galaburda, A. M. (1984). Anatomical asymmetries in the human brain. In N. Geschwind & A. M. Galaburda (Eds.), *Biological foundations of cerebral dominance* (pp. 11–25). Cambridge, MA: Harvard University Press.

Galaburda, A. M., & Eidelberg, P. (1982). Symmetry and asymmetry in the human posterior thalamus. II: Thalamic lesions in a case of developmental dyslexia. *Archives of Neurology, 39,* 333–336.

Galaburda, A. M., LeMay, M., Kemper, T. L., & Geschwind, N. (1978). Right-left asymmetries in the brain. *Science, 199,* 852–856.

Galaburda, A. M., Sanides, F., & Geschwind, N. (1978). Human brain: Cytoarchitectonic left–right asymmetries in the temporal speech region. *Archives of Neurology, 35,* 812–817.

Galaburda, A. M., Sherman, G. F., Rosen, G. D., Aboitiz, F., & Geschwind, N. (1985). Developmental dyslexia: Four consecutive patients with cortical anomalies. *Annals of Neurology, 18,* 222–233.

Galin, D. (1979). The two modes of consciousness and the two halves of the brain. In Goleman & Davidson (Eds.), *Consciousness: Brain, states of awareness, and mysticism* (pp. 19–23). New York: Harper & Row.

Galin, D., & Ellis, R. R. (1975). Asymmetry in evoked potentials as an index of lateralized cognitive processes: Relation to EEG alpha asymmetry. *Psychophysiology, 13,* 45–50.

Galin, D., & Ornstein, R. (1972). Lateral specialization of cognitive mode: An EEG study. *Psychophysiology, 9,* 412–418.

Galin, D., & Ornstein, R. (1974). Individual differences in cognitive style. I: Reflexive eye movements. *Neuropsychologia, 12*, 367–376.

Gardner, B. T., & Gardner, R. A. (1975a). Evidence for sentence constituents in the early utterances of child and chimpanzee. *Journal of Experimental Psychology: General, 104*, 244–267.

Gardner, H. (1978). What we know (and don't know) about the two halves of the brain. *Harvard Magazine, 80*, 24–27.

Gardner, R. A., & Gardner, B. T. (1975b). Early signs of language in child and chimpanzee. *Science, 187*, 752–753.

Garner, W. R. (1978). Aspects of a stimulus: Features, dimensions, and configurations. In E. Rosch & B. B. Lloyd (Eds.), *Cognition and categorization*. Hillsdale, NJ: Lawrence Erlbaum Associates.

Garren, R. B. (1980). Hemispheric laterality differences among four levels of reading achievement. *Perceptual and Motor Skills, 50*, 119–123.

Gates, A., & Bradshaw, J. L. (1977a). Music perception and cerebral asymmetries. *Cortex, 13*, 390–401.

Gates, A., & Bradshaw, J. L. (1977b). The role of the cerebral hemispheres in music. *Brain and Language, 4*, 403–431.

Gaziel, T., Obler, L., & Albert, M. (1978). A tachistoscopic study of Hebrew-English bilinguals. In M. Albert & L. Obler (Eds.), *The bilingual brain: Neuropsychological and neurolinguistic aspects of bilingualism*. New York: Academic Press.

Gazzaniga, M. (1967). The split brain in man. *Scientific American, 217*, 24–29.

Gazzaniga, M. (1970). *The bisected brain*. New York: Appleton-Century-Crofts.

Gazzaniga, M. (1983). Right hemisphere language following brain bisection: A 20-year perspective. *American Psychologist, 38*, 525–537.

Gazzaniga, M. (1989). Organization of the human brain. *Science, 245*, 947–952.

Gazzaniga, M., & Hillyard, S. A. (1971). Language and speech capacity of the right hemisphere. *Neuropsychologia, 9*, 273–280.

Gazzaniga, M., & LeDoux, J. E. (1978). *The integrated mind*. New York: Plenum Press.

Gazzaniga, M., & Sperry, R. W. (1966). Simultaneous double discrimination response following brain bisection. *Psychonomic Science, 4*, 261–262.

Gazzaniga, M., & Sperry, R. W. (1967). Language after section of the cerebral commissure. *Brain, 90*, 131–148.

Gebhardt, C. (1981). *Computer analysis of CT scans of chronic alcoholics: The relation of third ventricle region to memory and of frontal-parietal regions to perception*. Unpublished Ph.D. dissertation, Boston University.

Geffen, G., Bradshaw, J. L., & Wallace, G. (1971). Interhemispheric effects on reaction time to verbal and nonverbal visual stimuli. *Journal of Experimental Psychology, 87*, 415–422.

Geffen, G., & Caudrey, R. (1981). Reliability and validity of the dichotic monitoring test for language laterality. *Neuropsychologia, 19*, 413–423.

Geffen, G., & Traub, E. (1980). The effects of duration of stimulation, preferred hand, and familial sinistrality in dichotic monitoring. *Cortex, 16*, 83–96.

Geffner, D. S., & Dorman, M. F. (1976). Hemispheric specialization for speech perception in four-year-old children from low and middle socioeconomic classes. *Cortex, 12*, 71–73.

Genesee, F., Hamers, J., Lambert, W. E., Seitz, M., & Stark, R. (1978). Language processing in bilinguals. *Brain and Language, 5*, 1–12.

Geschwind, N. (1965). Disconnexion syndromes in animals and man. *Brain, 88*, 237–294.

Geschwind, N. (1972). Language and the brain. *Scientific American, 226*, 76–83.

Geschwind, N. (1984). Cerebral dominance in biological perspective. *Neuropsychologia, 22*, 675–683.

Geschwind, N. (1985). Implications for evolution, genetics, and clinical syndromes. In S. Glick (Ed.), *Cerebral lateralization in nonhuman species*. Orlando, FL: Academic Press.

Geschwind, N., & Behan, P. O. (1982). Left-handedness: Association with immune disease, migraine, and developmental learning disorder. *Proceedings of the National Academy of Sciences, 79,* 5097–5100.

Geschwind, N., & Behan, P. O. (1984). Laterality, hormones, and immunity. In N. Geschwind & A. M. Galaburda (Eds.), *Cerebral dominance: The biological foundations.* Cambridge, MA: Harvard University Press.

Geschwind, N., & Galaburda, A. M. (1987). *Cerebral lateralization: Biological mechanisms, associations and pathology.* Cambridge, MA: MIT Press.

Gesell, A., & Ames, L. B. (1947). The development of handedness. *Journal of Genetic Psychology, 70,* 155–175.

Ghent, L. (1961). Developmental changes in tactual thresholds on dominant and nondominant sides. *Journal of Comparative and Physiological Psychology, 54,* 670–673.

Gibson, W. (1962). Pioneers in localization of brain function. *Journal of the American Medical Association, 180,* 944–951.

Gilbert, J. H. V., & Climan, I. (1974). Dichotic studies in 2 to 3 year olds: A preliminary report. In *Speech communication seminar Stockholm* (Vol. 2). Uppsala, Sweden: Almquist & Wiksell.

Ginsberg, Y. P., & Hartwick, A. (1971). Directional confusion as a sign of dyslexia. *Perceptual and Motor Skills, 32,* 535–543.

Gladue, B. A., Green, R., & Hellman, R. E. (1984). Neuroendocrine response to estrogen and sexual orientation. *Science, 225,* 1496–1499.

Glanville, B. B., Best, C. T., & Levenson, R. (1977). A cardiac measure of cerebral asymmetries in infant auditory perception. *Developmental Psychology, 13,* 54–59.

Glick, S. D. (1983). Heritable determinants of left–right bias in the rat. *Life Science, 32,* 2215–2221.

Glick, S. D., Jerussi, T. P., & Zimmerberg, B. (1977). Behavioral and neuropharmacological correlates of nigrostriatal asymmetry in rats. In S. Harnad, R. W. Doty, L. Goldstein, J. Jaynes, & G. Krauthamer (Eds.), *Lateralization in the nervous system* (pp. 213–249). New York: Academic Press.

Glick, S. D., Meibach, R. C., Cox, R. D., & Maayani, S. (1979). Multiple and interrelated functional asymmetries in rat brain. *Life Sciences, 25,* 395–400.

Glick, S. D., & Ross, D. A. (1981). Lateralization of function in the rat brain. Basic mechanism may be operative in humans. *Trends in the Neurosciences, 12,* 196–199.

Glick, S. D., Ross, D. A., & Hough, L. B. (1982). Lateral asymmetry of neurotransmitters in human brain. *Brain Research, 234,* 53–63.

Golden, C. J., Graber, B., Blase, I., Berg, R., Coffman, J., & Bloch, S. (1981). Difference in brain densities between chronic alcoholic and normal control patients. *Science, 211,* 508–510.

Goodglass, H., & Calderon, M. (1977). Parallel processing of verbal and musical stimuli in right and left hemispheres. *Neuropsychologia, 15,* 397–407.

Goodglass, H., & Kaplan, E. (1979). Assessment of cognitive deficit in the brain-injured patient. In M. Gazzaniga (Ed.), *Handbook of behavioral neurobiology* (Vol. 2, pp. 3–22). New York: Plenum Press.

Goodman, D. M., Beatty, J., & Mulholland, T. B. (1980). Detection of cerebral lateralization of function using EEG alpha contingent visual stimulation. *Electroencephalography and Clinical Neurophysiology, 48,* 418–431.

Gordon, H. W. (1978). Left hemisphere dominance for rhythmic elements in dichotically presented melodies. *Cortex, 14,* 58–76.

Gordon, H. W. (1980). Cerebral organization in bilinguals: I. Lateralization. *Brain and Language, 9,* 255–268.

Gordon, H. W., & Bogen, J. E. (1974). Hemispheric lateralization of singing after intracarotid sodium amylobarbitone. *Journal of Neurology, Neurosurgery, and Psychiatry, 37,* 727–738.

Gordon, H. W., & Carmon, A. (1976). Transfer of dominance in speed of verbal response to visually presented stimuli from right to left hemisphere. *Perceptual and Motor Skills*, *42*, 1091–1100.

Gorski, R. A. (1980). Sexual differentiation in the brain. In D. T. Krieger & J. C. Hughes (Eds.), *Neuroendocrinology*. Sunderland, MA: Sinauer.

Gorski, R. A., Gordon, J. H., Shryne, J. E., & Southam, A. M. (1978). Evidence for a morphological sex difference within the medial preoptic area of the rat brain. *Brain Research*, *148*, 333–346.

Gott, P. S. (1973). Language after dominant hemispherectomy. *Journal of Neurology, Neurosurgery, and Psychiatry*, *36*, 1082–1088.

Gowers, W. R. (1893). *A manual of diseases of the nervous system*. London: Churchill.

Grady, M. P., & Luecke, E. A. (1978). *Education and the brain*. Bloomington, IN: Phi Delta Kappa Educational Foundation.

Grant, D. W. (1980). Visual asymmetries on a color-naming task: A developmental perspective. *Perceptual and Motor Skills*, *50*, 475–480.

Grant, D. W. (1981). Visual asymmetry on a color-naming task: A longitudinal study with primary school children. *Child Development*, *52*, 370–372.

Graves, R., Landis, T., & Goodglass, H. (1981). Laterality and sex differences for visual recognition of emotional and nonemotional words. *Neuropsychologia*, *19*, 95–102.

Gregory, R. J., Alley, P., & Morris, L. (1980). Left-handedness and spatial reasoning abilities: The deficit hypothesis revisited. *Intelligence*, *4*, 151–159.

Greenwood, P., Wilson, D. H., & Gazzaniga, M. S. (1977). Dream report following commissurotomy. *Cortex*, *13*, 311–316.

Grinder, J., & Bandler, R. (1976). *The structure of magic II: A book about communication and change*. Palo Alto, CA: Science and Behavior Books.

Grodzinsky, Y. (1990). *Theoretical perspectives on language deficits*. Cambridge, MA: MIT Press.

Gross, Y., Franko, R., & Lewin, I. (1978). Effects of voluntary eye movements on hemispheric activity and choice of cognitive mode. *Neuropsychologia*, *16*, 653–657.

Grow, M. F., & Johnson, N. (1983). Math learning: The two hemispheres. *Journal of Humanistic Education and Development*, *22*, 30–39.

Gruzelier, J. H., & Flor-Henry, P. (1979). *Hemisphere asymmetries of function in psychopathology*. Amsterdam: Elsevier/North-Holland Biomedical Press.

Gruzelier, J. H., & Hammond, N. V. (1976). Schizophrenia—a dominant hemisphere temporal lobe disorder? *Research Communications in Psychology, Psychiatry, and Behavior*, *1*, 33–72.

Gruzelier, J. H., & Hammond, N. V. (1979). Gains, losses, and lateral differences in the hearing of schizophrenic patients. *British Journal of Psychology*, *70*, 319–330.

Gruzelier, J. H., & Venables, P. H. (1973). Skin conductance responses to tones with and without attentional significance in schizophrenic and nonschizophrenic patients. *Neuropsychologia*, *11*, 221–230.

Guiard, Y. (1980). Cerebral hemispheres and selective attention. *Acta Psychologica*, *46*, 41–61.

Gulliksen, H., & Voneida, T. (1975). An attempt to obtain replicate learning curves in the split-brain cat. *Physiological Psychology*, *3*, 77–85.

Gur, R. C., & Gur, R. E. (1977). Correlates of conjugate lateral eye movements in man. In S. Harnad, R. W. Doty, L. Goldstein, J. Jaynes, & G. Krauthamer (Eds.), *Lateralization in the nervous system* (pp. 261–281). New York: Academic Press.

Gur, R. C., & Gur, R. E. (1980). Handedness and individual differences in hemispheric activation. In J. Herron (Ed.), *Neuropsychology of left-handedness* (pp. 211–231). New York: Academic Press.

Gur, R. C., Gur, R. E., Obrist, W. D., Hungerbuhler, J. P., Younkin, D., Rosen, A. D., Skolnick, B. E., & Reivich, M. (1982). Sex and handedness differences in cerebral blood flow during rest and cognitive activity. *Science, 217*, 659–661.

Gur, R. C., Packer, I. K., Hungerbuhler, J. P., Reivich, M., Obrist, W. D., Amarnek, W. S., & Sackheim, H. A. (1980). Differences in the distribution of gray and white matter in human cerebral hemispheres. *Science, 207*, 1226–1228.

Gur, R. C., & Reivich, M. (1980). Cognitive task effects on hemispheric blood flow in humans: Evidence for individual differences in hemispheric activation. *Brain and Language, 9*, 78–92.

Gur, R. E. (1979). Cognitive concomitants of hemispheric dysfunction in schizophrenia. *Archives of General Psychiatry, 36*, 269–274.

Gur, R. E., Gur, R. C., & Harris, L. J. (1975). Cerebral activation, as measured by subjects' lateral eye movements, is influenced by experimenter location. *Neuropsychologia, 13*, 35–44.

Habib, M. (1989). Anatomical asymmetries of the human cerebral cortex. *International Journal of Neuroscience, 47*, 67–79.

Haggard, M. P., & Parkinson, A. M. (1971). Stimulus and task factors as determinants of ear advantage. *Quarterly Journal of Experimental Psychology, 23*, 168–177.

Hahn, W. K. (1987). Cerebral lateralization of function: From infancy through childhood. *Psychological Bulletin, 101*, 376–392.

Hakuta, K. (1986). *Mirror of language.* New York: Basic Books.

Hall, C. (1979). The meaning of dreams. In Goleman & Davidson (Eds.), *Consciousness: Brain, states of awareness, and mysticism* (pp. 79–82). New York: Harper & Row.

Hall, J. L., & Goldstein, M. H. (1968). Representation of binaural stimuli by single units in primary auditory cortex of unaesthetized cats. *Journal of the Acoustical Society of America, 43*, 456–461.

Halperin, Y., Nachshon, I., & Carmon, A. (1973). Shift of ear superiority in dichotic listening to temporally patterned nonverbal stimuli. *Journal of the Acoustical Society of America, 53*, 46–50.

Halpern, D. F. (1986). *Sex differences in cognitive abilities.* Hillsdale, NJ: Lawrence Erlbaum Associates.

Halpern, D. F., & Coren, S. (1990). *Hand preference and life span.* Manuscript submitted for publication.

Halsey, J. H., Blaunstein, U. W., Wilson, E. W., & Wills, E. H. (1979). Regional cerebral blood flow comparison of right and left hand movement. *Neurology, 29*, 21–28.

Hamilton, C. R. (1977). An assessment of hemispheric specialization in monkeys. In S. Dimond and D. Blizzard (Eds.), *Evolution and lateralization of the brain.* New York: New York Academy of Sciences.

Hannay, H., & Malone, D. (1976). Visual field effects and short-term memory for verbal material. *Neuropsychologia, 14*, 203–209.

Hansch, E. C., & Pirozzolo, F. J. (1980). Task relevant effects on the assessment of cerebral specialization for facial emotion. *Brain and Language, 10*, 51–59.

Harburg, E. (1981). Handedness and drinking-smoking types. *Perceptual and Motor Skills, 52*, 279–282.

Harburg, E., Feldstein, A., & Papsdorf, J. (1978). Handedness and smoking. *Perceptual and Motor Skills, 47*, 1171–1174.

Hardyck, C. (1977). A model of individual differences in hemispheric functioning. In H. Whitaker & H. A. Whitaker (Eds.), *Studies in neurolinguistics* (Vol. 3, pp. 223–255). New York: Academic Press.

Hardyck, C., Chiarello, C., Dronkers, N. F., & Simpson, G. V. (1985). Orienting attention within visual fields: How efficient is interhemispheric transfer? *Journal of Experimental Psychology: Human Perception and Performance, 11*, 650–666.

Hardyck, C., Goldman, R., & Petrinovich, L. (1975). Handedness and sex, race, and age. *Human Biology, 47*, 369–375.

Hardyck, C., & Petrinovich, L. F. (1977). Left-handedness. *Psychological Bulletin, 84*, 385–404.

Harper, L. V., & Kraft, R. H. (1986). Lateralization of receptive language in preschoolers: Test–retest reliability in a dichotic listening task. *Developmental Psychology, 22*, 553–556.

Harris, L. J. (1977). Sex differences in the growth and use of language. In E. Donelson & J. Gullahorn (Eds.), *Women: A psychological perspective*. New York: Wiley.

Harris, L. J. (1978). Sex differences in spatial ability: Possible environmental, genetic, and neurological factors. In M. Kinsbourne (Ed.), *Asymmetrical function of the brain* (pp. 405–522). Cambridge, England: Cambridge University Press.

Harris, L. J. (1980). Which hand is the "eye" of the blind?—A new look at an old question. In J. Herron (Ed.), *Neuropsychology of left-handedness* (pp. 303–329). New York: Academic Press.

Harris, L. J. (1986). III. James Mark Baldwin on the origins of right- and left-handedness: The story of an experiment that mattered. *Monographs of the Society for Research in Child Development, 50*, 44–64.

Harris, L. J. (1988). Right brain training: Some reflections on the application of research on cerebral hemispheric specialization to education. In D. L. Molfese & S. J. Segalowitz (Eds.), *Brain lateralization in children: Developmental implications* (pp. 207–235). New York: Guilford Press.

Harris, L. J., & Carr, T. H. (1981). Implications of differences between perceptual systems for the analysis of hemispheric specialization. *Behavioral and Brain Sciences, 4*, 71–72.

Harris, M. (1989). *Our kind: Who we are, where we came from, where we are going.* New York: Harper Collins.

Harris, T. L., & Hodges, R. E. (1981). *A dictionary of reading and related terms.* Newark, NJ: International Reading Association.

Harshman, R. A., Hampson, E., & Berenbaum, S. E. (1983). Individual differences in cognitive abilities and brain organization, part I: Sex and handedness differences in ability. *Canadian Journal of Psychology, 37*, 144–192.

Harshman, R. A., Remington, R., & Krashen, S. (1975). *Sex, language, and the brain, part II: Evidence from dichotic listening for adult sex differences in verbal lateralization.* Unpublished manuscript. University of California, Los Angeles.

Hatta, T. (1977). Recognition of Japanese kanji in the left and right visual fields. *Neuropsychologia, 15*, 685–688.

Hatta, T. (1978). Recognition of Japanese kanji and hirakana in the left and right visual fields. *Japanese Psychological Research, 20*, 51–59.

Hatta, T., Yamamoto, M., Kawabata, Y., & Tsutui, K. (1981). Development of hemisphere specialization for tactile recognition in normal children. *Cortex, 17*, 611–616.

Hawn, P. R., & Harris, L. J. (1979). *Hand asymmetries in grasp duration and reaching in two- and five-month-old infants.* Paper presented at the biennial meeting of the Society for Research in Child Development, San Francisco, CA.

Hecaen, H., & Albert, M. L. (1978). *Human neuropsychology.* New York: Wiley.

Heilman, K., Scholes, R., & Watson, R. T. (1975). Auditory affective agnosia: Disturbed comprehension of affective speech. *Journal of Neurology, Neurosurgery, and Psychiatry, 38*, 69–72.

Heilman, K., & Watson, S. (1977). The neglect syndrome—a unilateral defect of the orienting response. In S. Harnad, R. W. Doty, L. Goldstein, J. Jaynes, & G. Krauthamer (Eds.), *Lateralization of the nervous system* (pp. 285–302). New York: Academic Press.

Heller, W., & Levy, J. (1981). Perception and expression of emotion in right-handers and left-handers. *Neuropsychologia, 19*, 263–272.

Hellige, J. B., & Cox, P. J. (1976). Effects of concurrent verbal memory on recognition of stimuli from left and right visual fields. *Journal of Experimental Psychology: Human Perception and Performance, 2*, 210–221.

Henriques, J., & Davidson, R. (1990). Regional brain electrical asymmetries discriminate between previously depressed and healthy control subjects. *Journal of Abnormal Psychology, 99*, 22–31.

Hermelin, B., & O'Connor, N. (1971a). Functional asymmetry in the reading of braille. *Neuropsychologia, 9*, 431–435.

Hermelin, B., & O'Connor, N. (1971b). Right- and left-handed reading of braille. *Nature, 231*, 470.

Herrman, D. J., & Van Dyke, K. (1978). Handedness and the mental rotation of perceived patterns. *Cortex, 14*, 521–529.

Herron, J., Galin, D., Johnstone, J., & Ornstein, R. (1979). Cerebral specialization, writing posture, and motor control of writing in left-handers. *Science, 205*, 1285–1289.

Hewes, G. W. (1949). Lateral dominance, culture, and writing systems. *Human Biology, 21*, 233–245.

Hewes, G. W. (1973). Primate communication and the gestural origin of language. *Current Anthropology, 14*, 5–24.

Hicks, E. E., & Kinsbourne, M. (1978). Human handedness. In M. Kinsbourne (Ed.), *Asymmetrical function of the brain* (pp. 523–549). Cambridge, England: Cambridge University Press.

Hicks, R. E. (1975). Intrahemispheric response competition between vocal and unimanual performance in normal adult human males. *Journal of Comparative and Physiological Psychology, 89*, 50–60.

Hicks, R. E., & Beveridge, R. (1978). Handedness and intelligence. *Cortex, 14*, 304–307.

Hier, D. B., & Kaplan, J. (1980). Are sex differences in cerebral organization clinically significant? *Behavioral and Brain Sciences, 3*, 238–239.

Hier, D. B., LeMay, M., Rosenberger, P. B., & Perlo, V. P. (1978). Developmental dyslexia: Evidence for a subgroup with a reversal of cerebral asymmetry. *Archives of Neurology, 35*, 90–92.

Hilliard, R. D. (1973). Hemispheric laterality effects on a facial recognition task in normal subjects. *Cortex, 9*, 246–258.

Hines, D. (1972). Bilateral tachistoscopic recognitions of verbal and nonverbal stimuli. *Cortex, 8*, 315–322.

Hines, D. (1978). Visual information processing in the left and right hemispheres. *Neuropsychologia, 16*, 593–600.

Hines, D., Fennell, E. B., Bowers, D., & Satz, P. (1980). Left-handers show greater test–retest variability in auditory and visual asymmetry. *Brain and Language, 10*, 208–211.

Hines, D., & Satz, P. (1971). Superiority of right visual fields in right-handers for free recall of digits presented at varying rates. *Neuropsychologia, 9*, 239–247.

Hiscock, M. (1977). Eye movement asymmetry and hemispheric function: An examination of individual differences. *Journal of Psychology, 97*, 49–52.

Hiscock, M. (1988). Behavioral asymmetries in normal children. In D. L. Molfese & S. J. Segalowitz (Eds.), *Brain lateralization in children: Developmental implications* (pp. 85–169). New York: Guilford Press.

Hiscock, M., Antoniuk, D., Prisciak, K., & van Hessert, D. (1985). Generalized and lateralized interference between concurrent tasks performed by children: Effects of age, sex, and skill. *Developmental Psychology, 21*, 29–48.

Hiscock, M., & Hiscock, C. K. (1988). An anomalous sex difference in auditory laterality. *Cortex, 24*, 595–599.

Hiscock, M., & Kinsbourne, M. (1980). Asymmetry of verbal–manual time-sharing in children: A follow-up study. *Neuropsychologia, 18*, 151–162.

Hiscock, M., Kinsbourne, M., Samuels, M., & Krause, A. E. (1987). Dual task performance in children: Generalized and lateralized effects of memory encoding upon the rate and variability of concurrent finger tapping. *Brain and Cognition, 6*, 24–40.

Hochberg, F., & LeMay, M. (1975). Arteriographic correlates of handedness. *Neurology, 25*, 218–222.

Hollandsworth, J. G., Jr. (1990). *The physiology of psychological disorders: Schizophrenia, depression, anxiety, and substance abuse.* New York: Plenum Press.

Holzman, P. S. (1985). Eye movement dysfunctions and psychosis. *International Review of Neurobiology, 27*, 179–205.

Honda, H. (1978). Shift of visual laterality differences by loading of auditory discrimination tasks. *Japanese Journal of Psychology, 49*, 8–14.

Humphrey, M. E., & Zangwill, O. L. (1951). Cessation of dreaming after brain injury. *Journal of Neurology, Neurosurgery, and Psychiatry, 14*, 322–325.

Huttenlocher, P. R. (1984). Synapse elimination and plasticity in developing human cerebral cortex. *American Journal of Mental Deficiency, 88*, 488–496.

Huxley, A. (1979). The doors of perception. In Goleman & Davidson (Eds.), *Consciousness: Brain, states of awareness, and mysticism* (pp. 102–104). New York: Harper & Row.

Hynd, G. W., & Cohen, M. (1983). *Dyslexia: Neuropsychological theory, research, and clinical differentiation.* New York: Grune & Stratton.

Hynd, G. W., & Obrzut, J. E. (1977). Effects of grade level and sex on the magnitude of the dichotic ear advantage. *Neuropsychologia, 15*, 689–692.

Hynd, G. W., Obrzut, J. E., Weed, W., & Hynd, C. R. (1979). Development of cerebral dominance: Dichotic listening asymmetry in normal and learning-disabled children. *Journal of Experimental Child Psychology, 28*, 445–454.

Hynd, G. W., & Semrud-Clikeman, M. (1989). Dyslexia and brain morphology. *Psychological Bulletin, 106*, 447–482.

Iaccino, J. F. (1990). Asymmetrical processing of tachistoscopic inputs in undergraduates across sex, handedness, field side, and fixation instructions. *Perceptual and Motor Skills, 70*, 1203–1213.

Iaccino, J. F., & Houran, J. (1989). Influence of stronger attentional manipulations on the processing of dichotic inputs in right-handers. *Perceptual and Motor Skills, 69*, 1235–1240.

Iaccino, J. F., & Houran, J. (1991). The influence of attentional bias on the asymmetrical processing of dichotic inputs in undergraduates. *Journal of Psychology and the Behavioral Sciences, 6*, 30–39.

Iaccino, J. F., & Houran, J. (in press). Further effects of attentional bias on the asymmetrical processing of tachistoscopic inputs in right-handed undergraduates. *Journal of Psychology and the Behavioral Sciences.*

Iaccino, J. F., & Sowa, S. J. (1989). Asymmetrical processing of dichotic inputs in undergraduates across sex, handedness, ear-side, and experimental instructions. *Perceptual and Motor Skills, 68*, 1003–1010.

Iaccino, J. F., & Sowa, S. J. (1990, May). *Cerebral asymmetries I: Asymmetrical processing of dichotic inputs as a function of sex, handedness, and instructions.* Paper presented at the 62nd annual meeting of the Midwestern Psychological Association, Chicago, IL.

Iacono, W. G. (1988). Eye movement abnormalities in schizophrenic and affective disorders. In C. W. Johnston & F. J. Pirozzolo (Eds.), *Neuropsychology of eye movements* (pp. 115–145). Hillsdale, NJ: Lawrence Erlbaum Associates.

Inglis, J. (1962). Dichotic stimulation, temporal lobe damage, and the perception and storage of auditory stimuli—a note on Kimura's findings. *Canadian Journal of Psychology, 16*, 11–17.

Inglis, J., & Sykes, D. H. (1967). Some sources of variation in dichotic listening performance in children. *Journal of Experimental Child Psychology*, *5*, 480–488.

Isaev, D. N., & Kagan, V. E. (1974). Autistic syndromes in children and adolescents. *Acta Paedopsychiatrica*, *40*, 182–190.

Jackson, J. H. (1958). *Selected writings of John Hughlings Jackson* (Vols. I & II). New York: Basic Books.

Jacobson, C. D., Csernus, V. J., Shryne, J. E., & Gorski, R. A. (1981). The influence of gonadectomy, androgen exposure, or a gonadal graft in the neonatal rat on the volume of the sexually dimorphic nucleus of the preoptic area. *Journal of Neuroscience*, *1*, 1142–1147.

Jeeves, M. H. (1965). Psychological studies of three cases of congenital agenesis of the corpus callosum. In A. U. S. de Reuck & R. Porter (Eds.), *Functions of the corpus callosum*. London: Churchill.

Jenkins, R. L., & Parsons, O. A. (1981). Neuropsychological effect of chronic alcoholism on tactual-spatial performance and memory in males. *Alcoholism: Clinical and Experimental Research*, *5*, 26–33.

Johnson, D. J., & Mykelbust, H. R. (1971). *Learning disabilities: Educational principles and practices*. New York: Grune & Stratton.

Johnson, E. S., & Meade, A. C. (1987). Developmental patterns of spatial ability: An early sex difference. *Child Development*, *58*, 725–740.

Johnson, P. (1977). Dichotically stimulated ear differences in musicians and nonmusicians. *Cortex*, *13*, 385–389.

Jones, B. (1979). Sex and visual-field effects on accuracy and decision-making when subjects classify male and female faces. *Cortex*, *15*, 551–560.

Jones, R. K. (1966). Observations on stammering after localized cerebral injury. *Journal of Neurology, Neurosurgery, and Psychiatry*, *29*, 192–195.

Kail, R. V., & Siegel, A. W. (1977). Sex differences in retention of verbal and spatial characteristics of stimuli. *Journal of Experimental Child Psychology*, *23*, 341–347.

Kallman, H. J. (1977). Ear asymmetries with monaurally presented sounds. *Neuropsychologia*, *15*, 833–835.

Kallman, H. (1978). Can expectancy explain reaction time ear asymmetries? *Neuropsychologia*, *16*, 225–228.

Kallman, H., & Corballis, M. C. (1975). Ear asymmetry in reaction time to musical sounds. *Perception and Psychophysics*, *17*, 368–370.

Kaplan, E. (1980). *A qualitative approach to clinical neuropsychological assessment*. Paper presented at the annual meeting of the American Psychological Association, Montreal, Canada.

Kasamatsu, A., & Hirai, T. (1972). An electroencephalographic study of Zen meditation (Zazen). In C. T. Tart (Ed.), *Altered states of consciousness* (pp. 501–514). New York: Doubleday.

Keefe, B., & Swinney, D. (1979). On the relationship of hemispheric specialization and developmental dyslexia. *Cortex*, *15*, 471–481.

Kellar, L. A., & Bever, T. G. (1980). Hemispheric asymmetries in the perception of musical interviews as a function of musical experience and family handedness background. *Brain and Language*, *10*, 24–38.

Kershner, J. R. (1977). Lateralization in normal six-year-olds as related to later reading disability. *Developmental Psychobiology*, *11*, 309–319.

Kershner, J. R., Thomae, R., & Callaway, R. (1977). Nonverbal fixation control in young children induces a left-field advantage in digit recall. *Neuropsychologia*, *15*, 569–576.

Kesner, R. (1990). Cognitive constructs in animal and human studies. In J. W. Rohrbaugh, R. Parasuraman, & R. Johnson, Jr. (Eds.), *Event-related brain potentials: Basic issues and applications*. Oxford: Oxford University Press.

Kiessling, L. S., Denckla, M. B., & Carlton, M. (1983). Evidence for differential hemispheric function in children with hemiplegic cerebral palsy. *Developmental Medicine and Child Neurology, 25,* 727–734.

Kimura, D. (1961). Some effects of temporal lobe damage on auditory perception. *Canadian Journal of Psychology, 15,* 156–165.

Kimura, D. (1963). Speech lateralization in young children as determined by an auditory test. *Journal of Comparative and Physiological Psychology, 56,* 899–902.

Kimura, D. (1967). Functional asymmetry of the brain in dichotic listening. *Cortex, 3,* 163–178.

Kimura, D. (1969). Spatial localization in left and right visual fields. *Canadian Journal of Psychology, 23,* 445–458.

Kimura, D. (1973a). Manual activity during speaking. I. Right-handers. *Neuropsychologia, 11,* 45–50.

Kimura, D. (1973b). Manual activity during speaking. II. Left-handers. *Neuropsychologia, 11,* 51–55.

Kimura, D. (1976). The neural basis of language qua gesture. In H. Whitaker & H. A. Whitaker (Eds.), *Studies in neurolinguistics* (Vol. 1). New York: Academic Press.

Kimura, D. (1985). Male brain, female brain: The hidden difference. *Psychology Today, 19,* 50–58.

Kimura, D., & Archibald, Y. (1974). Motor functions of the left hemisphere. *Brain, 97,* 337–350.

Kimura, D., & Folb, S. (1968). Neural processing of backwards speech sounds. *Science, 161,* 395–396.

Kimura, D., & Harshman, R. (1984). Sex differences in brain organization for verbal and nonverbal functions. In G. J. de Vries (Ed.), *Sex differences in the brain: Progress in brain research* (Vol. 61). New York: Elsevier.

Kinsbourne, M. (1972). Eye and head turning indicates cerebral lateralization. *Science, 176,* 539–541.

Kinsbourne, M. (1973). The control of attention by interaction between the cerebral hemispheres. In S. Kornblum (Ed.), *Attention and performance II.* New York: Academic Press.

Kinsbourne, M. (1974). The mechanisms of hemisphere asymmetry in man. In M. Kinsbourne & W. L. Smith (Eds.), *Hemispheric disconnection and cerebral function.* Springfield, IL: Charles C. Thomas.

Kinsbourne, M. (1975). The ontogeny of cerebral dominance. In D. Aaronson & R. W. Reiber (Eds.), *Developmental psycholinguistics and communication disorders.* New York: New York Academy of Sciences.

Kinsbourne, M., & Cook, J. (1971). Generalized and lateralized effects of concurrent verbalizations on a unimanual skill. *Quarterly Journal of Experimental Psychology, 23,* 341–345.

Kinsbourne, M., & McMurray, J. (1975). The effect of cerebral dominance on time-sharing between speaking and tapping by preschool children. *Child Development, 46,* 240–242.

Kirby, J. R., & Asman, A. F. (1984). Planning skills and mathematics achievement: Implications regarding learning disability. *Journal of Psychoeducational Assessment, 2,* 9–22.

Kirsner, K. H. (1980). Hemisphere specific processes in letter matching. *Journal of Experimental Psychology: Human Perception and Performance, 6,* 167–179.

Klein, D., Moscovitch, M., & Vigna, C. (1976). Attentional mechanisms and perceptual asymmetries in tachistoscopic recognition of words and faces. *Neuropsychologia, 14,* 55–66.

Klein, S. P., & Rosenfield, W. D. (1980). The hemispheric specialization for linguistic and nonlinguistic tactile stimuli in third grade children. *Cortex, 16,* 205–212.

Knopman, D. S., Rubens, A. B., Klassen, A. C., Meyer, M. W., & Niccum, N. (1980). Regional cerebral blood flow patterns during verbal and nonverbal auditory activation. *Brain and Language, 9,* 93–112.

Knox, C., & Kimura, D. (1970). Cerebral processing of nonverbal sounds in boys and girls. *Neuropsychologia, 8,* 227–237.

Kocel, K. M., Galin, D., Ornstein, R., & Merrin, E. (1972). Lateral eye movement and cognitive mode. *Psychonomic Science, 27,* 223–224.

Kolb, B., & Whishaw, I. Q. (1985). *Fundamentals of human neuropsychology.* New York: W. H. Freeman.

Konner, M. (1983). *The tangled wing: Biological constraints on the human spirit.* New York: Harper Colophon.

Kopp, N., Michel, F., Carrier, H., Biron, A., & Duvillard, P. (1977). Etude de certaines asymmetries hemispheriques du cerveau humain. *Journal of Neurological Sciences, 34,* 340–363.

Koslow, R. E. (1987). Sex-related differences and visual–spatial mental imagery as factors affecting symbolic motor skill acquisition. *Sex Roles, 17,* 521–527.

Kraft, R. H. (1984). Lateral specialization and verbal/spatial ability in preschool children: Age, sex, and familial handedness differences. *Neuropsychologia, 22,* 319–335.

Krashen, S. D. (1973). Lateralization, language learning, and the critical period: Some new evidence. *Language Learning, 23,* 63–74.

Krashen, S. D. (1975). The development of cerebral dominance and language learning: More new evidence. In D. P. Dato (Ed.), *Developmental psycholinguistics: Theory and applications.* Washington, DC: Georgetown University Press.

Krashen, S. D. (1976). Cerebral asymmetry. In H. Whitaker & H. A. Whitaker (Eds.), *Studies in neurolinguistics* (Vol. 1). New York: Academic Press.

Krashen, S. D. (1977). The left hemisphere. In M. C. Whitrock (Ed.), *The human brain.* Englewood Cliffs, NJ: Prentice-Hall.

Kriss, A., Blumhardt, L. D., Halliday, A. M., & Platt, R. T. C. (1975). Neurological asymmetries immediately after unilateral ECT. *Journal of Neurology, Neurosurgery, and Psychiatry, 41,* 1135–1144.

Krynicki, V. E., & Nahas, A. D. (1979). Differing lateralized perceptual-motor patterns in schizophrenic and nonpsychotic children. *Perceptual and Motor Skills, 49,* 603–610.

Kutas, M., & Donchin, E. (1974). Studies of squeezing: Handedness, responding hand, response force and asymmetry of readiness potential. *Science, 186,* 545–548.

Lacroix, J. M., & Comper, P. (1979). Lateralization in the electrodermal system as a function of cognitive/hemispheric manipulations. *Psychophysiology, 16,* 116–129.

Lake, D. A., & Bryden, M. P. (1976). Handedness and sex differences in hemispheric asymmetry. *Brain and Language, 3,* 266–282.

Landis, T., Assal, G., & Perret, C. (1979). Opposite cerebral hemispheric superiorities for visual associative processing of emotional facial expressions and objects. *Nature, 278,* 739–740.

Landsdown, R. (1978). Retardation in mathematics: A consideration of multifactorial determination. *Journal of Child Psychology and Psychiatry, 19,* 181–185.

Lansdell, H. (1969). Verbal and nonverbal factors in right-hemisphere speech: Relation to early neurological history. *Journal of Comparative and Physiological Psychology, 69,* 734–738.

Larsen, S. (1984). Developmental changes in the pattern of ear asymmetry as revealed by a dichotic listening task. *Cortex, 20,* 5–17.

Laschet, U. (1973). Antiandrogen in the treatment of sex offenders: Mode of action and therapeutic outcome. In J. Zubin & J. Money (Eds.), *Contemporary sexual behavior: Critical issues in the 1970s.* Baltimore: Johns Hopkins University Press.

Lassen, N. A., & Ingvar, D. H. (1972). Radioisotopic assessment of regional cerebral blood flows. In *Progress in nuclear medicine* (Vol. 1). Baltimore: University Park Press.

Lassen, N. A., Ingvar, D. H., & Skinhoj, F. (1978). Brain function and blood flow. *Scientific American, 239,* 50–59.

Lavadas, E., Nicoletti, R., Umilta, C., & Rizzolatti, G. (1984). Right hemisphere interference during negative affect: A reaction time study. *Neuropsychologia, 22,* 479–484.

Lavadas, E., Umilta, C. I., & Ricci-Bitti, P. E. (1980). Evidence for sex differences in right hemisphere dominance for emotions. *Neuropsychologia, 18,* 361–366.

LeDoux, J. E., Wilson, D. H., & Gazzaniga, M. S. (1977a). A divided mind: Observation on the conscious properties of the separated hemispheres. *Annals of Neurology, 2,* 417–421.

LeDoux, J. E., Wilson, D. H., & Gazzaniga, M. S. (1977b). Manipulo-spatial aspects of cerebral lateralization: Clues to the origin of lateralization. *Neuropsychologia, 15,* 743–750.

Lee, D. (1973). Codification of reality: Lineal and nonlineal. In R. E. Ornstein (Ed.), *The nature of human consciousness.* New York: Viking Press.

Lee, T., & Seeman, P. (1980). Elevation of brain neuroleptic/dopamine receptors in schizophrenia. *American Journal of Psychiatry, 137,* 191–197.

Leehey, S., Diamond, R., & Cahn, A. (1978). Upright and inverted faces: The right hemisphere knows the difference. *Cortex, 14,* 411–419.

Lehman, R. A. W. (1980). The handedness of rhesus monkeys III: Consistency within and across activities. *Cortex, 16,* 197–204.

Leiber, L. (1976). Lexical decisions in the right and left cerebral hemispheres. *Brain and Language, 3,* 443–450.

Leiber, L., & Axelrod, S. (1981). Not all sinistrality is pathological. *Cortex, 17,* 259–272.

LeMay, M. (1976). Morphological cerebral asymmetries of modern man, fossil man, and nonhuman primate. *Annals of the New York Academy of Sciences, 280,* 349–366.

LeMay, M. (1977). Asymmetries of the skull and handedness: Phrenology revisited. *Journal of the Neurological Sciences, 32,* 243–253.

LeMay, M. (1981). Are there radiological changes in the brains of individuals with dyslexia? *Bulletin of the Orton Society, 31,* 135–141.

LeMay, M. (1982). Morphological aspects of human brain asymmetry: An evolutionary perspective. *Trends in Neurosciences, 5,* 273–275.

LeMay, M., & Culebras, A. (1972). Human brain morphologic differences in the hemispheres demonstrated by carotid angiography. *New England Journal of Medicine, 287,* 168–170.

LeMay, M., & Geschwind, N. (1975). Hemispheric differences in the brains of great apes. *Brain, Behavior and Evolution, 11,* 48–52.

LeMay, M., & Geschwind, N. (1978). Asymmetries of the human cerebral hemisphere. In A. Caramazza & E. B. Zurif (Eds.), *Language acquisition and language breakdown.* Baltimore: Johns Hopkins University Press.

Lenneberg, E. H. (1967). *Biological foundations of language.* New York: Wiley.

Levander, M., & Levander, S. (1990). Cognitive performance among left-handers differing in strength of handedness and familial sinistrality. *Intelligence, 14,* 97–108.

Levin, S. (1984). Frontal lobe dysfunction in schizophrenia—I. Eye movement impairments. *Psychiatry Research, 18,* 27–55.

Levine, S. C. (1985). Developmental changes in right hemisphere involvement in face perception. In C. T. Best (Ed.), *Hemisphere function and collaboration in the child.* New York: Academic Press.

Levy, J. (1969). Possible basis for the evolution of lateral specialization of the human brain. *Nature, 224,* 614–615.

Levy, J. (1972). Lateral specialization of the human brain: Behavioral manifestations and possible evolutionary basis. In J. A. Kiger (Ed.), *The biology of behavior.* Corvallis: Oregon State University.

Levy, J. (1974). Psychobiological implications of bilateral asymmetry. In S. Dimond & S. Beaumont (Eds.), *Hemispheric function in the human brain.* New York: Halstead Press.

Levy, J. (1976). Cerebral lateralization and spatial ability. *Behavior Genetics, 6,* 171–188.

Levy, J. (1978). Lateral differences in the human brain in cognition and behavioral control. In P. Buser & A. Rougeul-Buser (Eds.), *Cerebral correlates of conscious experience*. New York: North-Holland.

Levy, J. (1985). Interhemispheric collaboration: Single mindedness in the asymmetrical brain. In C. T. Best (Ed.), *Hemispheric function and collaboration in the child*. New York: Academic Press.

Levy, J., & Nagylaki, T. (1972). A model for the genetics of handedness. *Genetics, 72,* 117–128.

Levy, J., & Reid, M. (1976). Variations in writing posture and cerebral organization. *Science, 194,* 337–339.

Levy, J., & Reid, M. (1978). Variations in cerebral organization as a function of handedness, hand posture in writing, and sex. *Journal of Experimental Psychology: General, 107,* 119–144.

Levy, J., & Trevarthen, C. (1976). Metacontrol of hemispheric function in human split-brain patients. *Journal of Experimental Psychology: Human Perception and Performance, 2,* 299–312.

Levy, J., & Trevarthen, G. (1977). Perceptual, semantic language processes in split-brain patients. *Brain, 100,* 105–118.

Levy, J., Trevarthen, C. B., & Sperry, R. W. (1972). Perception of bilateral chimeric figures following hemispheric deconnexion. *Brain, 95,* 61–78.

Levy-Agresti, J., & Sperry, R. W. (1968). Differential perceptual capacities in major and minor hemispheres. *Proceedings of the National Academy of Sciences, 61,* 1151.

Levy, R. S. (1977). The question of electrophysiological asymmetries preceding speech. In H. Whitaker & H. A. Whitaker (Eds.), *Studies in neurolinguistics* (Vol. 3). New York: Academic Press.

Lewandowski, L. (1982). Hemispheric asymmetries in children. *Perceptual and Motor Skills, 54,* 1011–1019.

Ley, R. G., & Bryden, M. P. (1977). Hemispheric differences in processing emotional stimuli? *Bulletin of the Psychonomic Society, 10,* 239–261.

Ley, R. G., & Bryden, M. P. (1979). Hemispheric differences in processing emotions and faces. *Brain and Language, 7,* 127–138.

Lieberman, P. (1984). *The biology and evolution of language*. Cambridge, MA: Harvard University Press.

Lieberman, P. (1985). On the evolution of human syntactic ability: Its preadaptive bases— motor control and speech. *Journal of Human Evolution, 14,* 657–668.

Liederman, J., & Kinsbourne, M. (1980a). The mechanism of neonatal rightward turning bias: A sensory or motor asymmetry? *Infant Behavior and Development, 5,* 223–238.

Liederman, J., & Kinsbourne, M. (1980b). Rightward turning biases in neonates reflect a single neural asymmetry in motor programming: A reply to Turkewitz. *Infant Behavior and Development, 3,* 245–251.

Limber, J. (1977). Language in child and chimp? *American Psychologist, 32,* 280–295.

Linn, M. C., & Petersen, A. C. (1985). Emergence and characterization of sex differences in spatial ability: A meta-analysis. *Child Development, 56,* 1479–1498.

Linnville, S. E. (1984, May). *Electrophysiological correlates of handedness and speech perception contrasts*. Paper presented at the Midwestern Psychological Association Conference, Chicago, IL.

Lisk, R. D. (1978). The regulation of sexual "heat." In J. B. Hutchison (Ed.), *Biological determinants of sexual behavior*. New York: Wiley.

London, W. P. (1986). Handedness and alcoholism. *Alcohol: Clinical and Experimental Research, 10,* 357.

Loo, R., & Schneider, R. (1979). An evaluation of the Briggs-Nebes modified version of Annett's handedness inventory. *Cortex, 15,* 683–686.

Lynes, S. (1987, April). *Components in hemispheric lateralization.* Paper presented at the 67th annual meeting of the Western Psychological Association, Long Beach, CA.

Majkowski, J., Bochenek, Z., Bochenek, W., Knapik-Fijalkowska, D., & Kopec, J. (1971). Latency of averaged evoked potentials to contralateral and ipsilateral auditory stimulation in normal subjects. *Brain Research, 25,* 416–419.

Mancuso, R. P., Lawrence, A. F., Hintze, R. W., & White, C. T. (1979). Effect of altered central and peripheral visual field stimulation on correct recognition and visual evoked response. *International Journal of Neuroscience, 9,* 113–122.

Mandell, A. (1980). Toward a psychology of transcendence: God in the brain. In J. M. Davidson & R. J. Davidson (Eds.), *Psychobiology of consciousness.* New York: Plenum Press.

Manning, A. A., Goble, W., Markman, R., & LaBreche, T. (1977). Lateral cerebral differences in the deaf in response to linguistic and nonlinguistic stimuli. *Brain and Language, 4,* 309–321.

Marsh, G. R. (1978). Asymmetry of electrophysiological phenomena and its relation to behavior in humans. In M. Kinsbourne (Ed.), *Asymmetrical function of the brain* (pp. 292–317). Cambridge, England: Cambridge University Press.

Marshall, J. C. (1980). Clues from neurological deficits. In U. Bellugi & M. Studdert-Kennedy (Eds.), *Signed and spoken language: Biological constraints on linguistic form.* Weinheim and Deerfield Beach, FL: Verlag Chernie.

Marshall, J. C., Caplan, D., & Holmes, J. M. (1975). The measure of laterality. *Neuropsychologia, 13,* 315–321.

Marzi, C. A., Brizzolara, D., Rizzolatti, G., Umilta, C., & Berlucchi, G. (1974). Left hemisphere superiority for the recognition of well known faces. *Brain Research, 66,* 358.

Marzi, I. A., & Berlucchi, G. (1977). Right visual field superiority for accuracy of recognition of famous faces in normals. *Neuropsychologia, 15,* 751–756.

Mazur, A. (1983). Hormones, aggression and dominance in humans. In B. B. Svare (Ed.), *Hormones and aggressive behavior.* New York: Plenum Press.

McGee, M. G. (1979). Human spatial abilities: Psychometric studies and environmental, genetic, hormonal, and neurological influences. *Psychological Bulletin, 86,* 889–918.

McGee, M. G. (1980). The effect of brain asymmetry on cognitive functions depends upon what ability, for which sex, at what point in development. *Behavioral and Brain Sciences, 3,* 243–244.

McGlone, J. (1978). Sex differences in functional brain asymmetry. *Cortex, 14,* 122–128.

McGlone, J. (1980). Sex differences in human brain asymmetry: A critical survey. *Behavioral and Brain Sciences, 3,* 215–263.

McKeever, W. F. (1971). Lateral word recognition: Effects of unilateral and bilateral presentation, asynchrony of bilateral presentation, and forced order of report. *Quarterly Journal of Experimental Psychology, 23,* 410–416.

McKeever, W. F. (1979). Handwriting posture in left handers: Sex, familial sinistrality, and language laterality correlates. *Neuropsychologia, 17,* 429–444.

McKeever, W. F. (1981). Evidence against the hypothesis of right-hemisphere language dominance in the native American Navajo. *Neuropsychologia, 19,* 595–598.

McKeever, W. F., & Dixon, M. S. (1981). Right-hemisphere superiority of discriminating memorized from nonmemorized faces: Affective imagery, sex, and perceived emotional effects. *Brain and Language, 12,* 246–260.

McKeever, W. F., & Gill, K. M. (1972). Visual half-field differences in the recognition of bilaterally presented single letters and vertically spelled words. *Perceptual and Motor Skills, 34,* 815–818.

McKeever, W. F., & Hurling, M. D. (1970). Lateral dominance in tachistoscopic word recognition of children at two levels of ability. *Quarterly Journal of Experimental Psychology, 22,* 600–604.

McKeever, W. F., & Hurling, M. D. (1971). Lateral dominance in tachistoscopic word recognition performance obtained with simultaneous bilateral input. *Neuropsychologia, 9*, 15–20.

McKeever, W. F., & Van Deventer, A. D. (1975). Dyslexic adolescents: Evidence of impaired visual and auditory language processing associated with normal lateralization and visual responsivity. *Cortex, 11*, 361–378.

McKeever, W. F., & Van Deventer, A. D. (1977). Visual and auditory language processing asymmetries: Influence of handedness, familial sinistrality and sex. *Cortex, 13*, 225–241.

McKeever, W. F., & Van Deventer, A. D. (1980). Inverted handwriting position, language laterality, and the Levy–Nagylaki model of handedness and cerebral organization. *Neuropsychologia, 18*, 99–102.

McKeever, W. F., Van Deventer, A. D., & Suberti, M. (1973). Avowed, assessed, and familial handedness on differential hemispheric processing of brief sequential and nonsequential visual stimuli. *Neuropsychologia, 11*, 235–238.

McManus, I. C. (1976). Scrotal asymmetry in man and ancient sculpture. *Nature, 259*, 426.

McManus, I. C. (1979). *Human laterality.* Unpublished doctoral dissertation. Cambridge University, Cambridge, England.

McManus, I. C. (1985). Handedness, language dominance and aphasia: A genetic model. *Psychological Medicine, 15*, 1–14.

McManus, I. C., & Bryden, M. P. (1991). Geschwind's theory of cerebral lateralization: Developing a formal, causal model. *Psychological Bulletin, 110*, 237–253.

McQ. Reynolds, D., & Jeeves, M. A. (1978a). A developmental study of hemisphere specialization for alphabetic stimuli. *Cortex, 14*, 259–267.

McQ. Reynolds, D., & Jeeves, M. A. (1978b). A developmental study of hemisphere specialization for recognition of faces in normal subjects. *Cortex, 14*, 511–520.

Meece, J., Parsons, J., Kaczala, C., Goff, S., & Futterman, R. (1982). Sex differences in math achievement: Toward a model of academic choice. *Psychological Bulletin, 91*, 324–348.

Merola, J. L., & Liederman, J. (1985). Developmental changes in hemisphere independence. *Child Development, 56*, 1184–1194.

Miglioli, M., Buchtel, H. A., Campanini, T., & DeRisio, C. (1979). Cerebral hemispheric lateralization of cognitive deficits due to alcoholism. *Journal of Nervous and Mental Diseases, 167*, 212–217.

Milberg, W. P., Whitman, R. D., Rourke, D., & Glaros, A. G. (1981). Role of subvocal motor activity in dichotic speech perception and selective attention. *Journal of Experimental Psychology: Human Perception and Performance, 7*, 231–239.

Mills, L., & Rollman, G. B. (1980). Hemispheric asymmetry for auditory perception of temporal order. *Neuropsychologia, 18*, 41–47.

Milner, A. D., & Jeeves, M. A. (1979). A review of behavioural studies of agenesis of the corpus callosum. In I. Steele Russell, M. W. Hof, & G. Berlucchi (Eds.), *Structure and function of cerebral commissures.* London: Macmillan.

Milner, B. (1962). Laterality effects in audition. In V. Mountcastle (Ed.), *Interhemispheric relations and cerebral dominance.* Baltimore: Johns Hopkins University Press.

Milner, B. (1974). Hemispheric specialization: Scope and limits. In F. O. Schmitt & F. G. Warden (Eds.), *The neurosciences: Third study program.* Cambridge, MA: MIT Press.

Mirabile, P. J., Porter, R. J., Jr., Hughes, L. F., & Berlin, C. I. (1978). Dichotic lag effect in children 7 to 15. *Developmental Psychology, 14*, 277–285.

Mishkin, M., & Forgays, D. G. (1952). Word recognition as a function of retinal locus. *Journal of Experimental Psychology, 43*, 43–48.

Moir, A. (1991). *Brain sex: The real difference between men and women.* Secaucus, NJ: Lyle Stuart.

Molfese, D. L. (1972). *Cerebral asymmetry in infants, children and adults: Auditory evoked responses to speech and music stimuli.* Unpublished Ph.D. dissertation, Pennsylvania State University.

Molfese, D. L. (1973). Cerebral asymmetry in infants, children and adults: Auditory evoked responses to speech and noise stimuli. *Dissertation Abstracts International, 34,* 1298.

Molfese, D. L. (1978). Neuroelectrical correlates of categorical speech perception in adults. *Brain and Language, 5,* 25–35.

Molfese, D. L. (1980). The phoneme and the engram: Electrophysiological evidence for the acoustic invariant in stop consonants. *Brain and Language, 9,* 372–376.

Molfese, D. L., & Best, J. C. (1988). Electrophysiological indices of the early development of lateralization for language and cognition, and their implications for predicting later development. In D. L. Molfese & S. J. Segalowitz (Eds.), *Brain lateralization in children: Developmental implications* (pp. 171–190). New York: Guilford Press.

Molfese, D. L., Freeman, R. B., Jr., & Palermo, D. S. (1975). The ontogeny of the brain lateralization for speech and nonspeech stimuli. *Brain and Language, 2,* 356–368.

Molfese, D. L., & Hess, T. M. (1978). Speech perception in nursery school children: Sex and hemisphere differences. *Journal of Experimental Child Psychology, 26,* 71–84.

Molfese, D. L., & Molfese, V. J. (1979a). Hemisphere and stimulus differences as reflected in the cortical responses of newborn infants to speech stimuli. *Developmental Psychology, 15,* 505–511.

Molfese, D. L., & Molfese, V. J. (1979b). Infant speech perception: Learned or innate? In H. A. Whitaker & H. Whitaker (Eds.), *Advances in neurolinguistics* (Vol. 4, pp. 225–238). New York: Academic Press.

Molfese, D. L., & Molfese, V. J. (1980). Cortical responses of preterm infants to phonetic and nonphonetic speech stimuli. *Developmental Psychology, 16,* 574–581.

Molfese, D. L., & Molfese, V. J. (1985). Electrophysiological indices of auditory discrimination in newborn infants: The bases for predicting later language development? *Infant Behavior and Development, 8,* 197–211.

Molfese, D. L., & Molfese, V. J. (1988). Right hemisphere responses from preschool children to temporal cues contained in speech and nonspeech materials: Electrophysiological correlates. *Brain and Language, 33,* 245–249.

Montgomery, G. (1989). The mind in motion. *Discover, 10,* 58–66.

Moore, W. H. (1976). Bilateral tachistoscopic word perception of stutterers and normal subjects. *Brain and Language, 3,* 434–442.

Moore, W. H., & Lang, M. K. (1977). Alpha symmetry over the right and left hemispheres of stutterers and control subjects preceding massed oral readings: A preliminary investigation. *Perceptual and Motor Skills, 44,* 223–230.

Morais, J., & Landercy, M. (1977). Listening to speech while retaining music: What happens to the right ear advantage? *Brain and Language, 4,* 295–308.

Moscovitch, M. (1976). On the representation of language in the right hemisphere of right-handed people. *Brain and Language, 3,* 47–71.

Moscovitch, M., & Olds, J. (1982). Asymmetries in spontaneous facial expressions and their possible relation to hemispheric specialization. *Neuropsychologia, 20,* 71–81.

Myers, R. E., & Sperry, R. W. (1958). Interhemispheric communication through the corpus callosum: Mnemonic carry-over between the hemispheres. *Archives of Neurology and Psychiatry, 80,* 298–303.

Myslobodsky, M. S., & Horesh, N. (1978). Bilateral electrodermal activity in depressive patients. *Biological Psychology, 6,* 111–120.

Myslobodsky, M. S., & Rattok, J. (1975). Asymmetry of electrodermal activity in man. *Bulletin of the Psychonomic Society, 6,* 501–502.

Myslobodsky, M. S., & Rattok, J. (1977). Bilateral electrodermal activity in waking man. *Acta Psychologica, 41,* 273–282.

Nachshon, I., & Carmon, A. (1975). Hand preference in sequential and spatial discrimination tasks. *Cortex, 11,* 123–131.

Naeser, M. A., Levine, H. L., Benson, D. F., Stuss, D. T., & Weir, W. S. (1981). Frontal leukotomy size and hemispheric asymmetries on computerized tomographic scans of schizophrenics with variable recovery. *Archives of Neurology, 38*, 30–37.

Nagae, S. (1983). Development of hand-eye dominance in relation to verbal self-regulation of motor behavior. *American Journal of Psychology, 96*, 539–552.

Naidoo, S. (1972). *Specific dyslexia*. London: Pitman.

Nass, R. D., Sadler, A. E., & Sidtis, J. J. (1984). Differential effects of congenital right and left hemisphere injury on dichotic tests of specialized auditory function. *Annals of Neurology, 16*, 388.

Naylor, H. (1980). Reading disability and lateral asymmetry: An information-processing analysis. *Psychological Bulletin, 87*, 531–545.

Nebes, R. D. (1978). Direct examination of cognitive function in the right and left hemispheres. In M. Kinsbourne (Ed.), *Asymmetrical function of the brain* (pp. 99–137). Cambridge, England: Cambridge University Press.

Nebes, R. D. (1989). Semantic memory in Alzheimer's disease. *Psychological Bulletin, 106*, 377–394.

Neilsen, J. M. (1946). *Agnosia, apraxia, aphasia: Their value in cerebral localization.* New York: Hafner.

Newcombe, N. (1982). Sex-related differences in spatial ability: Problems and gaps in current approaches. In M. Potegal (Ed.), *Spatial abilities: Development and physiological foundations.* New York: Academic Press.

Nicholas, M., Obler, L. K., Albert, M. L., & Helm-Estabrooks, N. (1985). Empty speech in Alzheimer's disease and fluent aphasia. *Journal of Speech and Hearing Research, 28*, 405–410.

Nilsson, J., Glencross, D., & Geffen, G. (1980). The effects of familial sinistrality and preferred hand on dichaptic and dichotic tasks. *Brain and Language, 10*, 390–404.

Nottebohm, F. (1977). Asymmetries in neural control of vocalization in the canary. In S. Harnad, R. W. Doty, L. Goldstein, J. Jaynes, & G. Krauthamer (Eds.), *Lateralization in the nervous system* (pp. 23–44). New York: Academic Press.

Nottebohm, F. (1979). Origins and mechanisms in the establishment of cerebral dominance. In M. S. Gazzaniga (Ed.), *Handbook of behavioral neurobiology: Volume 2, neuropsychology.* New York: Plenum.

Obler, L. (1979). Right hemisphere participation in second language acquisition. In K. C. Diller (Ed.), *Individual differences and universals in language learning aptitude* (pp. 53–64). Rowley, MA: Newbury House.

Obler, L., Albert, M., & Gordon, H. (1975). *Asymmetrical cerebral dominance in bilinguals.* Paper presented at the Academy of Aphasia, Victoria, British Columbia, Canada.

Obrzut, J. E., Hynd, G. W., Obrzut, A., & Leitgeb, J. L. (1980). Time-sharing and dichotic listening asymmetries in normal and learning-disabled children. *Brain and Language, 11*, 181–194.

Obrzut, J. E., Hynd, G. W., Obrzut, A., & Pirozzolo, F. J. (1981). Effect of directed attention on cerebral asymmetries in normal and learning disabled children. *Developmental Psychology, 17*, 118–125.

Ogiela, D. A. (1990, December). *Tapping the human language capacity.* Unpublished master's thesis, Illinois Benedictine College, Lisle, IL.

Ogiela, D. A. (1991, May). *Language and lateralization of cerebral functions.* Paper presented at the annual Psi-Chi Initiation Ceremony, Illinois Benedictine College Chapter, Lisle, IL.

Ohgishi, M. (1978). Hemispheric differences in the mode of information processing. *Japanese Journal of Psychology, 49*, 257–264.

Ojemann, G. A. (1974). Mental arithmetic during human thalamic stimulation. *Neuropsychologia, 12*, 1–10.

Ojemann, G. A. (1979). Individual variability in cortical localization of language. *Journal of Neurosurgery, 50,* 164–169.

Ojemann, G. A. (1983). Brain organization for language from the perspective of electrical stimulation mapping. *Behavioral and Brain Sciences, 2,* 189–230.

Ojemann, G. A., & Whitaker, H. A. (1978). The bilingual brain. *Archives of Neurology, 35,* 409–412.

Oke, A., Keller, R., Mefford, I., & Adams, R. N. (1978). Lateralization of norepinephrine in the human thalamus. *Science, 200,* 1411–1413.

Oldfield, R. C. (1971). The assessment and analysis of handedness: The Edinburgh inventory. *Neuropsychologia, 9,* 97–114.

O'Leary, M. R., Donovan, D. M., Chaney, E. F., Walker, R. D., & Schau, E. J. (1979). Application of discriminant analysis to level of performance of alcoholics and nonalcoholics on Wechsler-Bellevue and Halstead-Reitan subtests. *Journal of Clinical Neuropsychology, 35,* 204–208.

Olson, M. E. (1973). Laterality differences in tachistoscopic word recognition in normal and delayed readers in elementary school. *Neuropsychologia, 11,* 343–350.

Ornstein, R. E. (1977). *The psychology of consciousness* (2nd ed.). Chicago: Harcourt, Brace, Jovanovich.

Ornstein, R. E. (1978). The split and whole brain. *Human Nature, 1,* 76–83.

Orton, J. L. (1966). "Word-blindedness" in school children and other papers on strephosymbolia (specific language disability—dyslexia). *Orton Society Monograph* (Towson, MD: Orton Society, No. 2).

Orton, S. T. (1925). "Word-blindedness" in school children. *Archives of Neurology and Psychiatry, 14,* 581–615.

Orton, S. T. (1928). Specific reading disability—strephosymbolia. *Journal of the American Medical Association, 90,* 1095–1099.

Orton, S. T. (1937). *Reading, writing and speech problems in children.* New York: W. W. Norton.

Oscar-Berman, M., & Bonner, R. T. (1985). Matching- and delayed matching-to-sample performance as measures of visual processing, selective attention, and memory in aging and alcoholic individuals. *Neuropsychologia, 23,* 639–651.

Oscar-Berman, M., Goodglass, H., & Cherlow, D. G. (1973). Perceptual laterality and iconic recognition of visual materials by Korsakoff patients and normal adults. *Journal of Comparative and Physiological Psychology, 82,* 316–321.

Oscar-Berman, M., Rehbein, L., Porfert, A., & Goodglass, H. (1978). Dichaptic hand-order effects with verbal and nonverbal tactile stimuli. *Brain and Language, 6,* 323–333.

Ozols, E. J., & Rourke, B. P. (1985). Dimensions of social sensitivity in two types of learning disabled children. In B. P. Rourke (Ed.), *Neuropsychology of learning disabilities* (pp. 281–301). New York: Guilford.

Papanicolaou, A. C., Levin, H. S., Eisenberg, H. M., & Moore, B. D. (1983). Evoked potential indices of selective hemispheric engagement in affective and phonetic tasks. *Neuropsychologia, 21,* 401–405.

Papanicolaou, A. C., Schmidt, A. L., Moore, B. D., & Eisenberg, H. M. (1983). Cerebral activation patterns in an arithmetic and a visuospatial processing task. *International Journal of Neuroscience, 20,* 283–288.

Parkins, R., Roberts, R. J., Reinarz, S. J., & Varney, N. R. (1987). *CT asymmetries in adult developmental dyslexics.* Paper presented at the annual convention of the International Neuropsychological Society, Washington, DC.

Parsons, O. A. (1987). Neuropsychological consequences of alcohol abuse: Many questions— some answers. In O. A. Parsons, M. Butters, & P. Nathan (Eds.), *Neuropsychology of alcoholism: Implications for diagnosis and treatment* (pp. 153–178). New York: Guilford.

Patterson, K., & Bradshaw, J. L. (1975). Differential hemispheric mediation of nonverbal visual stimuli. *Journal of Experimental Psychology: Human Perception and Performance, 1,* 246–252.

Pavlidis, G. T. (1981). Do eye movements hold the key to dyslexia? *Neuropsychologia, 19,* 57–64.

Penfield, W. (1975). *The mystery of the mind.* Princeton, NJ: Princeton University Press.

Penfield, W., & Roberts, L. (1959). *Speech and brain mechanisms.* Princeton, NJ: Princeton University Press.

Perris, C., & Monakhou, K. (1979). Depressive symptomatology and systematic structural analysis of the EEG. In J. H. Gruzelier & P. Flor-Henry (Eds.), *Hemisphere asymmetries of function in psychopathology.* Amsterdam: Elsevier/North Holland Biomedical Press.

Peters, M., & Durding, B. M. (1979). Footedness of left- and right-handers. *American Journal of Psychology, 92,* 133–142.

Peters, M., & Petrie, B. F. (1979). Functional asymmetries in the stepping reflex of human neonates. *Canadian Journal of Psychology, 33,* 198–200.

Petersen, M. R., Beecher, M. D., Zoloth, S. R., Moody, D. B., & Stebbins, W. C. (1978). Neural lateralization of species-specific vocalizations by Japanese macaques. *Science, 202,* 324–326.

Petersen, S. E., Fox, P. T., Mintun, M. A., Posner, M. I., & Raichle, M. E. (1989). Studies of the processing of single words using averaged positron emission tomographic measurements of cerebral blood flow changes. *Journal of Cognitive Neuroscience, 1,* 153–170.

Petersen, S. E., Fox, P. T., Posner, M. I., Mintun, M. A., & Raichle, M. E. (1988). Positron emission tomographic studies of the cortical anatomy of single-word processing. *Nature, 331,* 585–589.

Pfaff, D. W., & Schwartz-Giblin, S. (1988). Cellular mechanisms of female reproductive behaviors. In E. Knobil & J. Neill (Eds.), *The physiology of reproduction.* New York: Raven Press.

Piazza, D. M. (1980). The influence of sex and handedness in the hemispheric specialization of verbal and nonverbal tasks. *Neuropsychologia, 18,* 163–176.

Pinel, J. (1990). *Biopsychology.* Boston: Allyn & Bacon.

Pirozzolo, F. J. (1979). *The neuropsychology of developmental reading disorders.* New York: Holt, Rinehart & Winston.

Poizner, H., Klima, E. S., & Bellugi, U. (1990). *What the hands reveal about the brain.* Cambridge, MA: MIT Press.

Polich, J. M. (1980). Left hemisphere superiority for visual search. *Cortex, 16,* 39–50.

Porac, C., & Coren, S. (1976). The dominant eye. *Psychological Bulletin, 83,* 880–897.

Porac, C., & Coren, S. (1981). *Lateral preferences and human behavior.* New York: Springer-Verlag.

Porac, C., Coren, S., & Duncan, P. (1980a). Lateral preference in retardates: Relationships between hand, eye, foot, and ear preference. *Journal of Clinical Neuropsychology, 2,* 173–187.

Porac, C., Coren, S., & Duncan, P. (1980b). Life-span age trends in laterality. *Journal of Gerontology, 35,* 715–721.

Porac, C., Coren, S., & Searleman, A. (1986). Environmental factors in hand preference formation: Evidence from attempts to switch the preferred hand. *Behavior Genetics, 16,* 251–261.

Porter, R. J., & Berlin, C. I. (1975). On interpreting developmental changes in the dichotic right-ear advantage. *Brain and Language, 2,* 186–200.

Posluszny, R., & Barton, K. (1981). Dichaptic task performance as a function of pattern, sex, and hand preference. *Perceptual and Motor Skills, 53,* 435–438.

Preilowski, B. (1979). Consciousness after complete surgical section of the forebrain commissures in man. In I. Steele Russell, M. W. Hof, & G. Berlucchi (Eds.), *Structure and function of cerebral commissures.* London: Macmillan.

Pribram, K. H., & McGuinness, D. (1975). Arousal, activation, and effort in the control of attention. *Psychological Review, 82,* 116–149.

Prince, G. (1978). Putting the other half of the brain to work. *Training: The Magazine of Human Resources Development, 15,* 57–61.

Prior, M. R., & Bradshaw, J. L. (1979). Hemispheric functioning in autistic children. *Cortex, 15,* 73–81.

Prohovnik, I., Hakansson, K., & Risberg, J. (1980). Observations of the functional significance of regional cerebral blood flow in "resting" normal subjects. *Neuropsychologia, 18,* 203–217.

Puccetti, R. (1981a). The alleged manipulospatiality explanation of right-hemisphere visuospatial superiority. *Behavioral and Brain Sciences, 4,* 75–76.

Puccetti, R. (1981b). The case for mental duality: Evidence from split-brain data and other considerations. *Behavioral and Brain Sciences, 4,* 93–123.

Qalker, A. E., & Jablon, S. (1961). *A follow-up study of head wounds in World War II.* Washington, DC: Government Printing Office.

Querishi, R., & Dimond, S. J. (1979). Calculation and the right hemisphere. *Lancet, 1,* 322–323.

Quinn, P. (1972). Stuttering, cerebral dominance, and the dichotic word test. *Medical Journal of Australia, 2,* 639–643.

Rada, R. T., Porch, B. E., Dillingham, C., Kellner, R., & Porec, J. B. (1977). Alcoholism and language function. *Alcoholism: Clinical and Experimental Research, 1,* 199–205.

Raichle, M. E. (1987). Circulatory and metabolic correlates of brain function in normal humans. In J. B. Brookhart & V. B. Mountcastle (Eds.), *Handbook of physiology: The nervous system* V. Bethesda, MD: American Physiological Society.

Rainbow, R. C., Parsons, B., & McEwen, B. S. (1982). Sex differences in rat brain estrogen and progestin receptors. *Nature, 300,* 648–649.

Ramaley, F. (1913). Inheritance of left-handedness. *American Naturalist, 47,* 730–738.

Ramsay, D. S. (1980). Beginnings of bimanual handedness and speech in infants. *Infant Behavior and Development, 3,* 67–77.

Rasmussen, T., & Milner, B. (1977). The role of early left-brain injury in determining lateralization of cerebral speech functions. *Annals of the New York Academy of Sciences, 299,* 353–369.

Rebert, C. S. (1978). Neuroelectric measures of lateral specialization in relation to performance. *Contemporary Clinical Neurophysiology, 34,* 231–238.

Regelski, T. A. (1977). Music education and the human brain. *Music Educators Journal, 63,* 30–38.

Reivich, M., & Gur, R. C. (1985). Cerebral metabolic effects of sensory stimuli. In M. Reivich & Alavi (Eds.), *Positron emission tomography.* New York: Alan R. Liss.

Rice, T., & Plomin, R. (1983). Hand preferences in the Colorado adoption project. *Behavior Genetics, 13,* 550.

Risberg, J., Halsey, J. H., Wills, E. L., & Wilson, E. M. (1975). Hemispheric specialization in normal man studied by bilateral measurements of the regional cerebral blood flow: A study with the ^{133}Xe inhalation technique. *Brain, 98,* 511–524.

Riva, D., & Cazzaniga, L. (1986). Late effects of unilateral brain lesions before and after the first year of age. *Neuropsychologia, 24,* 423–428.

Rizzolatti, G., & Buchtel, H. (1977). Hemispheric superiority in reaction time to faces: A sex difference. *Cortex, 13,* 300–305.

Rizzolatti, G., Umilta, C., & Berlucchi, G. (1971). Opposite superiorities of the right and left cerebral hemispheres in discriminative reaction time to physiognomical and alphabetical material. *Brain, 94,* 431–442.

Robin, D. E., & Shortridge, R. T. J. (1979). Lateralization of tumors of the nasal cavity and paranasal sinuses and its relation to aetiology. *Lancet, 8118*, 695–696.

Robinson, G. M., & Solomon, D. J. (1974). Rhythm is processed by the speech hemisphere. *Journal of Experimental Psychology, 102*, 508–511.

Robinson, J. S., & Voneida, T. J. (1973). Hemispheric differences in cognitive capacity in the split-brain cat. *Experimental Neurology, 38*, 123–134.

Rogers, L. J. (1980). Lateralization in the avian brain. *Bird Behavior, 2*, 1–12.

Rogers, L. J., TenHouten, W. Kaplan, C., & Gardiner, M. (1977). Hemispheric specialization of language: An EEG study of bilingual Hopi Indian children. *International Journal of Neuroscience, 8*, 1–6.

Rose, S. A. (1984). Developmental changes in hemispheric specialization for tactual processing in very young children: Evidence from cross-modal transfer. *Developmental Psychology, 20*, 568–574.

Rose, S. A. (1985). Influence of concurrent auditory input on tactual processing in very young children. *Developmental Psychology, 21*, 168–175.

Rosen, G. D., Berrebi, A. S., & Yutzey, D. A. (1983). Prenatal testosterone causes shift of asymmetry in neonatal tail posture of the rat. *Developmental Brain Research, 9*, 99–101.

Rosenberg, B. A. (1980). Mental-task instructions and optokinetic nystagmus to the left and right. *Journal of Experimental Psychology: Human Perception and Performance, 6*, 459–472.

Rosenberger, P. B., & Hier, D. B. (1980). Cerebral asymmetry and verbal intellectual deficits. *Annals of Neurology, 8*, 300–304.

Ross, E. D. (1981). The aprosodias: Functional-anatomic organization of the affective components of language in the right hemisphere. *Archives of Neurology, 38*, 561–569.

Ross, E. D. (1984). Right hemisphere's role in language, affective behavior and emotion. *Trends in Neurosciences, 7*, 342–345.

Rossi, G. F., & Rosadini, G. (1967). Experimental analysis of cerebral dominance in man. In C. H. Milikan & F. L. Danley (Eds.), *Brain mechanisms underlying speech and language*. New York: Grune & Stratton.

Rourke, B. P. (1982). Central processing deficiencies in children: Toward a developmental neuropsychological model. *Journal of Clinical Neuropsychology, 4*, 1–18.

Rourke, B. P., & Finlayson, M. A. J. (1978). Neuropsychological significance of variations in patterns of academic performance: Verbal and visual–spatial abilities. *Journal of Abnormal Child Psychology, 6*, 121–133.

Rubens, A. B. (1977). Anatomical asymmetries of human cerebral cortex. In S. Harnad, R. W. Doty, L. Goldstein, J. Jaynes, & G. Krauthamer (Eds.), *Lateralization in the nervous system* (pp. 503–516). New York: Academic Press.

Rubin, D. A., & Rubin, R. T. (1980). Differences in asymmetry of facial expression between right- and left-handed children. *Neuropsychologia, 18*, 373–377.

Ryan, C. (1980). Learning and memory deficits in alcoholics. *Journal of Studies on Alcohol, 41*, 437–447.

Ryan, C., & Butters, N. (1986). Neuropsychology of alcoholism. In D. Wedding, A. M. Horton, & J. S. Webster (Eds.), *The neuropsychology handbook* (pp. 376–409). New York: Springer-Verlag.

Ryan, W. J., & McNeil, M. (1974). Listener reliability for a dichotic task. *Journal of the Acoustical Society of America, 56*, 1922–1923.

Sackheim, H. A., Greenberg, M. S., Weiman, A. L., Gur, R. C., Hungerbuhler, J. P., & Geschwind, N. (1982). Hemispheric asymmetry in the expression of positive and negative emotions: Neurological evidence. *Archives of Neurology, 39*, 210–218.

Sackheim, H. A., & Gur, R. C. (1978). Lateral asymmetry in intensity of emotional expression. *Neuropsychologia, 16*, 473–482.

Sackheim, H. A., Gur, R. C., & Saucy, M. (1978). Emotions are expressed more intensely on the left side of the face. *Science, 202,* 434–436.

Safer, M. A. (1981). Sex and hemisphere differences in access to codes for processing emotional expressions and faces. *Journal of Experimental Psychology: General, 110,* 86–100.

Sagan, C. (1977). *The dragons of Eden.* New York: Random House.

Sanders, B., Wilson, J. R., & Vandenberg, S. G. (1982). Handedness and spatial ability. *Cortex, 18,* 79–90.

Sasanuma, S. (1980). Acquired dyslexia in Japanese: Clinical features and underlying mechanisms. In M. Coltheart, K. Patterson, & J. C. Marshall (Eds.), *Deep dyslexia.* London: Routledge & Kegan Paul.

Sasanuma, S., Itoh, M., Mori, K., & Kobayashi, Y. (1977). Tachistoscopic recognition of Kana and Kanji words. *Neuropsychologia, 15,* 547–553.

Sasanuma, S., & Kobayashi, Y. (1978). Tachistoscopic recognition of line orientation. *Neuropsychologia, 16,* 239–242.

Sass, K. J., Novelly, R. A., Spencer, D. D., & Spencer, S. S. (1988). Mnestic and attention impairments following corpus callosum section for epilepsy. *Journal of Epilepsy, 1,* 61–66.

Satz, P. (1973). Left-handers and early brain insult: An explanation. *Neuropsychologia, 11,* 115–117.

Satz, P., Achenbach, K., Patishall, E., & Fennell, E. (1965). Ear asymmetry and handedness in dichotic listening. *Cortex, 1,* 377–396.

Satz, P., Bakker, D. J., Teunissen, J., Goebel, R., & Van der Vlugt, H. (1975). Developmental parameters of the ear asymmetry: A multivariate approach. *Brain and Language, 2,* 171–185.

Satz, P., Orsini, D. L., Saslow, E., & Henry, R. (1985a). Early brain injury and pathological left-handedness: Clues to a syndrome. In E. Zaidel (Ed.), *The dual brain.* New York: Guilford.

Satz, P., Orsini, D. L., Saslow, E., & Henry, R. (1985b). The pathological left-handedness syndrome. *Brain and Cognition, 4,* 27–46.

Satz, P., & Sparrow, S. (1970). Specific developmental dyslexia: A theoretical formulation. In D. J. Bakker & P. Satz (Eds.), *Specific reading disability: Advances in theory and method* (pp. 17–39). Rotterdam: Rotterdam University Press.

Saxby, L., & Bryden, M. P. (1984). Left-ear superiority in children for processing auditory emotional material. *Developmental Psychology, 20,* 72–80.

Saxby, L., & Bryden, M. P. (1985). Left visual-field advantage in children for processing visual emotional stimuli. *Developmental Psychology, 21,* 253–261.

Schiff, B. B., & Lamon, M. (1989). Inducing emotion by unilateral contraction of facial muscles: A new look at hemispheric specialization and the experience of emotion. *Neuropsychologia, 27,* 923–935.

Schmuller, J., & Goodman, R. (1979). Bilateral tachistoscopic perception, handedness, and laterality. *Brain and Language, 8,* 81–91.

Schmuller, J., & Goodman, R. (1980). Bilateral tachistoscopic perception, handedness, and laterality: II. Nonverbal stimuli. *Brain and Language, 11,* 12–18.

Schneider, S. J. (1983). Multiple measures of hemispheric dysfunction in schizophrenia and depression. *Psychological Medicine, 13,* 287–297.

Schwartz, G. E., Davidson, R. J., & Maer, F. (1975). Right hemisphere lateralization for emotion in the human brain: Interactions with cognition. *Science, 190,* 286–288.

Schwartz, J., & Tallal, P. (1980). Rate of acoustic change may underlie hemispheric specialization for speech perception. *Science, 207,* 1380–1381.

Schwartz, M. (1988). Handedness, prenatal stress, and pregnancy complications. *Neuropsychologia, 15,* 341–344.

Schwartz, M., & Smith, M. L. (1980). Visual asymmetries with chimeric faces. *Neuropsychologia, 18,* 103–106.

Schweitzer, L. (1979). Differences in cerebral lateralization among schizophrenic and depressed patients. *Biological Psychiatry, 14,* 721–733.

Schweitzer, L., Becker, E., & Welsh, H. (1978). Abnormalities of cerebral lateralization in schizophrenic patients. *Archives of General Psychiatry, 35,* 982–985.

Scott, S., Hynd, G., Hunt, L., & Weed, W. (1979). Cerebral speech lateralization in the native American Navajo. *Neuropsychologia, 17,* 89–92.

Searleman, A. (1977). A review of right hemisphere linguistic abilities. *Psychological Bulletin, 84,* 503–528.

Searleman, A., & Fugagli, A. K. (1987). Suspected autoimmune disorders and left-handedness: Evidence from individuals with diabetes, Crohn's disease and ulcerative colitis. *Neuropsychologia, 25,* 367–374.

Searleman, A., Herrmann, D. J., & Coventry, A. K. (1984). Cognitive abilities and left-handedness: An interaction between familial sinistrality and strength of handedness. *Intelligence, 8,* 295–304.

Searleman, A., Porac, C., & Coren, S. (1982). The relationship between birth stress and writing hand posture. *Brain and Cognition, 1,* 158–164.

Segalowitz, S. J., & Cohen, H. (1989). Right hemispheric EEG sensitivity to speech. *Brain and Language, 37,* 220–231.

Selnes, O. A. (1974). The corpus callosum: Some anatomical and functional considerations with special reference to language. *Brain and Language, 1,* 111–139.

Seltzer, B., & Sherwin, I. (1983). A comparison of clinical features in early- and late-onset primary degenerative dementia. *Archives of Neurology, 40,* 143–146.

Semmes, J. (1968). Hemispheric specialization: A possible clue to mechanism. *Neuropsychologia, 6,* 11–26.

Semrud-Clikeman, M., & Hynd, G. W. (1990). Right hemisphere dysfunction in nonverbal learning disabilities: Social, academic, and adaptive functioning in adults and children. *Psychological Bulletin, 107,* 196–209.

Seth, G. (1973). Eye-hand coordination and "handedness": A developmental study of visuomotor behavior in infancy. *British Journal of Educational Psychology, 43,* 35–49.

Shakhnovich, A. R., Serbinenko, F. A., Razumousky, A. Ye., Rodionov, I. M., & Oskolok, L. N. (1980). The dependence of cerebral blood flow on mental activity and on emotional state in man. *Neuropsychologia, 18,* 465–476.

Shankweiler, D., & Studdert-Kennedy, M. (1967). Identification of consonants and vowels presented to left and right ears. *Quarterly Journal of Experimental Psychology, 19,* 59–63.

Shankweiler, D., & Studdert-Kennedy, M. (1975). A continuum of lateralization for speech perception? *Brain and Language, 2,* 212–225.

Shanon, B. (1980). Lateralization effects in musical decision tasks. *Neuropsychologia, 18,* 21–31.

Sheenan, J. G. (1970). *Stuttering: Research and therapy.* New York: Harper & Row.

Sherman, G. F., Garbanati, J. A., Rosen, G. D., Yutzey, D. A., & Denenberg, V. H. (1980). Brain and behavioral asymmetries for spatial preference in rats. *Brain Research, 192,* 61–67.

Shevrin, H., Smokler, I. A., & Wolf, E. (1979). Field independence, lateralization, and defensive style. *Perceptual and Motor Skills, 49,* 195–202.

Sidtis, J. J. (1980). On the nature of the cortical function underlying right hemisphere auditory perception. *Neuropsychologia, 18,* 321–330.

Sidtis, J. J. (1981). The complex tone test: Implications for the assessment of auditory laterality effects. *Neuropsychologia, 19,* 103–112.

Sidtis, J. J., & Bryden, M. P. (1978). Asymmetrical perception of language and music: Evidence for independent processing strategies. *Neuropsychologia, 16,* 627–632.

Silberman, E. K., & Weingartner, H. (1986). Hemispheric lateralization of functions related to emotion. *Brain Cognition, 5,* 322–353.

Silverberg, R., Gordon, H. W., Pollack, S., & Bentin, S. (1980). Shift of visual field preference for Hebrew words in native speakers learning to read. *Brain and Language, 11,* 99–105.

Smith, A. (1966). Speech and other functions after left (dominant) hemispherectomy. *Journal of Neurology, Neurosurgery, and Psychiatry, 29,* 467–471.

Smith, A., & Burklund, C. W. (1966). Dominant hemispherectomy: Preliminary report on neuropsychological sequelae. *Science, 153,* 1280–1282.

Smith, A., & Sugar, O. (1975). Development of above normal language and intelligence. 21 years after left hemispherectomy. *Neurology, 25,* 813–818.

Smith, J. (1987). Left-handedness: Its association with allergic disease. *Neuropsychologia, 25,* 665–674.

Smith, L. C., & Moscovitch, M. (1979). Writing posture, hemispheric control of movement, and cerebral dominance in individuals with inverted and noninverted hand postures during writing. *Neuropsychologia, 17,* 637–644.

Smith, V., & Chyatte, C. (1983). Left-handed versus right-handed alcoholics: An examination of relapse patterns. *Journal of Studies in Alcoholism, 44,* 553–555.

Snyder, S. H. (1986). *Drugs and the brain.* New York: Scientific American Books.

Sommers, R. K., Brady, W., & Moore, W. H., Jr. (1975). Dichotic ear preferences of stuttering children and adults. *Perceptual and Motor Skills, 41,* 931–938.

Southgate, V., & Roberts, G. R. (1970). *Reading—Which approach?* London: University of London Press.

Spellacy, F. (1970). Lateral preferences in the identification of patterned stimuli. *Journal of the Acoustical Society of America, 47,* 574–578.

Spellacy, F., & Blumstein, S. (1970). The influence of language set on ear preference in phoneme recognition. *Cortex, 6,* 430–439.

Sperry, R. W. (1964). The great cerebral commissure. *Scientific American, 210,* 42–52.

Sperry, R. W. (1968). Mental unity following surgical disconnection of the cerebral hemispheres. In *The Harvey lectures: Series 62.* New York: Academic Press.

Sperry, R. W. (1985). Consciousness, personal identity, and the divided brain. In D. F. Benson & E. Zaidel (Eds.), *The dual brain: Hemispheric specialization in humans* (pp. 11–26). New York: Guilford.

Sperry, R. W., Gazzaniga, M. S., & Bogen, J. E. (1969). Interhemispheric relationships: The neocortical commissures, syndromes of hemispheric disconnection. In P. J. Vinken & G. W. Bruyn (Eds.), *Handbook of clinical neurology, volume 4: Disorders of speech, perception, and symbolic behavior.* Amsterdam: Elsevier/North-Holland Biomedical Press.

Sperry, R. W., Zaidel, E., & Zaidel, D. (1979). Self-recognition and social awareness in the deconnected minor hemisphere. *Neuropsychologia, 17,* 153–166.

Springer, S. P., & Deutsch, G. (1989). *Left brain, right brain.* New York: W. H. Freeman.

Springer, S. P., & Searleman, A. (1980). Left-handedness in twins: Implications for the mechanisms underlying cerebral asymmetries of function. In J. Herron (Ed.), *Neuropsychology of left-handedness* (pp. 139–158). New York: Academic Press.

Stanish, B. (1989). *The ambidextrous mind book: Creative and inventive adventures for the curriculum.* Carthage, IL: Good Apple.

Stanish, B., & Singletary, C. (1987). *Inventioneering: Nurturing intellectual talent in the classroom.* Carthage, IL: Good Apple.

Stefan, M. S., Milea, S., & Magureanu, S. (1981). The autistic syndrome and epileptic seizures, clinical and etiopathogenetic interference. *Neurological Psychiatrique, 26,* 205–211.

Stein, J., & Fowler, S. (1981). Visual dyslexia. *Trends in the Neurosciences, 4,* 77–80.

Strang, J. D., & Rourke, B. P. (1985). Arithmetic disability subtypes: The neuropsychological significance of specific arithmetic impairments in childhood. In B. P. Rourke (Ed.), *Neuropsychology of learning disabilities* (pp. 302–330). New York: Guilford.

Studdert-Kennedy, M., & Shankweiler, D. (1970). Hemispheric specialization for speech perception. *Journal of the Acoustical Society of America, 48,* 579–594.

Suberi, M., & McKeever, W. F. (1977). Differential right hemisphere memory storage of emotional and nonemotional faces. *Neuropsychologia, 15,* 757–768.

Summers, W. K., Majovski, L. V., Marsh, G. M., Tachiki, K., & Kling, A. (1986). Oral tetrahydroaminoacridine in long-term treatment of senile dementia, Alzheimer type. *The New England Journal of Medicine, 315,* 1241–1245.

Sussman, H. M., & MacNeilage, P. F. (1975a). Hemispheric specialization for speech production and perception in stutterers. *Neuropsychologia, 13,* 19–26.

Sussman, H. M., & MacNeilage, P. F. (1975b). Studies of hemispheric specialization for speech production. *Brain and Language, 2,* 131–151.

Swaab, D. F., & Hofman, M. A. (1988). Sexual differentiation of the human hypothalamus: Ontogeny of the sexually dimorphic nucleus of the preoptic area. *Developmental Brain Research, 44,* 314–318.

Takeda, M., & Yoshimura, H. (1979). Lateral eye movement while eyes are closed. *Perceptual and Motor Skills, 48,* 1227–1231.

Tart, C. T. (1971). *On being stoned: A psychological study of marijuana intoxication.* Palo Alto, CA: Science and Behavior Books.

Tart, C. T. (1976). *Learning to use extrasensory perception.* Chicago: University of Chicago Press.

Tart, C. T. (1990). *Altered states of consciousness.* San Francisco: Harper.

Tarter, R. E. (1976). Neuropsychological investigations of alcoholism. In G. Goldstein & C. Neuringer (Eds.), *Empirical studies of alcoholism* (pp. 231–256). Cambridge, MA: Ballinger.

Tegano, D. W. (1982, March). *Assessment of hemispheric dominance for language at three ages.* Paper presented at the annual conference of the Southern Association for Children Under Six, Tulsa, OK.

Teng, E. L. (1980). Dichotic pairing of digits with tones: High performance level and lack of ear effect. *Quarterly Journal of Experimental Psychology, 32,* 287–293.

Ternes, J., Woody, R., & Livingston, R. (1987). A child with right hemisphere deficit syndrome responsive to carbamazepine treatment. *Journal of the American Academy of Child and Adolescent Psychology, 26,* 586–588.

Terrace, H. S. (1980). *Nim: A chimpanzee who learned sign language.* New York: Knopf.

Terrace, H., Petitto, L. A., Sanders, R. J., & Bever, T. G. (1979). Can an ape create a sentence? *Science, 206,* 891–902.

Terry, R. D., & Davies, P. (1980). Dementia of the Alzheimer type. *Annual Review of Neuroscience, 3,* 77–96.

Terzian, H. (1964). Behavioral and EEG effects of intracarotid sodium amytal injection. *Acta Neurochirurgia (Wein), 12,* 230–239.

Thistle, A. (1975). Performance of males and females on a dichotic listening task. *Journal of the Acoustical Society of America, 58,* S76.

Thomas, J. H. (1989, August). *Implications of being left-handed as related to being right-handed.* Paper presented at the Research Colloquia, "Issues in Education," Murray, KY.

Thomson, M. E. (1976). Comparison of laterality effects in dyslexics and controls using verbal dichotic listening tasks. *Neuropsychologia, 14,* 243–246.

Time-Life Books. (1987). Beyond the five senses. In G. Constable (Ed.), *Mysteries of the unknown: Psychic powers* (pp. 14–34). Alexandria, VA: Time-Life.

Tomarken, A. J., & Davidson, A. J. (1988). *Resting anterior EEG asymmetry predicts affective response to emotional films.* Unpublished manuscript.

Tomer, R., Mintz, M., Levi, A., & Myslobodsky, M. S. (1979). Reactive gaze laterality in schizophrenic patients. *Biological Psychology, 9,* 115–127.

Tomlinson-Keasey, C., & Kelly, R. R. (1979). A task analysis of hemispheric functioning. *Neuropsychologia, 17,* 345–351.

Tomlinson-Keasey, C., Kelly, R. R., & Burton, J. K. (1978). Hemispheric changes in information processing during development. *Developmental Psychology, 14,* 214–223.

Torrance, E. P., & Reynolds, C. (1980). *Norms-technical manual for "your style of learning and thinking."* Athens, GA: Department of Educational Psychology, University of Georgia.

Trevarthen, C. B. (1972). Brain bisymmetry and the role of the corpus callosum in behavior and conscious experience. In *Cerebral interhemispheric relations.* Bratislava, Czechoslovakia: Publishing House of the Slovak Academy of Sciences.

Trevarthen, C. B. (1974a). Analysis of cerebral activities that generate and regulate consciousness in commissurotomy patients. In S. J. Dimond & J. G. Beaumont (Eds.), *Hemisphere function in the human brain.* London: Elek Science.

Trevarthen, C. B. (1974b). Cerebral embryology and the split brain. In M. Kinsbourne & W. L. Smith (Eds.), *Hemispheric disconnection and cerebral function.* Springfield, IL: Charles C. Thomas.

Trevarthen, C. B., & Kinsbourne, M. (1974). Cerebral asymmetries as manifested in split-brain man. In M. Kinsbourne & W. L. Smith (Eds.), *Hemispheric disconnection and cerebral function.* Springfield, IL: Charles C. Thomas.

Tucker, D. M. (1976). Sex differences in hemispheric specialization for synthetic visuospatial functions. *Neuropsychologia, 14,* 447–454.

Tucker, D. M., Stenslie, C. E., Roth, R. S., & Shearer, S. L. (1981). Right frontal lobe activation and right hemisphere performance. *Archives of General Psychiatry, 38,* 169–174.

Tucker, D. M., Watson, R. T., & Heilman, K. M. (1977). Affective discrimination and evocation in patients with right parietal disease. *Neurology, 27,* 947–950.

Tucker, D. M., & Williamson, P. A. (1984). Asymmetric neural control systems in human self-regulation. *Psychological Review, 91,* 185–215.

Turkewitz, G. (1977). The development of lateral differences in the human infant. In S. Harnad, R. W. Doty, L. Goldstein, J. Jaynes, & G. Krauthamer (Eds.), *Lateralization in the nervous system* (pp. 251–259). New York: Academic Press.

Turkewitz, G. (1988). A prenatal source for the development of hemispheric specialization. In D. L. Molfese & S. J. Segalowitz (Eds.), *Brain lateralization in children: Developmental implications* (pp. 73–81). New York: Guilford.

Turkewitz, G., & Creighton, S. (1974). Changes in lateral differentiation of head posture in the human neonate. *Developmental Psychology, 8,* 85–89.

Turkewitz, G., & Ross-Kossak, P. (1984). Multiple modes of information processing: Age and sex differences in facial recognition. *Developmental Psychology, 20,* 95–103.

Umilta, C., Brizzolara, D., Tabossi, P., & Fairweather, H. (1978). Factors affecting face recognition in the cerebral hemispheres: Familiarity and naming. In J. Requin (Ed.), *Attention and performance VII.* Hillsdale, NJ: Lawrence Erlbaum Associates.

Umilta, C., Frost, N., & Hyman, R. (1972). Interhemispheric effects on choice reaction times to one-, two-, and three-letter displays. *Journal of Experimental Psychology, 93,* 198–204.

Umilta, C., Salmaso, D., Bagnara, S., & Simion, F. (1979). Evidence for a right-hemisphere superiority and for a serial search strategy in a dot detection task. *Cortex, 15,* 597–608.

Vaid, J., & Genesee, F. (1980). Neuropsychological approaches to bilingualism: A critical review. *Canadian Journal of Psychology, 34,* 419–447.

Van Duyne, H. J., Gargiulo, R. M., & Gonter, M. A. (1984). The effect of word presentation rate on monaural and dichotic ear-asymmetry in school age children. *International Journal of Clinical Neuropsychology, 6,* 175–183.

Van Riper, C. (1971). *Nature of stuttering.* New York: Prentice-Hall.

van Strien, J. W., Bouma, A., & Bakker, D. J. (1987). Birth stress, autoimmune diseases, and handedness. *Journal of Clinical and Experimental Neuropsychology, 9,* 775–780.

Van Wagenen, W., & Herren, R. (1940). Surgical division of commissural pathways in the corpus callosum. *Archives of Neurology and Psychiatry, 44,* 740–759.

Vargha-Khadem, F. (1983). Visual-field asymmetries in congenitally deaf and hearing children. *British Journal of Developmental Psychology, 1,* 375–387.

Vargha-Khadem, F., & Corballis, M. C. (1979). Cerebral asymmetry in infants. *Brain and Language, 8,* 1–9.

Vargha-Khadem, F., O'Gorman, A. M., & Watters, G. V. (1985). Aphasia and handedness in relation to hemispheric side, age at injury, and severity of cerebral lesion during childhood. *Brain, 108,* 677–696.

Vernon, M. D. (1979). Variability in reading retardation. *British Journal of Psychology, 70,* 7–16.

Voeller, K. K. S. (1986). Right hemisphere deficit syndrome in children. *Journal of Psychiatry, 143,* 1004–1009.

Volpe, B. T., LeDoux, J. E., & Gazzaniga, M. S. (1979). Information processing of visual stimuli in an "extinguished field." *Nature, 282,* 122–124.

von Saal, F. S. (1983). Models of early hormonal effects on intrasex aggression in mice. In B. B. Svare (Ed.), *Hormones and aggressive behavior.* New York: Plenum.

Waber, D. P. (1976). Sex differences in cognition: A function of maturation rate? *Science, 192,* 572–574.

Wada, J. A., Clarke, R., & Hamm, A. (1975). Cerebral hemispheric asymmetry in humans. *Archives of Neurology, 32,* 239–246.

Wada, J. A., & Davis, A. (1977). Fundamental nature of human infants' brain asymmetry. *Canadian Journal of Neurological Sciences, 4,* 203–207.

Wada, J. A., & Rasmussen, T. (1960). Intracarotid injection of sodium amytal for the lateralization of cerebral speech dominance: Experimental and clinical observations. *Journal of Neurosurgery, 17,* 266–282.

Walker, S. F. (1980). Lateralization of functions in the vertebrate brain: A review. *British Journal of Psychology, 71,* 329–367.

Walsh, K. W. (1978). *Neuropsychology: A clinical approach.* Edinburgh: Churchill Livingstone.

Walter, J., Bryden, M., & Allard, F. (1976). *Hemispheric differences for nonverbal visual material.* Paper presented at the Canadian Psychological Association, Toronto.

Warren, J. M., Abplanalp, J. M., & Warren, H. B. (1967). The development of handedness in cats and rhesus monkeys. In H. W. Stevenson, E. H. Hess, & H. L. Reingold (Eds.), *Early behavior: Comparative and developmental approaches* (pp. 73–101). New York: Wiley.

Warren, J. M., & Nonneman, A. J. (1976). The search for cerebral dominance in monkeys. *Annals of the New York Academy of Sciences, 280,* 732–744.

Warrington, E. K., & Pratt, R. T. C. (1973). Language laterality in left-handers assessed by unilateral ECT. *Neuropsychologia, 11,* 423–428.

Webb, W. B. (1979). The nature of dreams. In Goleman & Davidson (Eds.), *Consciousness: Brain, states of awareness, and mysticism* (pp. 76–78). New York: Harper & Row.

Weber, A. M., & Bradshaw, J. L. (1981). Levy and Reid's neurological model in relation to writing hand/posture: An evaluation. *Psychological Bulletin, 90,* 74–88.

Webster, W. G. (1977). Territoriality and the evolution of brain asymmetry. In S. J. Dimond & D. A. Blizzard (Eds.), *Evolution and lateralization of the brain.* New York: New York Academy of Sciences.

Webster, W. G., & Thurber, A. D. (1978). Problem-solving strategies and manifest brain asymmetry. *Cortex, 14,* 474–484.

Weisenberg, T., & McBride, K. E. (1935). *Aphasia: A clinical and psychological study.* New York: Commonwealth Fund.

Wernicke, C. (1874). *Der aphasische symptomenkomplex.* Breslau, Germany: Cohn Weigert.

Wexler, B. E., & Heninger, G. R. (1980). Effects of concurrent administration of verbal and spatial visual tasks on a language-related dichotic listening measure of perceptual asymmetry. *Neuropsychologia, 18,* 379–382.

Wheatley, G. H. (1977). The right hemisphere's role in problem solving. *Arithmetic Teacher, 25,* 36–39.

White, K. (1986). Are some of your students "left" out? *Business Education Forum, 40,* 14–17.

Wile, I. S. (1934). *Handedness: Right and left.* Boston: Lothrop, Lee, & Shepard.

Williams, R. H., & Stockmyer, J. (1987). *Unleashing the right side of the brain: The LARC creativity program.* Lexington, MA: Stephen Greene.

Willis, W. G., & Hynd, G. W. (1987). Lateralized interference effects: Evidence for a processing style by modality interaction. *Brain and Cognition, 6,* 112–126.

Wilson, D. (1872). Right-handedness. *The Canadian Journal, 75,* 193–230.

Wing, L. (1985). Early childhood autism and Asperger's syndrome. In P. Pichot, B. Berner, R. Wolf, & K. Thau (Eds.), *Psychiatry: The state of the art* (pp. 47–52). New York: Plenum.

Witelson, S. F. (1974). Hemispheric specialization for linguistic and nonlinguistic tactual perception using a dichotomous stimulation technique. *Cortex, 10,* 3–17.

Witelson, S. F. (1976). Sex and the single hemisphere: Specialization of the right hemisphere for spatial processing. *Science, 193,* 425–427.

Witelson, S. F. (1977a). Anatomic asymmetry in the temporal lobes: Its documentation, phylogenesis, and relationship to functional asymmetry. *Annals of the New York Academy of Sciences, 299,* 328–354.

Witelson, S. F. (1977b). Developmental dyslexia: Two right hemispheres and none left. *Science, 195,* 309–311.

Witelson, S. F. (1977c). Early hemisphere specialization and interhemispheric plasticity: An empirical and theoretical review. In S. J. Segalowitz & F. A. Gruber (Eds.), *Language development and neurological theory* (pp. 213–287). New York: Academic Press.

Witelson, S. F. (1977d). Neural and cognitive correlates of developmental dyslexia: Age and sex differences. In C. Shaguss, S. Gershon, & A. J. Friedhoff (Eds.), *Psychopathology and brain dysfunction* (pp. 15–49). New York: Raven Press.

Witelson, S. F., & Kigar, D. L. (1988). Anatomical development of the corpus callosum in humans: A review with reference to sex and cognition. In D. L. Molfese & S. J. Segalowitz (Eds.), *Brain lateralization in children: Developmental implications* (pp. 35–57). New York: Guilford.

Witelson, S. F., & Pallie, W. (1973). Left hemisphere specialization for language in the newborn: Neuroanatomical evidence of asymmetry. *Brain, 96,* 641–646.

Witelson, S. F., & Rabinovich, M. (1972). Hemispheric speech lateralization in children with auditory-linguistic deficits. *Cortex, 8,* 412–426.

Wolff, S., & Barlow, A. (1979). Schizoid personality in childhood: A comparative study of schizoid, autistic, and normal children. *Journal of Child Psychology and Psychiatry, 20,* 29–46.

Wood, F. (1980). Theoretical, methodological, and statistical implications of the inhalation *rCBF* technique for the study of brain-behavior relationships. *Brain and Language, 9,* 1–8.

Woods, B. T. (1980a). Observations on the neurological basis for initial language acquisition. In D. Caplan (Ed.), *Biological studies of mental processes.* Cambridge, MA: MIT Press.

Woods, B. T. (1980b). The restricted effects of right-hemisphere lesions after age one: Wechsler test data. *Neuropsychologia, 18*, 65–70.

Woods, B. T., & Carey, S. (1979). Language deficits after apparent clinical recovery from childhood aphasia. *Annals of Neurology, 6*, 405–409.

Woods, B. T., & Teuber, H. L. (1978). Changing patterns of childhood aphasia. *Annals of Neurology, 3*, 273–280.

Woods, D. L. (1990). The physiological basis of selective attention: Implications of event-related potential studies. In J. W. Rohrbaugh, R. Parasuraman, & R. Johnson, Jr. (Eds.), *Event-related brain potentials: Basic issues and applications*. Oxford, England: Oxford University Press.

Woodward, S. H. (1988). An anatomical model of hemispheric asymmetry. *Journal of Clinical and Experimental Neuropsychology, 10*, 68.

Wurtman, R. S. (1985). Alzheimer's disease. *Scientific American, 252*, 62–74.

Yakovlev, P. I., & Lecours, A. (1967). The myelogenetic cycles of regional maturation of the brain. In A. Minkowski (Ed.), *Regional development of the brain in early life* (pp. 3–65). London: Blackwell.

Yamamoto, M. (1980). Developmental changes for hemispheric specialization of tactile recognition by normal children. *Perceptual and Motor Skills, 51*, 325–326.

Yamamoto, M. (1984). Intra- and inter-hemispheric tactile identification matching in young children. *Japanese Psychological Research, 26*, 120–124.

Yen, W. M. (1975). Independence of hand preference and sex-linked genetic effects on spatial performance. *Perceptual and Motor Skills, 41*, 311–318.

Yeni-Komshian, G. H., & Benson, D. (1976). Anatomical study of cerebral asymmetry in the temporal lobes of humans, chimpanzees, and rhesus monkeys. *Science, 192*, 387–389.

Yeni-Komshian, G. H., Isenberg, D., & Goldberg, H. (1975). Cerebral dominance and reading disability: Left visual field deficit in poor readers. *Neuropsychologia, 13*, 83–94.

Young, A. W. (1981). Methodological and theoretical bases of visual hemifield studies. In J. G. Beaumont (Ed.), *Divided visual field studies of cerebral organization*. New York: Academic Press.

Young, A. W. (1982). Asymmetry of cerebral hemisphere function during development. In J. W. T. Dickerson & H. McGurk (Eds.), *Brain and behavioural development* (pp. 168–202). Glasgow: Blackie.

Young, A. W., & Bion, P. J. (1979). Hemispheric laterality effects in the enumeration of visually presented collections of dots by children. *Neuropsychologia, 17*, 99–102.

Young, A. W., & Bion, P. J. (1980). Absence of any developmental trend in right hemisphere superiority for face recognition. *Cortex, 16*, 213–221.

Young, A. W., & Bion, P. J. (1981). Identification and storage of line drawings presented to the left and right cerebral hemispheres of adults and children. *Cortex, 17*, 459–464.

Young, A. W., & Ellis, A. W. (1981). Asymmetry of cerebral hemispheric function in normal and poor readers. *Psychological Bulletin, 89*, 183–190.

Young, G. (1977). Manual specialization in infancy: Implications for lateralization of brain function. In S. J. Segalowitz & F. A. Gruber (Eds.), *Language development and neurological theory*. New York: Academic Press.

Yund, E. W., Efron, R., & Nichols, D. R. (1990). Detectability gradients as a function of target location. *Brain and Cognition, 12*, 1–16.

Zaidel, D., & Sperry, R. W. (1973). Performance on the Raven's coloured progressive matrices test by subjects with cerebral commissurotomy. *Cortex, 9*, 34–39.

Zaidel, E. (1973). *Linguistic competence and related functions in the right cerebral hemisphere of man following commissurotomy and hemispherectomy*. Unpublished Ph.D. dissertation, California Institute of Technology.

Zaidel, E. (1975). A technique for presenting lateralized visual input with prolonged exposure. *Vision Research, 15*, 283–289.

Zaidel, E. (1978a). Auditory language comprehension in the right hemisphere following cerebral commissurotomy and hemispherectomy: A comparison with child language and aphasia. In A. Caramazza & E. Zurif (Eds.), *Language acquisition and language breakdown* (pp. 229–275). Baltimore: Johns Hopkins University Press.

Zaidel, E. (1978b). Concepts of cerebral dominance in the split brain. In P. A. Buser & A. Rougeul-Buser (Eds.), *Cerebral correlates of conscious experience*. Amsterdam: Elsevier/North Holland Biomedical Press.

Zaidel, E. (1978c). Lexical organization of the right hemisphere. In P. A. Buser & A. Rougeul-Buser (Eds.), *Cerebral correlates of conscious experience*. Amsterdam: Elsevier/North Holland Biomedical Press.

Zaidel, E. (1983a). A response to Gazzaniga: Language in the right hemisphere, convergent perspectives. *American Psychologist, 38*, 342–346.

Zaidel, E. (1983b). Disconnection syndrome as a model for laterality effects in the normal brain. In J. B. Hellige (Ed.), *Cerebral hemisphere asymmetry: Method, theory, and application* (pp. 95–151). New York: Praeger.

Zaidel, E. (1985). Introduction. In F. D. Benson & E. Zaidel (Eds.), *The dual brain: Hemispheric specialization in humans* (pp. 47–63). London: Guilford.

Zaidel, E., & Sperry, R. W. (1974). Memory impairment following commissurotomy in man. *Brain, 97*, 263–272.

Zangwill, O. L. (1978). Dyslexia and cerebral dominance: A reassessment. In L. Oettinger, Jr., & E. V. Majouski (Eds.), *The psychologist, the school, and the child with MBD/LD*. New York: Grune & Stratton.

Zenhausen, R. (1978). Imagery, cerebral dominance and style of thinking: A unified field model. *Bulletin of the Psychonomic Society, 12*, 381–384.

Zook, J. A., & Dwyer, J. H. (1976). Cultural differences in hemisphericity: A critique. *Bulletin of the Los Angeles Neurological Societies, 41*, 87–90.

Zurif, E. B. (1980). Language mechanisms: A neuropsychological perspective. *American Scientist, 68*, 305–311.

Zurif, E. B., & Bryden, M. P. (1969). Familial handedness and left–right differences in auditory and visual perception. *Neuropsychologia, 7*, 179–187.

Zurif, E. B., & Mendelsohn, M. (1972). Hemispheric specialization for the perception of speech sounds: The influence of intonation and structure. *Perception and Psychophysics, 11*, 329–332.

Zurif, E. B., & Sait, P. E. (1969). The role of syntax in dichotic listening. *Neuropsychologia, 8*, 239–244.

Author Index

Subject Index